POPULAR FRESHWATER
TROPICAL FISH

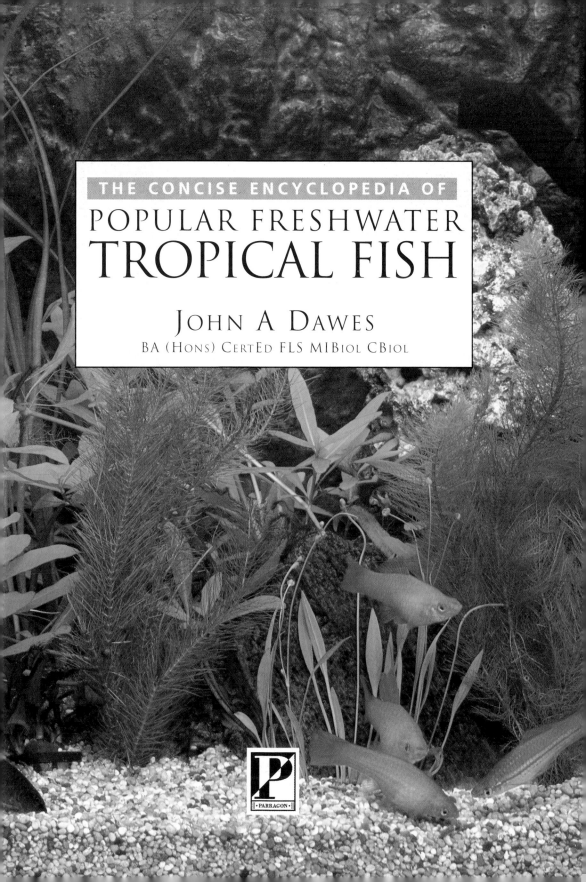

THE CONCISE ENCYCLOPEDIA OF
POPULAR FRESHWATER
TROPICAL FISH

JOHN A DAWES
BA (Hons) CertEd FLS MIBiol CBiol

P
·PARRAGON·

Photography credits

All photographs © Parragon by Peter Gathercole with
the exception of the following:

© Peter Gathercole, pages: 13-15, 17-33.
© Photomax, pages: 34b, 37, 65, 81, 111, 123b, 127, 132,
136t, 137, 138, 152, 155, 158, 170, 172, 174, 182, 184, 197,
206, 212, 214, 215, 222, 223, 225, 226, 227.
© David Allison, pages: 198, 236.
© Dennis Barrett, pages: 40b, 41.
© John Dawes, pages: 21tl, 38, 69b, 161.
© Aaron Norman, page: 159.
© Gina Sandford, page: 112.
© Bill Tomey, page: 95.
© K. A. Webb, page 169.

Author's Acknowledgements

A heartfelt vote of thanks is due to several people,
without whom this book would not have appeared in
print. Sue Pressley and Paul Turner of Stonecastle
Graphics have been the very essence of professionalism
during this project, taking even our permanent move
from the UK to Spain – which we undertook while the
book was already under way – in their stride and
offering constructive support throughout. Thanks are
due to Derek Lambert, who made his outstanding
collection of livebearing fishes available to Peter
Gathercole our photographer, and also to the various
photographers who submitted their valuable pictures for
our selection. Thanks. also, to John Chalmers of
Hobbyfish, where many of the photographs were taken.
Finally, special thanks to Vivian, my wife and eagle-eyed
critic, who can always spot my omissions, especially
when I fail to see the wood for the trees... and who
unfailingly gives me morale-boosting, ego-inflating
encouragement when I need it most.

CONTENTS

INTRODUCTION	6	INTRODUCTION TO FISH SPECIES	46
INTRODUCTION TO PRACTICAL SECTION	8	CYPRINIDS	48
TANKS	10	CHARACINS	69
HEATING	13	CATFISH	98
LIGHTING	14	CICHLIDS	121
AERATION	15	ANABANTOIDS/LABRYNTHFISHES	156
FILTRATION	16	LOACHES	180
ACCESSORIES	19	RAINBOWFISHES	187
FURNISHINGS & DECORATIONS	20	GOBIES AND SLEEPERS	195
WATER CHEMISTRY	22	KILLIFISH	201
SETTING UP THE AQUARIUM	24	EELS AND REEDFISH	212
SELECTING AND INTRODUCING FISH	29	GLASSFISHES, PUFFERS AND ARCHERS	216
FEEDING	31	MONOS AND SCATS	220
AQUARIUM MAINTENANCE	32	MISCELLANEOUS SPECIES	224
FISH HEALTH	34	LIVEBEARERS	230
BREEDING FISH	38	INDEX	254
AQUARIUM PLANTS	42	BIBLIOGRAPHY	256

INTRODUCTION

I F YOU HAVE never kept fish before, the chances are that you will know someone who has...or does, such is the worldwide popularity of the aquarium hobby. The reasons for this huge following are many. They are also as varied as those who decide to take the plunge and become aquarists.

Some of us come into the hobby as children and never look back, to the extent that life without some form of involvement in fishkeeping is, quite simply, almost unthinkable. Many others join as adults and often wonder how they managed to live their lives up to that point without the many pleasures that aquarium keeping brings.

Some people enter and remain within the hobby as single-tank owners all their lives. Others begin with one aquarium and end up building special rooms or separate buildings for their ever-expanding collections.

Some of us develop a hunger for aquatically-related knowledge that can only be satisfied through studying, investigating, travelling to the jungles and other places where our fish originate, visiting fish farms, attending conferences, writing articles and books, presenting lectures and films and so on. Others take a more laid-back approach and concentrate on enjoying their community aquarium and occasionally visiting their local dealer.

One of the pleasures of keeping freshwater tropical fish is that it brings the exotic colours of the tropics into our living rooms, wherever we happen to live.

A well planted aquarium, stocked with colourful fish is the basis for an enjoyable and rewarding hobby.

The great beauty of our hobby is that all these approaches, plus countless others, are equally 'valid'. There's room for all our various and varying tastes, with space to spare!

It is my hope that if this is the first aquarium book you have ever looked at, the impression it gives will be sufficiently positive and favourable to encourage you to take your initial interest further and, as a result, decide to join us. If, on the other hand, you are already an established aquarist, I hope that you, too, will find value in this book, which I have written both with the first-time aquarist and the 'veteran' in mind.

I have included basic information for those who require such guidance, along with the latest thinking on many of the families, genera, species and varieties that make up the extensive fish section. Here and there, I have also added personal details that I have gathered during my travels and collecting trips, and which hardly ever – if ever – find their way into aquarium books.

This project has been a challenging and hugely enjoyable one for me. I hope that some of this enjoyment shines through in the pages that follow.

Happy aquarium keeping!

John Dawes

INTRODUCTION TO PRACTICAL SECTION

SETTING UP a freshwater tropical aquarium is always an exciting and enjoyable activity. Setting up your first aquarium is even more special. It is also a journey of discovery and a time of mounting expectation as you prepare your tank – and yourself – for the first fish and plants.

It is now some 45 years since – as a seven-year old – I set up my first aquarium. It was an old-style all-glass battery tank, the uneven sides of which distorted the shape of the inhabitants. Even so, it obviously left a lasting impression on me, since I am still setting up aquaria and getting a thrill from doing so.

One thing that I learned very early on was that we can't rush Nature. We can help it along, but if we demand too much, too quickly, the inevitable consequence is disaster and disappointment.

Above: Balance between fish and plants is essential for the long-term well-being of both.

This does not mean that there is only one method of successfully setting up an aquarium. Not at all. Indeed, the guidelines that are established in the pages that follow are only that, i.e., guidelines. They represent a technique that has worked well for me over the years and which, I hope, will help you negotiate the early stages of your new life as an aquarist without any major mishaps.

What are inflexible and must be observed are Nature's laws. If conditions inside an aquarium are such that they will only accommodate a certain number or type of fish and/or plants, then there's very little that can be done about this, unless the conditions are modified.

For example, if a particular type of fish can only tolerate a certain level of waste products in its water, then trying to coax it (or force it) into tolerating a higher concentration by introducing one or more additional fish will just not work. In fact, what will happen sooner or later (usually sooner!) is that all the fish will suffer. However, if we can find a way of keeping toxin levels under control, for instance, by installing an effective water treatment system, then all the fish are likely to survive.

It is with this overriding consideration in mind – that the well-being of our fish and plants is paramount – that this section of the book approaches the various essential practical aspects of aquarium keeping.

Left: A well-planted aquarium offers a natural-looking environment for your fish.

TANKS

MANY YEARS ago, goldfish bowls were all the rage. Then, as so often happens, fashions changed and, as they did, the popularity of this once-ubiquitous fish 'container' waned. Other factors have contributed to the decline, prominent among these being the oft-quoted declaration that goldfish bowls are 'torture chambers'.

This, I am afraid, is one of several myths relating to our hobby, that are repeated so often that they are in danger of becoming accepted as self-evident truths. The reality is somewhat different.

If you buy a small goldfish bowl and attempt to keep several (even moderately sized) fish in it, then – without a shadow of doubt – it will become a genuine torture chamber. If, however, you install a proper goldfish bowl aeration/filtration kit, and keep just one or, at most, two small fish, and if you establish a sensible maintenance regime, there is no reason why your fish should not live a healthy, happy life.

It's all a matter – as I emphasized in the previous section – of not demanding from a system something that it cannot deliver. In truth, the emotive 'torture chamber' label can be attached to any aquarium, irrespective of size, if we ignore the basic principles of successful husbandry.

BIGGER IS BETTER

This said, it pays to choose the largest aquarium that you can afford, and that will meet the needs of the fish and plants you plan to keep. There are several reasons for this, and all are linked, either directly or indirectly, to water quality.

Contrary to common belief, smaller volumes of water are more difficult to maintain in a healthy state than larger ones. The problem with small volumes is that, by their very nature, they cannot easily accommodate fluctuating conditions. Therefore, just as they react more quickly to heating and cooling, they also deteriorate in

Small volumes of water are more difficult to control than larger ones.

A six-sided tank.

overall quality far more rapidly than larger volumes if and when, for example, a fish dies and goes unnoticed for some time, or if so much food is provided in one go that some of it remains uneaten and begins to rot, or if a slight overdose of medication is administered, or if stocking levels are exceeded, or if a partial water change is carried out...and so on.

Larger volumes have greater in-built buffering (cushioning) capacity and, consequently, offer the aquarist – particularly the newcomer to the hobby – a wider margin of error. This is an especially important 'safety net' to have during the early days of aquarium keeping when slip-ups are more likely to occur.

If your intention is to specialize in small species like killifish or livebearers, most of which are small or moderately sized, and if your ultimate aim is to attempt to keep as many species or varieties of these as possible

in numerous small aquaria, you would be well advised to start off with one of the standard-sized aquaria (see following section) and 'graduate' down to the smaller ones once you have mastered the basics of successful aquarium husbandry. The minimum size that I would recommend for a first aquarium, not just to such aquarists but also to those who intend to restrict their activities to a single tank, is to opt for a 60 x 30 x 30cm (24 x 12 x 12in) aquarium.

STANDARD OR CUSTOMIZED TANK?

Nowadays, it is perfectly feasible to construct aquaria of virtually any shape or size. Further, the quality of modern silicone-based sealants is such, that we now only rarely – if ever – use the metal frames that were so popular (and essential) in the past. As a result, an aquarium can be customized to fit into virtually any

An all-glass aquarium with fitted hood and stand.

available space, or in accordance with the owner's personal whims and preferences.

This situation has both advantages and disadvantages. On the upside, you end up with precisely the shape and size you want. On the downside, this flexibility carries with it potential dangers in that unsuitable shapes, designs and sizes can result if careful thought is not put into the planning phase. In particular, an aquarium should provide the maximum surface area:volume ratio, since gaseous exchange occurs via the water surface (see section on Aeration).

Not surprisingly, most new aquarists opt for an all-glass, commercially constructed, standard, rectangular tank. Of the many sizes that are available, the three most popular are:

Natural plants.

- 60 x 30 x 30cm   (24 x 12 x 12in)
- 90 x 30 x 37cm   (36 x 12 x 15in)
- 120 x 37 x 37cm   (48 x 15 x 15in)

These are offered either as free-standing models which can be located on top of a suitably strong unit or metal stand, or as 'cabinet aquaria' which rest on top of a specially constructed unit. Cabinet aquaria tend to come with a hood.

Ultimately, it is a question of personal preferences and circumstances, since both free-standing and cabinet aquaria can be operated equally successfully.

Open spaces provide easy viewing.

HEATING

ALTHOUGH, BY definition, tropical fish come from tropical regions of the world, aquaria even in the tropics very often require additional heating. This has nothing to do with the ambient temperature, of course, but, rather, with the temperatures that exist inside many air-conditioned houses and offices in such parts of the world. Therefore, a freshwater tropical aquarium in, say, Singapore is just as likely to require the provision of additional heating as an aquarium in a heated house or office in Sydney, or Syracuse... or Sittingbourne!

At the more sophisticated end of the market, there are superb heating systems that allow for very accurate temperature monitoring and adjustment. There are also canister filters which incorporate a heating element, undergravel heating cables or plates, and various other in-tank approaches to temperature control.

Among specialist hobbyists, space heating – the heating of a room set aside specifically for aquaria – is very popular. Yet even these specialists tend to have a back-up in the form of a traditional heater-thermostat unit in each aquarium.

These traditional units have been around for years and have been progressively refined so that they are not only highly efficient, but also long-lasting and easy to adjust. At the heart of each heater is a coiled heating element which is switched on or off, depending on the temperature of the water, by a thermostat (either an electronic one, or one based on the old tried-and-tested bi-metallic strip principle) that can be adjusted to meet

Above and above right: Eheim's Thermofilter.

An under-gravel heater.

the requirements of the fish and plants. Both the heating unit and the thermostat are usually housed together in a heat-dissipating tube.

When choosing a heater-thermostat, always aim for one that provides the required heat, with some spare capacity to cope with unforeseen conditions, such as the breakdown of the house's heating system during winter.

The accompanying table lists some approximate wattage requirements for the three most popular sizes of standard aquaria housed in a reasonably well-heated room. For cool rooms, add 50 percent to the listed wattages, and for cold rooms, double it to be on the safe side.

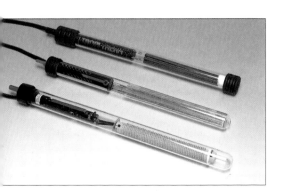

Three different heater-thermostats.

Aquarium Size		Wattage Required
Centimetres	(Inches)	
60 x 30 x 30	(24 x 12 x 12)	75-100
90 x 30 x 37	(36 x 12 x 15)	100-150
120 x 37 x 37	(48 x 15 x 15)	120-180

LIGHTING

AQUARIUM LIGHTING serves two main purposes: firstly it allows us to view the tank occupants, and it is essential for healthy plant growth.

If all you want is to be able to appreciate the colours of your fish, and if you are willing to replace plants as they die, or are damaged, or fail to grow luxuriantly, then choosing appropriate lighting is, basically, a question of obtaining a lighting unit that shows up colours to best effect.

If, however, you also want to grow plants successfully, then other considerations come into play. Prominent among these is the desirability of matching the intensity and quality of light emitted by the chosen unit with the needs of the plants you are buying.

Selecting such a unit requires some thought, of course, but, unless you so wish, it is not necessary to understand scientific aspects of lighting, such as lumens, lux or light temperature in any great depth. They are all vitally important from the point of view of plant health,

but, thankfully, leading manufacturers have researched the subject thoroughly on our behalf, and therefore provide their own guidelines regarding the suitability of their units for aquaria of all sizes.

Nowadays, ordinary tungsten bulbs are not used as frequently as they were in the past. Instead, their place has been largely taken by fluorescent tubes of numerous types, offering the aquarist a wide range of so-called 'white' colours, with varying amounts of ultra-violet and blue light. Generally speaking, these tubes can be fitted inside hoods (some with in-built reflectors) which, in turn, fit over the tank, thus ensuring that no stray light escapes. Tubes can also be fitted into suspended hoods, the best of which carry adjustable flaps to allow you to direct the light as desired.

Pendant lights have also become quite popular with aquarists who prefer open-top tanks and are particularly interested in plants. The quality of light emitted by these units is usually very good indeed.

Whatever your preferences, read the details supplied by the manufacturers and seek advice before you make your final decision.

SUGGESTED MINIMUM (FLUORESCENT) LIGHTING REQUIREMENTS:

Aquarium Length		Number of Tubes
Centimetres	(Inches)	& Wattage
60	(24)	1 x 15
90	(36)	2 x 20
120	(48)	2 x 30

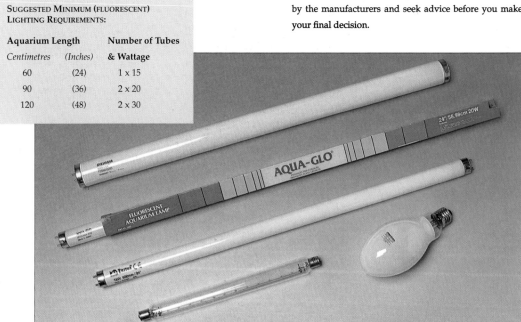

Fluorescent tubes, tungsten tubes and mercury vapour bulbs.

AERATION

WITH FEW exceptions, living things require oxygen to survive. This is just as true of green aquatic plants as it is of fish, despite what some aquarium books and articles say, for example, that green plants 'breathe in' carbon dioxide and 'breathe out' oxygen during the day and reverse the process at night.

This is another of those myths that have become widely accepted as truths. What, in essence, happens is that green plants take in carbon dioxide during the hours of daylight, not for respiratory purposes, but for use in a food-building process known as photosynthesis, a by-product of which is oxygen.

When photosynthesis progresses at full speed, it generates more oxygen than a plant requires for respiration, so the surplus is released. At night, photosynthesis stops, but respiration continues, so there is then a net intake of oxygen by plants, with an accompanying net output of carbon dioxide. Animals cannot photosynthesize, so they are strict users of oxygen and producers of carbon dioxide.

Unless we find a way of balancing the levels of these gases at all times, the aquarium occupants will experience difficulties at some stage during each day or night. This is where aeration plays such a vital role.

However, it is not the bubbles produced as aerators pump out their air via diffuser stones or venturis (special devices attached to power filters and power heads) that aerate the water. In fact, very little oxygen actually dissolves out of these bubbles as they rise through the water column. Their primary function is to agitate the water surface, thus facilitating the entry of oxygen and escape of carbon dioxide.

If the air flow from a diaphragm- or piston-driven aerator can be channelled through certain types of filter, it is also possible to carry out two essential processes simultaneously: aeration and filtration. A similar result can be obtained by using the venturi or spray-bar facility of many power heads and filters currently available, so it is worth checking all these possibilities before making your final choice.

Venturi action on powerfilter.

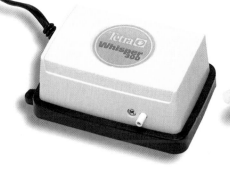

Two examples of air pumps.

FILTRATION

A S PREVIOUSLY mentioned in the introduction to the practical section (see page 10), fish must be provided with clean, 'healthy' water. In fact, this aspect of aquarium-keeping is so important that there is an old saying among experienced aquarists which states: 'Look after the water, and the water will look after your fish.' It would be quite accurate to think of ourselves primarily as 'water' keepers, rather than 'fish' keepers, since without mastering the control of water conditions in our aquaria, successful fishkeeping is totally impossible.

In the wild, water volumes are large, and physical (mechanical), chemical and biological purification processes are part and parcel of the natural cycles that maintain living conditions in a state of equilibrium. Usually, if and when imbalances occur, they are the result of some form of human intervention that disrupts the natural status quo.

However, when water is enclosed in an aquarium – no matter how large the aquarium may be – this relatively small volume of water is cut off from many of the natural purification processes that would normally keep it in a healthy state. Under such circumstances, we have to learn to manage this confined water properly, or the fish will perish. This is why it is so important for every aquarist to learn about filtration and how to employ it to optimal effect.

TYPES OF FILTRATION

Strictly speaking, the term 'filtration' implies a process which involves the passing of water (or other fluid)

It is important to learn about filtration and how to create the perfect environment to maintain healthy fish.

A range of filter media.

External canister filters.

through some form of sieve. If this is applied to what actually takes place in aquaria, however, then only one of the three main processes involved can be genuinely regarded as constituting filtration.

Mechanical Filtration

Strictly speaking, this is the only true filtration relating to aquaria, since it consists of passing water through a barrier of one kind or other that traps suspended particles of debris as the stream of water flows through. A wide range of media can be used for this purpose, including foam, filter wool, gravel, woven mats of inert material and so on.

Physical removal of suspended particles does not change the chemical composition of the water in any way, however. So, if it contains dissolved toxins, these will pass unaltered right through the filter medium.

Chemical Filtration

Although I have used the traditional term 'filtration' here, in reality, what we are talking about here is chemical detoxification or purification. Some materials, like activated charcoal and zeolite, can adsorb certain chemicals onto their surfaces (note that adsorption is quite different from absorption, in that it involves the adhesion of molecules – in this case, some dissolved toxins – as a thin layer on the surface of the medium employed).

It is always useful to incorporate this type of purification in a water-treatment system, but particularly so when dealing with a newly set up aquarium in which the beneficial bacterial population has not yet become established.

After a time, depending on the stocking and waste product levels, chemical media become exhausted and, either need to be re-activated or discarded. Zeolite can be easily re-activated by soaking the granules in saline

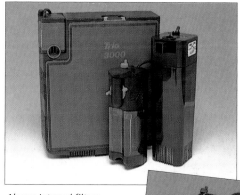

Above: Internal filters.
Right: Fitting a sponge cartridge into an internal filter.

solution, which has the effect of removing or 'unsticking' ammonia molecules from the medium, thus allowing it to be re-used. Activated charcoal can, in theory, be re-activated in an oven, but, realistically, the process is not as simple as it sounds and is not really worth the effort.

Biological Filtration

This type of purification/detoxification takes advantage of the remarkable ability which some bacteria possess to convert toxic ammonia (one of the waste compounds which fish produce) into somewhat less toxic nitrites and then to relatively harmless nitrates.

Traditionally, all aquarium and pond book authors (including myself) have referred to bacteria belonging to the genus *Nitrosomonas* as being responsible for converting ammonia into nitrites, and to *Nitrobacter* bacteria subsequently converting nitrites into nitrates. In 1996, however, research carried out by Timothy Hovanec and Edward DeLong in the US, raised doubts about the validity of this widely accepted belief. The results of their investigations throw up the very interesting possibility that neither *Nitrosomonas* nor *Nitrobacter* bacteria may be involved at all in biological water detoxification in freshwater aquaria. Although further study is required at the time of writing, it may well be that we will need to revise our thinking in due course.

Whatever the outcome, the fact remains that bacteria of some kind are involved in a most effective way in purifying toxin-laden aquarium water. Not only do they convert ammonia into nitrates, but some types can convert nitrates into free nitrogen, which can then escape from the water. The former process, known as nitrification, requires oxygen, i.e., it is aerobic, while the latter, denitrification, does not, i.e., it is anaerobic.

CHOOSING FILTERS AND FILTER MEDIA

Ideally, when choosing a filtration system, it is best to install one that can simultaneously perform all three types of water treatment: mechanical, chemical and biological.

This is where things can begin to get a little complicated, particularly for new aquarists. There are so many types of filter, and such a wide range of filter media available today, that choosing between them can seem a daunting task.

At the simpler (and less expensive) end of the spectrum, there are basic box filters which can do a perfectly adequate job, provided they are not required to filter large volumes of heavily polluted water. At the other end, there are fully integrated sophisticated (and more expensive) systems – sometimes with inbuilt heating and pumping units – that can be as large as the aquarium itself. Between the two extremes, are a whole host of designs available at a range of prices, including undergravel filter-plate systems, internal power filters, external power (canister) filters, wet/dry trickle filters and others.

Similarly, when it comes to filter media, there are numerous types, perhaps the simplest of which is filter

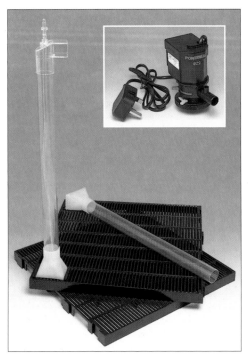

An undergravel filter and (above right) a powerhead for undergravel filter.

wool. Among the others, foam; ceramic granules, hoops and cylinders; sintered glass hoops and cylinders; intricate hollow plastic balls, pyramids and other shapes; filter ribbons and mats, offer a wide choice, especially when several are combined as part of a 'sandwich' inside a filter.

Ultimately, personal preferences and finances, the type and size of the aquarium, stocking levels and the types of fish and plants chosen, the feeding regime and several other factors, all play a role in determining which system should or can be bought.

In general terms, choose the most efficient system that you can afford. It is also sensible to seek advice before you buy. The staff of specialist shops are, of course, excellent sources of information but – to be fair, both to yourself and the shop staff – try to avoid particularly busy periods when time is short. Alternatively, take a friend who is experienced in the hobby with you.

Finally, follow the manufacturer's instructions to the letter when installing a filter...and be patient. It takes months for a fully operational biological system to become established.

ACCESSORIES

S O FAR, the book has discussed the essential requirements without which it would be virtually impossible to run a successful freshwater tropical aquarium. However, even if we approach the aquarium itself, along with its heating, lighting, aeration and filtration requirements, with the attention and care they deserve, it would still be difficult to cater for day-to-day and occasional maintenance needs without a back-up of appropriate accessories.

What actually constitutes an accessory and what is deemed essential is a matter of debate from aquarist to aquarist and also depends on levels of expertise. What I have therefore done in the following list is group together a selection of items (some more obviously 'aquatic' than others) which I have found particularly useful as my own back-up survival kit.

Aeration: a spare aerator (a battery-powered model is particularly useful during power cuts); a length of air line, plus air-line clips, a non-return valve and T and Y pieces for multiple connections (above); spare diffuser stones/ blocks; a spare diaphragm.

Electrical: a range of plugs and fuses; a cable tidy – a small contraption that keeps wiring safe and tidy (pictured above right); insulating and waterproof tape.

Heating: a spare heater-thermostat fully wired up and ready for immediate use; heater-thermostat clips; a spare thermometer; a heater-thermostat protector (a means of

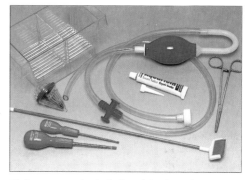

Various accessories, including siphoning tube, tongs, breeding trap, algae scraper and sealant.

preventing boisterous fish from dislodging the heating unit, and of preventing sedentary fish from burning themselves by lying against the heater).

Routine Maintenance: a siphon tube; an algae cleaner/ scraper; a gravel cleaner/ dip-tube; planting sticks; long forceps; a range of nets.

Feeding: reserve stocks of food of various types; automatic feeder (pictured right); a feeding ring which keeps food confined to a particular area.

Chemical Products: a range of water-testing kits (although included here, test kits should – in my view – be considered essentials); a medicine chest containing proprietary preparations for all common diseases; pH adjusters (just in case you need to alter the acidity/ alkalinity of the water – see section on Water Chemistry for further details).

Miscellaneous: a tube of silicone sealant for repairing leaks, attaching pieces of rock or bogwood to a firm base, etc; a breeding trap to house livebearer females while giving birth; scissors; waterproof marker pens; jam jars; a notebook; screwdrivers, etc; a selection of plastic plants to offer immediate shelter if required; suitable pieces of slate, rockwork and bogwood (natural or synthetic) for similar reasons, or to change the decor.

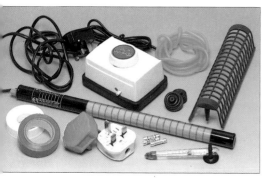

A range of accessories, including heater-thermostat, thermometer, plug, aerator, air line and heater guard.

FURNISHINGS & DECORATIONS

THE TYPES of furnishings and decorations you choose, and how you arrange them, is, of course, a matter of personal choice. I cannot hope to provide a comprehensive guide as to what is, and what is not, acceptable, and so will confine myself to pointing out a few general useful do's and don'ts that should help you to avoid the major pitfalls.

Furnishings come in various forms, the main ones being aquarium gravel, rocks, bogwood, backgrounds and ornaments.

AQUARIUM GRAVEL

Gravel is widely available in various grain sizes. Although gravel is often referred to as a rooting medium, this does not mean that it provides plants with a source of inorganic nutrients. In fact, gravel is totally sterile in this sense, so when it is called a rooting medium, its root-anchoring, rather than its 'nutritional', properties are being alluded to.

With regard to grain size, the finer this is, the more compacted it will become with time and the better suited it will be for plants with shallow roots. Burrowing species of fish, such as some of the Spiny Eels (*Macrognathus* and *Mastacembelus* species) will find fine-grained gravel/coarse sand much more suitable than coarse-grained types; species like *Corydoras* catfish also prefer a fine-grained substratum.

When using fine-grained gravel or coarse sand, regularly disturb the surface to prevent stagnant spots from developing and acting as focal points where organic matter, e.g., uneaten food, can rot.

Unless you need to establish hard-water, alkaline conditions, check that the gravel you buy is lime-free. Also – particularly if you are opting for synthetic (as opposed to natural) gravel – make sure that the grains are rounded. Sharp-edged grains can cause injury if a fish scratches its body against the gravel (as fish tend to do to relieve an itch), or when a foraging fish takes in gravel into its mouth.

Right: Cobbles.

Left: Lava rock.

Right: Tiered artificial rock

ROCKS

Rocks come in all sorts of shapes and sizes. They are also available as natural rocks or synthetic equivalents. Either way – as with gravel – it is important to avoid lime-rich types (unless your fish require hard, alkaline conditions) and jagged-edged pieces.

BOGWOOD

This term covers all types of suitable wood, including well matured and clean driftwood, etc. In addition to its decorative properties, natural bogwood can also perform a very useful role in aquaria that contain species of fish and plants that like a little tannic acid in the water. Tannins tend to colour the water yellow or brown, giving it the colour of weak tea, and form part of the natural environment from which many of our fish – including such popular types as the Cardinal Tetra (*Paracheirodon axelrodi*) – originate.

It is quite possible to prevent tannins from leaching out of bogwood by painting it with several coats of non-toxic polyurethane varnish. Alternatively, all the aesthetic properties of bogwood, plus many of its

Above: Bogwood.
Below left:
Decorative wood.
Right: Decorative
artificial wood

The Rio Negro showing black tannin-stained water.
Photograph © John Dawes.

especially when they begin to 'mature' – that it is very difficult to distinguish them from the real thing.

Between the two types, there is a growing range of variously priced choices, all of which have their positive points and are well worth considering.

DECORATIONS

While all the different furnishings mentioned above are also decorative, the term 'decoration' is generally reserved for ornamental items that are not strictly aquatic. Therefore, skulls, treasure chests, skeletons, frogs, bridges, castles and numerous other subjects are classified as aquarium decorations or ornaments.

As already stressed, aquarium keeping involves a great deal of personal preference. This applies just as much to aquarium decorations as to anything else, so if ornaments of the above types appeal to you, then – as long as they are safe in terms of composition and design – you will not be short of choice.

functional ones (like offering shelter or resting sites to those species and individuals that require them), can be just as effectively met by the very realistic and safe artificial types which are commonly available.

BACKGROUNDS

Traditionally, aquarium backgrounds were primarily available as aquascapes which could be bought off a roll and stuck onto the outside of the tank, thus creating an immediate underwater scene. Such types of background are still as widely available as ever and offer aquarists an inexpensive and very effective way of providing an attractive backdrop for their aquaria.

More recently, three-dimensional backgrounds have become available on a much larger scale than previously and some of the latest models are so realistic –

Some aquarium decorations are also functional, usually providing an inlet and outlet for an air line. As a result, such decorations have an added bonus in that they can open and close rhythmically, emitting air bubbles every time they open and adding a little extra attraction to the underwater scene in the process.

A wide range of novelty tank decorations are available.

WATER CHEMISTRY

DESPITE ITS simple chemical nature, pure water is a remarkable substance which, given time, will dissolve almost anything. As it does so, these dissolved substances give water its chemical characteristics. For example, water containing dissolved organic acids will tend to be soft and acidic, while certain calcium and magnesium salts will make it hard and alkaline.

The seas and oceans of the world, the eventual destination of all the water on the planet, are all more or less confluent with each other, and so all have the same basic composition. There are some local differences, particularly where a body of seawater is restricted in some way as, for example, in the Red Sea, but – overall – seawater is high in sodium chloride and other salts – which are derived not just from the inflow of dissolved terrestrial substances, but also from emissions from the thermal vents that exist along the deep-sea ridges. Together, these factors make it denser than freshwater and distinctly alkaline.

The character of bodies of freshwater, however, is determined by the nature of the terrain over, or through, which the water flows. If the rocks are neutral in terms of acidic/alkalinic compounds (as in most silica sandstones), the water will be soft. Further, if the water flow passes through an area overgrown with trees whose leaves eventually drop into the water, the level of organic acids in it will rise, as we find in some of the major freshwater basins of the world like the Amazon. Conversely, water that flows over, or through, strata such as limestone, will be hard and alkaline.

Right: Various water treatment kits are readily available from good stockists.

The water chemistry of the aquarium is vital to the well-being of its inhabitants.

From the aquarium standpoint, it is the acidity/alkalinity of water (its pH), its hardness, plus its ammonia/ammonium and nitrite/nitrate content that are most directly relevant. Do, therefore, make certain that you buy water-testing kits to determine, at least, the above properties. They are all widely available and easy to use.

Left: Water conditioners

Right: Quick test tablets – nitrate

Left: Chemical strip test kits. Buffering capacity/hardness.

ACIDITY/ALKALINITY

Acidity and alkalinity are measured on a scale of 1 to 14, with 1 representing extreme acidity and 14 representing extreme alkalinity. Both extremes are lethal to fish and plants, particularly when we bear in mind that each unit represents a ten-fold increase or decrease. In other words, water having an acidity of 6 is ten times as acid as water with an equivalent value of 7.

Acidity/alkalinity is denoted by the symbol pH, with pH7 representing neutral conditions. All values below pH7 represent increasing levels of acidity, while those above indicate rising alkalinity. Most freshwater fish prefer pH values between 6 and 7.5. Specific requirements will be referred to in each entry in the Species Section.

HARDNESS

The most straightforward way of representing hardness is in terms of milligrams per litre (mg/l) or parts per million (ppm).

The total hardness of a water sample is the sum of its temporary or bicarbonate hardness ('hardness' that can be eliminated by boiling) and general or permanent hardness which cannot be boiled off. Temporary hardness is important because, when it is low, water loses much of its buffering capacity and is therefore susceptible to rapid fluctuations in quality. Permanent hardness is important in a different way. For example,

WATER HARDNESS CHART

Description	mg/l (ppm)
Very Soft	0-50
Moderately Soft	50-100
Slightly Hard	100-150
Moderately Hard	150-200
Hard	200-300
Very Hard	300+

fish that originate in soft-water regions, such as the Amazon, require low permanent hardness conditions, while those from high permanent hardness regions, such as the African Rift lakes, only do well in the long term in hard water. As with pH, specific requirements will be highlighted in the Species Section.

AMMONIA/AMMONIUM

Ammonia is a highly toxic waste product excreted by fish and other aquatic animals. Even levels as low as 0.025mg/l (ppm) can be toxic to some species. However, in neutral or acidic conditions, ammonia is converted into ammonium ions which are not toxic. Therefore, aquaria whose water is neutral or slightly acid provide a considerably wider safety margin, in terms of ammonia content, than alkaline ones.

NITRITES/NITRATES

During natural biological purification, ammonia is converted into nitrites (see Filtration for further details) which are, in themselves, also toxic to fish at concentrations as low as 0.1mg/l (ppm). However, the presence of a good population of filter bacteria will ensure that these nitrites are promptly converted to nitrates, whose concentration needs to rise above 50mg/l (ppm) before even the more delicate fish species begin to show any sign of discomfort of distress.

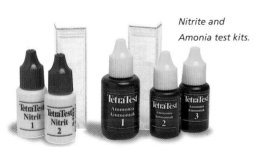

Nitrite and Amonia test kits.

SETTING UP THE AQUARIUM

ASK TWENTY experienced aquarists how to set up an aquarium, and you are likely to end up with twenty different answers. However, examine these in detail and you will find that, despite their differences, they all observe the same basic rules. This is not because anyone has forced these aquarists to sit down and learn the rules, but, rather, because experience has taught them that, without due attention to certain key elements, the exercise just cannot be completed successfully.

What follows in this section of the book is a step-by-step guide to setting up a community aquarium, i.e., one housing a selection of compatible, hardy species. In general, it can be applied to most other set-ups. It is an approach which I have found successful over the many years that I have been building and setting up aquaria and one which I still employ, with modifications to suit individual circumstances (for instance, omitting undergravel filters in aquaria that are going to house burrowing or vigorous bottom-foraging species).

Read through the complete set of guidelines before you make a start. You should find that they will answer most of your queries. However, if the aquarium arrangement you have in mind requires additional features or steps, do seek advice before getting under way. It is always preferable to avoid hiccups, rather than make mistakes and then be faced with the need to retrace your steps.

Imperial/metric conversions
*1 Imperial gallon = 1.2 US gallon
1 Imperial gallon = 4.55 litres
1 US gallon = 3.8 litres

1   Check that you have all the equipment you need. The minimum should include: the aquarium; a suitable stand or cabinet (alternatively you need a sufficiently sturdy piece of furniture on which to rest the tank – water weighs 1kg/litre or 10lb/Imperial gallon*); polystyrene strips, sheet or other forms of cushioning material on which to rest the tank; an aquarium hood and lights, including starter units for fluorescent tubes if these are being used; light fittings; a condensation tray or glass tank cover; a heater-thermostat; an undergravel or other type of filter; a gravel tidy (this useful option consists of a net-like sheet which can be placed on top of the undergravel filter to prevent fine grains of substratum from blocking the filter plate); a thermometer; an aerator, an air line, a non-return valve (to prevent water from siphoning back into the pump when it is switched off) and diffuser stone/block; alternatively, a power head (an electric pump) with a venturi (aerating facility) or a spray bar attachment for a power filter; gravel, rocks, bogwood and other furnishings, whether natural or synthetic; a good selection of plants, which must be kept moist at all times; a cable tidy if you wish to connect all your electrical equipment into a single unit; water testing/monitoring kits. (**No fish must be bought at this stage!**).

2

3

6

2   Bearing in mind the weight of water mentioned above, plus the considerable weight of natural rocks (synthetic ones are often lighter), choose a suitably robust site for the aquarium away from direct sunlight, fluctuating temperature sources, such as central heating radiators, draughts and constant disturbance from frequently used doorways, etc. If using a metal aquarium stand to support one of the larger standard aquaria, it is worth considering the use of a weight-spreading plate under each leg of the stand.

3   Check the tank for leaks. This operation performs two functions in that it allows you to detect this problem at the very outset, while at the same time acting as a dust-removing rinse for the tank. Repair any leaks or replace the tank.

4   You are now ready to begin installation – the first step is to rest the tank on the polystyrene sheet/ strips or other appropriate cushioning material.

5

5   If you are using an in-tank background – whether two- or three-dimensional – now is a good time to install it.

6   If you are using an undergravel filter, place this in position and lay the gravel tidy on top of the filter plate, cutting it to size if necessary. Fit the airlift(s) to the filter plate.

7   Rinse the gravel in a bucket, preferably under running water, and stir continuously until the water runs clear.

7

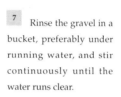

8   Spread the gravel on the filter plate, or gravel tidy, or directly onto the bottom of the tank if you have chosen not to use an undergravel filter. The layer should be several centimetres thick (7.5cm/ 3in should be enough if

8b

8a

you are using an undergravel filter; slightly less should still be adequate if you are not).

The general advice given is to create a gentle slope from the back to the front of the aquarium so that debris will collect at the front for easy removal. In practice, this doesn't always work once you plant the aquarium and furnish it with rocks, bogwood, etc.

9a

9b

9   Rinse rocks, bogwood and other furnishings in running water (**Don't under any circumstances use detergents – they are toxic to fish if not thoroughly removed.**) Arrange the furnishings in a way that appeals to you while, at the same time, providing some form of shelter for the fish. A useful tip is to avoid symmetrical arrangements, since these will make an already-artificial aquascape look even more unnatural.

Make sure that heavy rocks are well bedded into the substratum so that they don't topple over later on, trapping fish or damaging the aquarium.

10   Fix the thermometer and heater-thermostat into position making sure that the bottom tip of the heater-thermostat is clear of the gravel, otherwise, this will create a 'hot spot' that can damage the heater, with serious consequences for the tank occupants. Heater-

thermostats can be sited strategically in relation to furnishings so that they are not visible from the front of the aquarium. (**Do not switch the heater-thermostat on!**)

10a

10b

11

11   Connect the air line to the aerator, making sure that you insert the non-return valve the right way round (valves usually have an arrow indicating their correct alignment). Attach a diffuser to the free end of the air line and locate it somewhere along the back of the aquarium. Alternatively, if an undergravel filter is being used, the free end (either with a small diffuser stone, or without one), should be inserted into the top of the filter airlift and pushed down until it reaches gravel level.

It is also possible, using T and Y connections and air line clips and flow adjusters, to split the air supply between two airlifts or between an airlift and a diffuser stone or suitable aquarium ornament, or between a diffuser and an air-operated internal or external box-type filter. (**Do not switch the aerator on at this point.**)

12

13a

12 If an internal power filter or power head is being used, this can be placed in position, once the filter has been filled with an appropriate medium or media. Power heads should be firmly pushed into the top of the undergravel filter airlift(s). External power filters can be prepared and installed at this stage. Power head installation can also be left until the aquarium has been filled, thus using the water itself to support some of the weight. (**Do not switch the filter or power heads on at this point.**)

13 It is now time to start filling the tank. Use either a hose whose flow you can control from the nozzle end, or simply pour water into the tank from a bucket or other suitable receptacle. Whichever method you employ, the essential thing is to pour the water in gently and in a way that does not disturb the gravel.

There are many ways of doing this. For example, you can spread a sheet of newspaper, or a clear plastic sheet, or even greaseproof baking paper, on the bottom and direct the water flow onto this. Or you can pour the water onto a plate or saucer, or into a jam jar standing on a plate. Stop filling the tank when it is half full and remove the newspaper, etc.

14

14 Add a little warm water, not hot, to raise the temperature by a few degrees, thus avoiding giving the plants (Step 15) a cold-water shock.

15

15 It's planting time! Arrange your plants in a display that appeals to you, but provides both densely vegetated areas and open swimming spaces. As a general, but highly flexible, rule, short plants look best near the front, with taller ones along the sides and back of the aquarium. As with furnishings, it is usually a good idea to avoid symmetrical designs.

13b

16 Complete filling the tank to within about 2.5cm (1in) of the top.

17 If you did not install the power head(s) during Step 12, do so now. At this point, also adjust the position of the outflow tube from the power filter, so that it will not create major turbulence. If the outflow is being directed via a spray bar attachment, ensure that this is placed above water level and that the outlet holes are directed towards the water surface.

18 Place the condensation tray or glass cover in position.

19 Place the aquarium hood in position, having first fitted the lights, starter unit connections and the electrical leads from other equipment, and having threaded the air line and filter tubes neatly through the holes or slits in the condensation tray, or appropriate gaps in the glass tank cover.

20 Having checked everything thoroughly, switch on the electrical equipment and adjust the water/air flows as necessary.

If possible, aim to switch on during the morning or early afternoon, thus allowing yourself some time to monitor and adjust conditions, including pH, hardness and temperature. If you need to adjust any of the electrical equipment, **switch it off beforehand**. In the case of the heater-thermostat, allow the unit to cool down for about ten minutes before handling it.

21 Run the aquarium for about a week on a 12- to 15-hour light period. This will allow things to settle down and the water to clear and begin maturing, although this can process be speeded up using suitable water treatments/conditioners. Do not, however, introduce any fish for at least several days (see section on Selecting and Introducing Fish).

SELECTING AND INTRODUCING FISH

ONCE A NEW aquarium has begun to settle down, either naturally or with the help of water conditioners and start-up solutions or tablets, it is ready to receive its first fish. However, a new aquarium is too 'raw' to be able to accommodate its full complement of fish. That will not be possible until the filter bacteria and other water-purifying micro-organisms and plants have become established, a process that will take at least several weeks.

During this time, fish stocks should be built up gradually, starting off with no more than half the eventual number and adding a few fish to this each week until the full stocking level has been reached (see accompanying Table). As stocking proceeds, regular water monitoring should take place and, if any of the important parameters like pH, ammonia or nitrite levels show deviations from the norm, no more fish should be introduced until safe conditions have been restored.

Transporting and introducing fish into a new aquarium can be very stressful for them, so great care is essential.

helleri), both the popular Platies (*Xiphophorus maculatus* and *X. variatus*), the Dwarf Gourami (*Colisa lalia*), the Siamese Fighter (*Betta splendens*) and the Bronze and Peppered Corydoras (*Corydoras aeneus* and *C. reticulatus*). There are also many tetras, barbs and others which are suitable as first fish for first aquaria, so take your time and choose carefully, always bearing in mind the needs of the fish in question and your own vision of the final fully stocked aquarium.

The signs to look for to identify healthy fish are many and varied. Here are some of the most important signs that you should consider when selecting fish:

- Full, solid-looking body
- Intact and erect fins
- 'Bright' eyes
- No missing scales, growths, wounds or ulcers
- High level of activity (except in sedentary bottom-dwelling species)
- Healthy appetite (ask about this, but don't request a demonstration; newly fed fish are likely to defecate in the bag water on the way home!)

APPROXIMATE FULL STOCKING CAPACITIES

Approx. Aquarium Size (Surface dimensions)		Number of Fish (Size excludes length of tail)		
Centimetres	(Inches)	Up to 5cm/2in	5–7.5cm/2–3in	7.5–10cm/3–4in
60 x 30	(24 x12)	22	16	14
90 x 30	(36 x 12)	33	24	21
120 x 30	(48 x 12)	44	32	29

SELECTING FISH

If this is the first time that you are to buy fish, seek advice from shop staff or an experienced aquarist before you start. As you will see from the wide selection of species profiled later in the book, the choice is huge. However, not all fish are suitable for a first aquarium, or a community one.

Of course, there are some good choices, such as the Guppy (*Poecilia reticulata*), the Swordtail (*Xiphophorus*

In addition, find out about specific requirements or characteristics so that you buy sensibly. For example, many fish live in shoals and should therefore not be bought singly or in pairs, while others hate the sight of rivals of their own species.

INTRODUCING FISH

Once you have selected your fish, they will be put in water-filled bags appropriately for the journey home. However careful one is, though, netting, bagging, transporting and introducing fish into new aquaria all represent stressful situations. Therefore, try to ensure that these stresses are minimized at every stage.

For example, carry the fish home wrapped up in a way that cuts out the light and keeps the warmth in, for instance, in newspaper or an insulated box. Try not to expose the bags suddenly to bright lights or knocks.

Having got them home, ease the fish into their new home as follows:

1 Switch off the aquarium lights.

2 Float the bags in the aquarium for about ten minutes so that they reach the same temperature as the aquarium water.

3 Untie the bags. Do not pop them!

4 Allow a little aquarium water to flow into each bag. This helps the fish to adapt to the chemistry of their new water.

5 Leave for another ten minutes and repeat the process once or twice more.

6 Gently tip the bags to allow fish to swim out. Do not pour the fish out.

7 Leave the aquarium lights switched off and don't feed the fish until the following morning.

FEEDING

PET FOOD technology has made enormous advances over the past couple of decades, so much so that we now have commercially produced foods to suit virtually all aquarium fishes. Even species that were once difficult to feed will accept one or another of today's excellent formulations and, although there are still exceptions, most fish of this type are generally kept by specialist aquarists who can provide for their particular needs.

TYPES OF FOOD

The principal types of available commercial food fall into one of five main groups. The range of formulations, however, is extensive to say the least:

Flakes: These range from fine powdered foods for very young fish, through small flakes, to large flakes for bigger fish. In terms of their formulation, they range from high-protein diets for baby and growing fish to lower-protein flakes for adults, from vegetable-based formulations for herbivores, to animal-based ones for carnivores and mixed ones for omnivores. In addition, there are conditioning flakes, colour-enhancing flakes and many other types.

Granules/Tablets/Sticks: These foods consist of a somewhat narrower range of formulations which are either compressed or extruded into various shapes. Some types float, while others sink slowly and others quickly,

> FIVE-MINUTE RULE: Only supply your fish with as much food as they can consume in about five minutes. One or two such feeds per day is a perfectly adequate rate for most types of fish. Remove all surplus food to prevent it from causing water pollution problems.

thus catering for the feeding habits of a wide variety of fish.

Freeze-dried Diets: These contain very little moisture, but retain their high nutritional value. Consisting of insect larvae/pupae, crustaceans, worms or other small creatures, these foods come either loose for sprinkling on the water surface, or in small compressed blocks for sticking onto the sides of the aquarium.

Deep-frozen Diets: These predominantly animal-based foods are usually gamma-irradiated to render them disease-free and they come in a wide range of single-component and multiple-component formulations, some including vegetable matter. Deep-frozen foods must be kept in a freezer at all times.

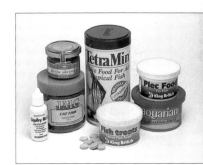

A variety of foods.

Livefoods: These come in all sizes, from microscopic rotifers (which can be cultured from a starter kit) and newly hatched brine shrimp to larger invertebrates, such as bloodworm, waterfleas, adult brine shrimp and others. Some types are best examined before feeding to ensure that no stray predators have been harvested along with the food. Tubifex worms should also be rinsed thoroughly beforehand to minimize the risk of introducing pathogenic (disease-causing) micro-organisms. Although, strictly speaking, liquid formulations are not livefoods, they are mentioned here because they are primarily designed to encourage the growth of micro-organisms (collectively referred to as 'infusoria'), which are particularly useful when attempting to feed egglayer fry during their first days of life.

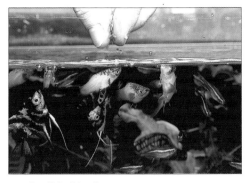

Feeding flaked food.

AQUARIUM MAINTENANCE

ONCE AN aquarium is fully stocked and has settled down, regular maintenance will be required to keep it in a healthy state. Some aspects of routine care consist of daily jobs, like feeding the fish, while others need only be carried out on an occasional basis. The important consideration, though, is not to neglect any single aspect of the routine care programme since, if you do so, remedial steps will probably have to be taken sooner or later.

Often, when such action becomes necessary, putting things right can result in such a significant and abrupt change in conditions that the fish will suffer, simply because they are being 'asked' to make metabolic adjustments that they cannot cope with. It is far better, therefore, to keep conditions finely tuned at all times. The guidelines that follow have been prepared precisely with this in mind.

Clean algae from the front glass every two weeks.

DAILY

• Switch the room lights on several minutes before switching on the aquarium lights to provide the fish with a gradual 'daybreak'. Alternatively, wait for natural daybreak and then switch on the aquarium lights.

• Check on the state of health of all the fish. If any fish show signs of illness, remove them to a separate hospital tank for treatment if whole-tank treatment is not feasible.

• Check the water temperature and adjust it if necessary.

• Feed the fish in the morning and, if necessary, again in the evening. Nocturnal fish should be offered food only a short while before lights out, or immediately after.

• Check for signs of spawning or birth and remove courting pairs or fry to separate quarters.

• Switch off aquarium lights several minutes before the room lights or before natural nightfall.

WEEKLY

• Check the heater-thermostat for signs of faults, such as leakages, and replace immediately if something is amiss.

• Check the pH, hardness, ammonia and nitrite levels of the water and adjust if necessary. If altering any of the parameters, do so gradually; usually, it is not the

Gravel cleaners are very useful for removing debris.

magnitude of a change that causes problems, but the abruptness with which it is carried out.

● Check your food and medication reserves and replenish if necessary.

● If desired, allow the fish to fast for one day per week, except in the case of growing fish or those being conditioned for breeding.

EVERY TWO WEEKS

● Switch off the aeration or power filtration. Rake or otherwise gently disturb the surface layer of the substratum (gravel cleaners are excellent for this).

● Scrape encrusting algae from the front glass of the aquarium.

● Wait for the debris to settle and siphon it off along with 20–25 percent of the aquarium water.

● Replace this with freshwater adjusted, if necessary, to meet the chemistry of the aquarium water. Try and match the temperature as closely as possible as well, and add a dechlorinator/dechloraminator and water conditioner if required.

● Switch on the aerator or power filtration.

N.B. If the partial water change is being carried out first thing in the morning, allow the tapwater to run for several minutes before drawing off what you require for the aquarium, thus eliminating the risk of introducing toxic chemicals, such as copper, from water standing in your household pipes.

Remove excess plants, dying or dead leaves and replace poor plants with new healthy specimens.

EVERY THREE/FOUR WEEKS

● Switch off the aeration or power filtration and rinse all non-biological media under a running tap, or replace them if necessary. Ideally, biological media should be rinsed in aquarium water so as not to destroy their cultures of beneficial bacteria and other helpful micro-organisms. **Under no circumstances must detergents be used – they are highly toxic**.

Wait for debris to settle and syphon it off together with 20-25% of the aquarium water.

● If an undergravel filter has been installed, remove the air line and clean the top of the airlift.

● Insert a siphon tube down the airlift until you reach gravel level and siphon out a small amount of the debris from under the filter plates.

● Clean all diffuser stones.

● Clean the condensation tray or glass aquarium cover.

● Check all other equipment, for instance, aerator, diaphragm, non-return valve, lights and fittings, etc.

● Remove dead leaves from plants, prune plants if necessary and replace poor or dead/dying specimens.

● Top up the aquarium if necessary.

FISH HEALTH

THE OLD adage 'Look after the water, and the water will look after your fish' resurfaces in connection with the broader subject of overall fish health. Like every saying or rule of thumb, this one applies most of the time but, predictably, there are situations where it will not (in fact, cannot) work.

For example, if you install an exceptionally efficient water-management system and back it up with a good water quality monitoring and maintenance programme, it may well be possible for you to stock your aquarium beyond recommended levels without deterioration in water conditions. However, this does not necessarily mean that your fish will remain healthy. Keeping fish in unnatural combinations, or in excessive numbers in a confined space like an aquarium, brings a number of factors (such as heightened aggression and competition) into play, some of which are likely to result in health problems.

This is another example of the pitfalls of making unreasonable demands of a particular set of conditions. Being unable to cope with these demands, the system will, sooner or later, begin to break down with distressing consequences for the health of the fish. It is therefore essential to maintain a balance between the fish, their environment and the inevitable pathogens (disease-causing agents) that are present if the water is going to stand a realistic chance of 'looking after our fish'.

PREVENTION IS BETTER THAN CURE

Without a doubt, preventive measures are preferable to remedial ones. You can safeguard fish against threats to their health by ensuring that appropriate stocking levels are adhered to, that only compatible species (and sexes) are kept together, and that an appropriate feeding and maintenance programme is established and followed on a long-term basis.

An additional step that is strongly recommended is the setting up of a separate acclimatization (usually referred to as quarantine) or hospital tank. This tank need not be as large as your show aquarium and does not need to be as expensively or extensively furnished. It must, however, be able to provide for all the needs of the fish.

When you buy your very first fish, your show tank acts as an acclimatization tank as well. However, once things have settled down and you have established a healthy community of fish, any new additions bring with them the risk, however small, of introducing disease.

White spot on a Harlequin fish.

Trichopsis vittatus (Croaking Gourami) with velvet disease.

By far the best way of eliminating this risk is by keeping all new fish for a while in a separate acclimatization tank where they can be monitored and remedial action taken if necessary. If, after about a week or two, there are no signs of disease, then gently transfer the fish into their permanent home, following the guidelines outlined earlier. If, however, even one new fish goes down with a disease, don't transfer any fish – however healthy they may look – until the problem has been resolved.

Acclimatization/hospital tanks are also especially valuable when a fish is suffering from a disease that warrants individual, rather than whole-tank, treatment. Once such treatment has been completed, the tank should be cleaned out, sterilized (with an aquarium disinfectant) and set up once more with all systems running.

If you think that it is too much trouble to set up and maintain an acclimatization/ hospital tank, it might help you to know that the vast majority of experienced aquarists, retailers, wholesalers and importers all have some way of reducing disease-transfer risks, having learned long ago that such risks are just not worth taking.

APPROACHES TO HEALTH CONTROL

If fish are kept in a healthy, stress-free environment and are fed properly, they will, as a rule, not succumb to disease. Therefore, at the first sign of trouble, check that nothing has changed in this environment. Sudden fluctuations in temperature, pH, levels of toxic wastes and other parameters can all have an adverse effect on a fish's health. Consequently, merely correcting the imbalance will often solve the problem.

Female Dwarf Gourami showing typical signs of terminal fin rot.

However, despite one's best efforts, some fish will, from time to time, suffer ill health. In many such cases, only one, or a few, fish in a whole community will be affected, indicating that, for some reason, these individuals are more susceptible to the pathogens in question than their tankmates. Anything from age to post-natal debility can prove a deciding factor, so, before happily pouring medications into the tank, try to isolate the underlying cause.

Red Eye Tetra with eye infection.

Treating symptoms will often be highly effective – at treating symptoms. However, unless the underlying cause of the problem is identified and corrected, it is likely to return, often with a vengeance. Fungus, for example, tends to affect fish that are already weakened in some way, perhaps as a result of injury or spawning stress, while white spot often affects fish that have been subjected to a sudden drop in temperature.

DISEASE DIAGNOSIS AND TREATMENT

It is quite unreasonable to expect a new aquarist to be able to handle any health crisis that may arise without some form of assistance. This can come from various sources, including experienced aquarists, staff at your local aquatic outlet, books and articles dedicated exclusively to fish health matters and – to a welcome and ever-increasing degree – vets who specialize in fish pathology. If in any doubt whatsoever, seek advice before you treat your fish or aquarium.

Fortunately, the most common fish diseases are easily diagnosed and the majority can be effectively treated with today's excellent proprietary preparations. The summaries that follow refer to just these most commonly encountered and (with the exception of bacterial diseases) easily treated diseases. Therefore, if your fish succumb to any of these, visit your local shop and obtain a bottle of the appropriate treatment, making sure that you closely follow instructions regarding its administration.

In addition to the 'environmental' diseases to which I referred earlier, fish diseases arise from a few major sources: parasites, fungi and bacteria.

Staff at your local aquatic outlet will be pleased to advise you on disease remedies.

Fungus infection on Corydorus rabauti.

White Spot or Ich: This disease is caused by *Ichthyophthirius multifiliis*, a protozoan (single-celled organism) which causes tiny white spots on the body and fins of the affected fish. These cause irritation, resulting in repeated scratching against the gravel, rock or furnishings which, in turn, can lead to injury and further secondary problems.

Slime Disease: There are three main protozoans (*Ichthyobodo, Trichodina, Chilodonella*) which can produce similar symptoms consisting of excessive mucus production (slimy skin), bluish-white coloration of the skin, awkward swimming movements, scratching, etc.

Gill Fluke Infection: Caused by parasitic worms (*Dactylogyrus spp*), this disease results in inflamed gills which produce excessive mucus, accelerated breathing movements and scratching of the gill covers.

Skin Fluke Infection: *Gyrodactylus spp* worms (related to *Dactylogyrus*) produce inflamed patches on the skin accompanied by excessive mucus secretion, some loss of body colour and scratching against objects.

Anchor Worm: Despite its name, the parasites, *Lernaea spp* are actually crustaceans. They cause nervous, jumping swimming movements, scratching and some loss of colour (in heavy infestations). The slim whitish parasites are clearly visible.

Velvet Disease: Regarded as dinoflagellate algae in some books, *Piscinoodinium* species cause a fine 'dusting' of tiny whitish or rust-coloured spots on the body and fins of affected fish, which can show gasping and scratching behaviour, as well as inflamed tissues.

Fungus or Cottonwool Disease: The usual causative agent is a fungus of the genus *Saprolegnia*. The symptoms usually appear on damaged tissue in the form of white or cream-coloured fluffy patches.

Mouth Fungus: Despite its name, this disease is caused by a bacterium, *Flexibacter columnaris*, which causes whitish growths around the mouth. In severe cases, the surrounding tissues can be eaten away, giving rise to further problems.

Other Bacterial Infections: Visible (variously) as ulcers, blood streaks in fins, loss of scales, sluggish behaviour, loss of colour or swollen body with 'pine cone' appearance (dropsy), such infections are only treatable (and not with guaranteed success) with antibiotics which, in many countries, are only available on prescription.

BREEDING FISH

IF THERE'S one thing, above all else, that separates living things from non-living ones, it is that living things reproduce. How each species goes about achieving this is one of the many great fascinations of Nature. As aquarists, we are privileged in that we can observe an amazingly wide variety of approaches to tackling this most basic of biological needs, even in modestly sized set-ups.

Fish either lay eggs or give birth to fully formed young (fry). The former are referred to as egglayers and the latter as livebearers. In egglayers, both eggs and sperm are released into the water and fertilization is therefore external. In livebearers, fertilization takes place internally and the eggs and developing embryos are retained inside the body of the female until the moment of birth.

There are some very interesting exceptions to this general 'rule' in which the eggs are fertilized internally and then released by the female prior to birth, but very few of these fish are ever encountered in the aquarium hobby, a notable exception being the Medaka, *Oryzias latipes*, which is profiled in the Miscellaneous Species section towards the end of this book.

EGGLAYERS

Although external fertilization is a characteristic of egglaying species, there are different ways in which this occurs, and what subsequently happens to the eggs and/or new-born young. Despite these differences, though, the ultimate biological objective is to provide the species with the best possible chance of ensuring its survival from one generation to the next.

Egg Scatterers: In egg-scattering aquarium species, which include most of the cyprinids, characins, rainbows and some killifish, pairs or shoals of mating fish simply scatter their eggs and sperm, either among fine-leaved vegetation, or along the bottom. In the wild, many egg-scattering species, especially

marine ones, also release their eggs and sperm in midwater, from where they float to the surface and are swept away by currents. The resulting fry then spend a shorter or longer period as part of the plankton.

Egg-scattering species which actively seek out fine-leaved vegetation in which to release their sticky eggs (like rainbows, some killies and many characins), are sometimes also referred to as egg depositors.

Egg Hiders and Buriers: Rather than simply scattering eggs and sperm and leaving their survival entirely up to chance, some species hide their eggs before abandoning them. This, clearly, gives each egg slightly better odds of surviving, and this is generally reflected in the smaller numbers of eggs laid by egg hiders/buriers compared to egg scatterers.

The most popular hiding place for eggs is the substratum itself, but other, more unusual, sites can also be chosen, such as the mantle cavity of freshwater mussels favoured by species of Bitterling, for example, *Rhodeus spp*. Among the egg buriers, the annual killifish which die when their ponds dry up in summer, are the best-known representatives.

Substrate Spawners: This reproductive strategy is common among cichlids, although it is not restricted to them. Typically, eggs are deposited on a surface, which can be an underwater log, the top or underside of a leaf, a flat or rounded stone, a depression in the substratum, a

Close up of Dwarf Gourami (Colisa lalia) nest. Photo © John Dawes.

Dwarf Gourami (Colisa lalia) with bubble nest.

cave, the inside of an empty snail shell, or any other suitable surface. In a few cases, like the Splashing Tetras (*Copella spp*), eggs can even be laid out of the water on the surface of overhanging leaves.

A characteristic feature of substrate spawners is parental care of both the eggs and fry. This increased level of protection, obviously, improves the chances of survival of each individual offspring which, in turn, makes it possible for these species to lay fewer, but larger, eggs. This results in new-born fry that may be more fully developed than those of egg-scattering species.

Nest Builders: Substrate spawners which actually dig a depression or excavate a tunnel or burrow in which to lay their eggs, can, equally justifiably, be regarded as nest builders, although they do not actually incorporate any materials into their nests.

Among aquarium fish, the most common type of nest consists of mucus-covered air bubbles, with or without incorporated vegetation. Such nests are built on the water surface, or under a broad leaf or other underwater structure which will trap the air. Eggs are either laid among the bubbles, or are released below them and

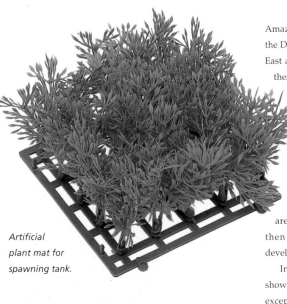

Artificial plant mat for spawning tank.

allowed to float up, or they are retrieved by one or both parents and deposited among the bubbles.

The best known nest builders are the gouramis and fighters, plus some catfish. Parental care of the eggs and fry is common in such species.

Mouth Brooders: If parental care is intensified even more, for example by one parent incubating the fertilized eggs in its mouth, the number of young produced in each brood can be significantly reduced, because those that are produced can be given an excellent headstart in life.

In most mouth brooders, protection extends beyond incubation and can last for several weeks following hatching. During this time, the fry are never far from their parent and, at the first sign of an external threat, they dive back into their parent's mouth where they are safe and can be quickly removed from the danger zone.

Mouth brooding is common among species of cichlid that inhabit the great African Rift lakes, in which the female is the brooding parent. In some other mouth brooders, like the Arowanas of the Amazon (*Osteoglossum bicirrhosum* and *O. ferreirai*) and the Dragon Fish and Saratogas (*Scleropages spp*) of the Far East and Australian regions, it is the male who takes on these parental duties.

LIVEBEARERS

In livebearing species, fertilization takes place internally, after which embryonic development proceeds along one of two main routes. The eggs either remain within their sacs (egg follicles) embedded in the surrounding ovarian tissue until embryonic development is complete, or else they are ejected into the mother's ovarian cavity (which then acts as a sort of womb) to complete their development bathed in nutrient-laden secretions.

In the former case, developing embryos generally show no weight increase at all, although there are a few exceptions. In fact, in many species, embryos actually experience weight loss between egg fertilization and birth. This type of incubation – referred to as ovoviviparity – is typical of the Poeciliids, the family to which all the most popular livebearers belong.

In the Goodeids and a few other types of livebearers, embryos can experience considerable weight gain during development as a result of their being surrounded by nutrients. This reproductive strategy in which the mother makes a substantial contribution to the growth of her young, is generally referred to as viviparity.

Livebearer, Brachyraphis sp. giving birth. Photo © Dennis Barrett.

Goodeid livebearer, Girardinichthys viviparus giving birth. Photo © Dennis Barrett.

Another difference between these two methods of livebearing is that, in ovoviviparous species, females can usually store sperm from a single mating and use them to fertilize a sequence of egg batches as they ripen. Therefore, once mated, such females can produce a number of broods without needing to mate again. In Goodeids, this is not possible, so each brood is the result of a separate mating.

AQUARIUM BREEDING

One of the many delights of aquarium keeping is being able to get our fish to breed. With the popular livebearers like guppies, swordtails, platies and mollies, this is very easy. In fact, we do not need to do anything at all to encourage these species to reproduce. As long as they are healthy, they will breed. Saving the fry is a different matter altogether, though, and very few – if any – are likely to survive for long in a community aquarium.

When it comes to egglayers, some of the hardier types will also attempt to breed in a community aquarium. However, if it is difficult to get livebearer fry to survive in such an environment, it is virtually impossible to achieve this with egglayers.

To raise any fry to adulthood, it is essential to provide adequate conditions, not just for them, but for the parents as well. There are many ways of doing this and most involve the setting up of a separate aquarium specifically for breeding purposes, taking into consideration the characteristics of the species in question as outlined in the individual species entries.

In the case of livebearers, breeding traps provide an alternative solution, which, while not being ideal, nevertheless offers a possible way of increasing stocks without needing to set up a separate aquarium. Breeding traps, which can be floated inside the aquarium, allow a female to be separated from her tankmates while she gives birth. Being double-chambered, with a slit or small holes separating the two chambers, they also provide an escape route for the fry, which may otherwise be eaten by their mother.

Once the female has finished giving birth, she can be returned to the main aquarium and the fry can then be kept in the trap until they are large enough to be released safely into the aquarium to fend for themselves.

Whatever approach you decide on if you wish to breed your fish, prepare thoroughly in advance. Failure to do so will, undoubtedly, result in disappointment, while adequate preparation will bring an added, educational dimension to your enjoyment of the hobby which is particularly fulfilling.

AQUARIUM PLANTS

PLANTS PERFORM many different functions in an aquarium, ranging from the purely aesthetic (important to us, as aquarists, but totally irrelevant to our fish), to the more 'useful', such as absorbing excess nitrates from the water, helping create balanced conditions, offering fish (both adults and young) shelter and providing suitable spawning sites.

CHOICES

Some of these functions, especially those that do not involve any biological processes, can be equally well performed by true 'aquatic' species, or by 'aquarium' species, or by artificial types. Those in which biological processes are involved (such as photosynthesis – see section on Aeration) can only be performed – at least in aquaria – by genuinely aquatic species.

Note that I am using two similar terms: 'aquatic' and 'aquarium'. The difference between them lies in that 'aquatic' plants – as their name suggests – have evolved to live and reproduce in water, while the term 'aquarium' plants can also be applied to marsh or even terrestrial plants which will either not grow or – if they do – will not reproduce if kept permanently submerged. There are many such plants available today and, although they are not true aquatics, they will, nevertheless, survive underwater for a shorter or longer period, during which they offer numerous decorative possibilities.

There are exceptions, as in virtually everything else, and some types, like the various Amazon Swords (*Echinodorus spp*), will grow permanently submerged or as marsh plants. Either way, when they are about to bloom, the flowering shoots project well above the water surface.

None of this applies to artificial plants, of course, and, while they do not serve any biological purpose, they do perform other useful roles. There is such a diversity of colours, sizes and models available these days that, with a little care and creativity, it is perfectly possible to create an instant aquascape of great beauty that is difficult to distinguish from a natural one without close examination. And if your preference is for a totally unnatural-looking aquascape made up of gaudily and cheerfully coloured vegetation, that, too, can be created

Praecox Rainbowfishes with artificial plants.

Egeria densa.

Bacopa sp.

Java fern.

Anubias lanceolata.

with artificial plants. There are other advantages as well – for example, artificial plants do not die and can be easily cleaned if and when they develop algal growth.

If you like the idea of growing natural plants, but also happen to like some of the artificial equivalents on offer, there is no rule that dictates that you must opt exclusively for one or the other. A 'mix-and-match' approach can produce spectacular results, with artificial and natural plants blending excellently with each other.

BUYING PLANTS

Plants are offered for sale in a variety of forms: unrooted single or bunched plants; rooted (but unplanted) specimens; rooted (potted) specimens; tubers, rhizomes or bulbs; portions (floating plants); or, more recently, plants which are rooted or attached to bogwood or rocks.

What you eventually select is a matter of personal choice, but give every type consideration. Some (the unrooted single or bunched plants) may be less expensive than most of the others, thus giving you the opportunity to buy more plants in one go than is otherwise possible. On the other hand, a good specimen that has already attached itself to a nice piece of bogwood may be more expensive, but it will also

constitute a much more impressive centrepiece.

Also important is the choice of 'aquatic' versus 'aquarium' plants mentioned earlier. If buying terrestrial 'aquarium' plants such as Dumb Cane (*Dieffenbachia*) or Spider Plants (*Chlorophytum*), keep a close watch on them and remove leaves as they begin to die, discarding the whole plant before it completely rots away in due course.

Some of the more aquatic types that can also grow in moist soil, like Amazon Swords (*Echinodorus spp*), Water Wisteria (*Hygrophila difformis*) and others, are often commercially cultivated under marsh conditions. Such plants will have stiff erect stems and/or leaves which are likely to die once they are fully submerged. This is quite a natural reaction, so don't despair. Given a little time, many such plants will begin to put out new underwater growth and develop into perfectly good specimens.

Plants which originate from bulbs, such as the Onion Plant (*Crinum thaianum*), tubers and rhizomes, such as Anubias (*Anubias spp*) and some *Aponogeton* species, are usually sold at least partially grown. They are either available unpotted, potted or, as is often the case in Anubias species, attached to a piece of bogwood or rock.

In recent years, plants grown in carefully controlled environments using the latest tissue-culture techniques, have been appearing in ever greater numbers. Such

Riccia fluitans (floating).

Salvinia auriculata (floating).

Myriophyllum sp.

SOME FLOATING PLANTS FOR THE TROPICAL FRESHWATER AQUARIUM

Common Name (Scientific Name)	Recommended Lighting	Recommended Water Conditions	Notes
Fairy Moss (Azolla caroliniana)	High	Medium hard	Fast-spreading. It is a fern, not a moss
Indian Fern (Ceratopteris spp)	High	Soft–Medium	Will also grow as a submerged rooted plant
Salvinia (Salvinia spp)	High	Medium hard	Another fern. Several species available
Crystalwort/Riccia (Riccia fluitans)	High	Medium hard	A liverwort that forms a thick mat
Water Lettuce/Nile Cabbage (Pistia stratiotes)	High	Not critical	Not suitable for small aquaria
Duckweed (Lemna spp)	High	Not critical	Fast-spreading. Often introduced accidentally, i.e., with other plants

plants are usually of very high quality and, while they may cost a little more than other types – not just because of the production methods, but also because of the species and varieties chosen – they offer us yet another possibility when it comes to planning our aquascapes.

GROWING AQUARIUM PLANTS

Successful cultivation of aquatic plants is not merely a question of pushing the roots into the substratum and hoping for the best. Light, pH, hardness, availability of nutrients and other factors all play a part. Despite this, plants with differing requirements can often be grown successfully in the same aquarium.

For example, if a plant possesses vigorous roots, which indicate that it uses these as a means of absorbing at least part of its food requirements, then inserting a fertilizer tablet or block close to such a plant will help it along. Equally, if a plant requires subdued light or partial shade, growing it close to a light-loving plant whose leaves extend over the surface, will provide it with acceptable conditions.

Adding fertilizers to the aquarium water (but only in the quantities prescribed by the manufacturers), supplying a continuous, but small, dose of carbon dioxide during the day (using a carbon dioxide diffuser)

and selecting light sources carefully, will all help plants obtain what they require for long-term health. Even without such assistance, though, some degree of success can be achieved. The accompanying table includes some of the best-known aquatic plants that are widely available, with an indication of their main requirements.

Artificial plants (above) can look very effective, especially when mixed with real plants.

SOME SUBMERGED/OXYGENATING PLANTS FOR THE TROPICAL FRESHWATER AQUARIUM

Common Name (Scientific Name)	Recommended Lighting	Recommended Water Conditions	Notes
Cabomba (Cabomba spp)	High	Soft	Several species, some bronze-red in colour. Fine-leaved
Milfoil (Myriophyllum spp)	High	Soft-Medium	Similar to Cabomba
Hornwort (Ceratophyllum spp)	High	Not critical	Two species: both rootless and fine-leaved
Argentine Water Weed/ Densa/Giant Elodea (Egeria densa)	High	Not critical	Vigorous grower. Two other similar species; Elodea canadensis and Lagarosiphon major
Indian Water Star (Hygrophila polysperma)	High	Not critical	Attractive stemmed and leaved plant. Easy to keep
Water Wisteria (Hygrophila difformis)	High	Not critical	Notched leaves. Attractive. Will not grow well if light is low
Ludwigia (Ludwigia spp)	High	Not critical	Some species have differently coloured top/underside of leaves
Bacopa (Bacopa spp)	Moderate–High	Not critical	Several species available. Some have fine hairs. Leaves usually with rounded tips
Vallis/Tape Grass (Vallisneria spiralis)	High	Not critical	Fast-spreading, grass-like plant. Crowns must not be buried. Twisted-Vallis ('Torta') may be a variety, rather than a separate species
Onion Plant (Crinum thaianum)	Not critical	Not critical	Bulb should be left half-exposed. Not suitable for small aquaria
Java Moss (Vesicularia dubyana)	Not critical	Not critical	Delicate-looking, but tough plant. May be sold attached to rocks/ bogwood
Java Fern (Microsorum pteropus)	Low–Moderate	Not critical	Some beautiful varieties available. May be sold attached to rocks/ bogwood
Anubias (Anubias spp)	Low–Moderate	Not critical	Several species available. May be sold attached to rocks/bogwood
Cryptos (Cryptocoryne spp)	Moderate	Not critical	Slow to establish, but magnificent when they do! Numerous species available
Amazon Sword (Echinodorus spp)	Moderate–High	Not critical	Many species (and some tissue-cultured varieties) available. First leaves may die – new ones will follow
Aponogetons (Aponogeton spp)	Moderate–High	Soft	Several species available. May show seasonal cessation of growth, followed by a 'rest' period

INTRODUCTION TO FISH SPECIES

THE PAGES that follow feature a large selection of freshwater tropical fish which we are likely to encounter in aquatic centres on a more or less regular basis. It includes all the popular 'easy' types, but also many which are considerably more challenging or unusual.

No selection of species and varieties can ever be complete, especially when there are over 2,000 kinds of fish to choose from. This particular selection is no exception. What I have tried to do is provide a representatively large sample aimed at meeting most new hobbyists' needs, with numerous 'added extras' to allow for flexibility of choice. Hopefully, established aquarists will also find value and interest in the range of species that I have chosen.

In determining what to include and what to leave out, I have had to make some difficult decisions, particularly in excluding species which, for one reason or other, require very specific aquaria or conditions. As a result, some of the larger catfishes, snakeheads, cichlids and other types, which are often available in shops, are not featured here. Similarly, where a genus contains numerous species, I have selected either one, or a few, representative examples, thus creating space for a wider overall choice.

Colisa lalia (Dwarf Gourami). See page 164.

CLASSIFYING FISH

Biologically, fish are classified into 'groups', depending on their degree of similarity. For instance, two types which are very similar to each other, such as the Dwarf Gourami and the Thick-lipped Gourami, are regarded as distinct, but closely related, **species**.

Along with two other species, the Honey Gourami and the Indian/Striped/Giant Gourami, they are deemed to form a group of closely related species which are distinct from other groups. Such groups of closely related species are referred to as **genera** (singular: **genus**).

As we move up and the similarities become more generalised, genera are grouped into **families**, families into **orders**, orders into **classes** and classes into **phyla** (singular: **phylum**). Finer divisions like **subfamilies**, **suborders**, **superorders**, etc., result in a hierarchical system that allows us to place any fish, or other living organism, for that matter, in a 'biological slot' dictated by strict international rules that help us make sense of a potentially chaotic situation.

NAMING FISH

Taking the Dwarf Gourami as an example, its **species** carries the name *lalia* (note that the species name is written in italics and in lower case). This species belongs to the **genus** *Colisa* (note that the generic name is also written in italics, but in upper and lower cases).

All the various *Colisa* species, along with their relations, the *Trichogaster* Gouramis, belong to the **subfamily**

Male Poecilia reticulata (Snakeskin Guppy). See page 240.

the Bony Fishes belong to the **superclass** Gnathostomata (Animals with Jaws) which, with many others, are part of the **subphylum** Vertebrata (Animals with Backbones) that, ultimately, constitute the **phylum** Chordata, the Chordates or Animals possessing a Notochord at some stage of their lives (this is later replaced by the spinal column in vertebrates), plus a hollow nerve cord.

Trichogasterinae (note: no italics) of the **family** Belontiidae which, in turn, belongs to the **suborder** Anabantoidei, known as the Anabantoids or Labyrinthfishes of the **order** Perciformes, the Perch-like Fishes.

As we move up, some leading ichthyologists differ regarding the actual categories. According to one of the more widely accepted classifications, the Perciformes form part of the **superorder** Teleostei, the so-called True Bony Fishes (as distinct from the Cartilaginous Fishes that include the true sharks and rays). Further. up the hierarchy, the True Bony Fishes, along with other superorders, belong to the **subclass** Actinopterygii, the Ray-finned Fishes, of the **class** Teleostomi (or Osteichthyes), the Bony Fishes. Still further up the chain,

From the aquarium hobby point of view, most of our needs are met by the bottom end of the classification hierarchy, from family level, down to species level.

One other aspect of the scientific nomenclature of fish that needs to be mentioned is the inclusion of a person's name and a date after the name of the fish. The name refers to the person who first described the fish (the author) and the date represents the year in which this was done.

If the person's name appears in brackets, it signifies that, while the fish was first described by that person, the name has been changed at some subsequent stage. In our example of the Dwarf Gourami, its full scientific 'label' is *Colisa lalia* (HAMILTON, 1822). For simplicity's sake, though, the author's name and the date are often omitted

Finally, in 'aquarium terms', fish are generally divided into **Egglayers** and **Livebearers**, depending on whether they lay eggs or give birth to fully formed young (see section on **Breeding** for fuller details).

In the pages that follow, I have adopted the Egglayer/Livebearer grouping and have omitted the author's name and date of original description, thus, hopefully, making the contents more easily accessible.

Paracheirodon axelrodi (Cardinal Tetras). See page 93.

CYPRINIDS

T HE FAMILY Cyprinidae is the largest of the fish
families, the members of which occur exclusively in
freshwater. With around 210 genera, incorporating some
2,010 species, it is also – with the possible exception of
the goby family (Gobiidae), which has freshwater,
brackish and marine representatives – the largest family
of vertebrates (backboned animals).

There are, in fact, so many and varied species
currently listed as cyprinids that some authorities believe
the family to be artificially large. As a result, there is
considerable debate regarding the subject, with
differences of opinion extending down to subfamily and
even generic levels. The classification followed here is
that which appears in Joseph S. Nelson's important
work, *Fishes of the World.**

In the pages that follow, representatives of two of the
seven subfamilies are featured: the Cyprininae and the
Rasborinae.

The Cyprininae contains around 700 species, most of
which possess mouth whiskers called barbels. Included
in this large subfamily are the barbs (*Barbus*), sharks and
foxes (*Labeo, Balantiocheilos* and *Epalzeorhynchus*), as well
as two old favourites of the coldwater hobby, the
Goldfish (*Carassius auratus*) and Koi (*Cyprinus carpio*).

In the Rasborinae (which is also frequently referred to
as the Danioninae), we find other popular aquarium fish,
such as the rasboras (*Rasbora*), the danios (*Brachydanio*

Barbus conchonius one of 700 Cyprininae species..

and *Danio*) and the White Cloud Mountain Minnow
(*Tanichthys albonubes*).

Despite the many differences that exist between the
various subfamilies of Cyprinidae, they all share several
important characteristics. They all, for example, possess
toothless jaws, although they do have grinding teeth
further back in the throat area (pharyngeal teeth). They
also possess a bony linkage (the Weberian apparatus)
between the double-chambered swim-bladder and the
inner ear which affords them excellent hearing ability.

In addition, the head region is, almost always,
scaleless, the dorsal (back) fin is single and there is no
adipose fin (a small rayless vestigial fin found behind the
dorsal in characins, for example).

*Nelson, Joseph S.
Fishes of the World, (3rd
edition) published by
John Wiley & Sons, Inc.
(1994), ISBN: 0-471
54713-1.

*Ruby Shark
(Epalzeorhynchus
frenatus).*

Balantiocheilos (Balantiocheilus) melanopterus
(Bala, Tri-colour, Malaysian or Silver Shark)

THIS ELEGANT cyprinid is, of course, not a true shark in any sense of the word. It merely bears a superficial (very superficial, some would say) physical resemblance to sharks. In every other sense, it could not be more different.

For a start, *Balantiocheilos melanopterus* is not a predatory fish, although it will eat smallish livefoods like *Tubifex* worms and waterfleas (*Daphnia*). In fact, among its many favourite foods are tender, juicy plant shoots, plus a whole host of other items, which makes it an omnivorous, rather than a carnivorous, species.

Bala Sharks are also, despite their relatively large size (see below), generally peaceful towards other species – although they are highly active – and can be kept with smaller fish. Ideally, this species should be kept in shoals, but, in practice, most home aquaria can only house a small shoal of juveniles.

At one time, all the Bala Sharks offered for sale were wild-caught, but concern for the continued survival of wild populations led to the setting up of commercial breeding programmes. Today, the aquarium trade in this species – consisting largely of beautifully marked specimens measuring 10cm (4in) or less – is based, almost entirely, on cultured fish from the Far East.

Natural Range: This is a southeast Asian species which is found in Borneo (Kalimantan), Sumatra, Thailand and peninsular Malaysia.

Size: Up to around 35cm (14in) in the wild, but usually considerably smaller than this in aquaria.

Food: Wide range of commercial dry, freeze-dried, deep-frozen and livefoods accepted; a regular vegetable dietary component is also recommended. Some specimens may show a distinct preference for livefoods.

Tank Conditions: A roomy tank with open swimming spaces should be provided, as well as a close-fitting cover (these fish are excellent jumpers). Water chemistry is not critical, but softish conditions with a pH around 6.5–7 are recommended.

Temperature: 22–28°C (72–82°F), with the middle of this range perhaps being most appropriate.

Breeding: Unknown in home aquaria, but this species is extensively cultured in commercial quantities in Far Eastern farms.

Balantiocheilos melanopterus (Bala Shark) is an elegant cyprinid that should ideally be kept in shoals.

Barbus conchonius
(Rosy Barb)

THE ROSY Barb (*Barbus conchonius*) is a popular aquarium species which has been extensively bred in fish farms in all the major fish-producing areas of the world. These commercial varieties, which account for the vast majority of the stocks available to followers of the hobby, often show intensified or modified colours and/or extended finnage when compared to the original wild type. Irrespective of the intensity of these modifications, males are invariably more colourful than females.

Coming from the northern regions of the Indian subcontinent, the Rosy Barb is tolerant of lower temperatures than many other aquarium species, particularly during the winter months. Some of this temperature tolerance is exhibited even by the longer-finned varieties, but it would seem sensible to avoid subjecting such fish to a prolonged low-temperature season. In any case, Rosy Barbs do perfectly well at normal tropical temperatures if the extreme upper range is avoided.

Natural Range: Northern India; Bengal; Assam.
Size: Reported to grow up to 15cm (6in) but aquarium specimens are considerably smaller than this.
Food: All commercial foods are accepted; livefoods are particularly favoured.

Tank Conditions: Thickly vegetated corners and ample swimming space should be provided. Although the composition of the water is not too critical (provided it is clean and toxin-free), soft, slightly acid conditions are recommended, particularly for breeding purposes.

Temperature: As low as 15°C (59°F) during winter (but possibly best avoided where long-finned varieties are concerned). At other times, anything from 18–25° (64–77°F) will be adequate (see main text for further details).

Breeding: This is a typical egg-scattering species in which eggs are released among vegetation and over the substratum. The adults are avid egg eaters, so they must be promptly separated from their spawn. Hatching takes about 30 hours and the fry must be fed on the smallest foods (rotifers and/or infusoria) as soon as they become free-swimming, moving on to newly-hatched brine shrimp after a few days.

Above: A pair of Barbus conchonius (Short-finned Rosy Barb). Top right: Rosy Barb, long-finned variety.

Barbus cumingi
(Cuming's Barb)

CUMING'S BARB (*Barbus cumingi*) is a delightful species which generally does well in community aquaria, particularly if kept in a small shoal and in an environment that offers both shaded and open swimming areas.

Although wild stocks are low in the mountain streams of its native Sri Lanka, Cuming's Barb is commercially bred in substantial numbers in several countries. Yet, despite the success of these breeding programmes, no colour or fin modifications appear to have been developed by commercial breeders. Perhaps the superficial similarity of the species with the easily-bred Rosy Barb (*B. conchonius*) and the number of fin and colour forms of the latter that have been developed, may have something to do with the apparent lack of 'fancy' varieties of Cuming's Barb. Whatever the reason, this species is beautiful enough as it is and is deservedly popular among aquarists.

B. cumingi is one of several similar-looking species which have been implicated as possible ancestors of the 'Odessa' Barb (see entry on page 54 for further details of other possible ancestral species).

Natural Range: Mountain streams in Sri Lanka.

Size: Around 5cm (2in).

Food: All commercial and small livefoods accepted.

Tank Conditions: This charming barb looks best in subdued light, but, as this is usually detrimental to plant growth, it is a good idea to arrange the planting so that it provides some shaded areas. There should also be open swimming spaces. Good-quality water with a pH around neutral suits this species well.

Temperature: 22–27°C (72–81°F).

Breeding: This is an egg-scattering species with an appetite for its own eggs. Although not one of the easiest species to breed in aquaria, success can be achieved once a compatible pair has been established (males are slightly slimmer and more colourful than females, especially when in breeding condition). Hatching and rearing: basically as for *B. conchonius*.

Barbus cumingi (Cuming's Barb) does well in community aquaria and is popular among aquarists.

Barbus filamentosus
(Black-Spot/Filament Barb)

T HE BLACK-SPOT BARB (*Barbus filamentosus*) has been known in the hobby for over 40 years and, despite the relatively large size it attains when fully grown, it is still popular today. This is not surprising, since its glistening scales and high level of activity make it a very attractive fish, particularly when a shoal is kept under subdued lighting conditions which show off their scales to optimum effect.

Of the two sexes, the males – with their elongated dorsal fin rays and brighter colours – are more impressive than the females, although they are smaller. When in breeding condition, males develop small white growths (nuptial tubercles) around the mouth and gill plates (operculi). These indicate that such a male is ready to spawn and must, therefore, not be mistaken for signs of disease!

Juvenile *B. filamentosus* look quite different from the adults in that they possess three vertical black bands on their bodies, while mature specimens lack bands but have a black spot near the caudal peduncle (i.e., slightly in front of the tail fin). A further interesting feature about this species is that, unlike other members of the genus *Barbus*, it lacks mouth barbels.

Natural Range: Sri Lanka, south and southwest India.
Size: Up to 15cm (6in), but generally smaller; females are larger than males.
Food: All foods accepted.
Tank Conditions: Being somewhat larger than most other 'aquarium' barbs, this active species needs a roomy tank with plenty of open swimming space and thickly planted areas. It is, therefore, not suitable for small aquaria, except during its juvenile stages. As with *B. cumingi*, subdued lighting is recommended. The water should be soft and slightly acid.
Temperature: 20–24°C (68–75°F), but slightly higher temperatures will also be tolerated, particularly for breeding purposes.
Breeding: Eggs will be scattered among fine-leaved vegetation, following which either the parents or the eggs should be removed to separate quarters. Hatching takes from $1\frac{1}{2}-2$ days, depending on temperature.

The smaller, but more colourful male Barbus filamentosus (Black-Spot Barb) is more impressive than the female.

Barbus nigrofasciatus
(Ruby/Purple-Headed Barb)

THE RUBY BARB (*Barbus nigrofasciatus*) is one of the best-loved and most beautiful of all the barbs. The males, in particular, develop an intense coloration – especially around their head and 'shoulders' – during the breeding season, that is truly amazing. At such times, a shoal of Rubies swimming around in subdued light is hard to beat as the males spar with each other and display in front of the smaller, drabber, but nonetheless, attractive females.

One thing to watch out for when transferring Ruby Barbs between shop and home is that these fish appear to be somewhat highly-strung and can suffer seizures if they are handled roughly or if the introduction procedures are not carried out carefully and in as stress-free a manner as possible. In particular, avoid introducing Ruby Barbs into a brightly lit aquarium containing raw water (see guidelines for fish introductions on page 29 for further details).

This species is always in great demand and is bred in large numbers in many of the fish-producing regions of the world, where careful selection over many generations has led to some beautiful varieties which exhibit intense coloration and/or extended fins.

Natural Range: Sri Lanka.

Size: Around 6cm (2.4in).

Food: All foods accepted, particularly livefoods. Diet should include a vegetable component.

Tank Conditions: This is yet another species of Sri Lankan barb that looks best in subdued light. It is also, like its relatives, an active swimmer that likes vegetated areas with open swimming spaces in between. Soft, slightly acid water is recommended.

Temperature: 22–26°C (72–79°F); slightly higher for breeding.

Breeding: This is another egg-scattering, egg-eating species which spawns among fine-leaved vegetation, usually in the morning. As with many other barbs from the region, hard water appears to impair fertilization of the eggs. Hatching can be expected after about one day, with feeding commencing once the fry become free-swimming several days later.

The colourful Barbus nigrofasciatus (Ruby Barb) is bred in large numbers as it is always in great demand.

Barbus 'odessa'
(Odessa Barb)

A fine Barbus 'odessa' male (Odessa Barb) demonstrating how beautiful this controversial 'species' can be.

EVERYONE WHO sets eyes on this lively barb agrees that, by any standards, it is a beautiful fish. Few people, however, agree on its identity, although most are of the opinion that the Odessa Barb is not a naturally occurring species.

In 1971/72, news broke out that a new barb had been discovered in a fish bazaar in Odessa, Russia. Within a few years, the new 'species' had become popular in the hobby and was being bred in reasonable numbers. Despite this, its true identity remained (and still remains) a mystery. Indeed, the scientific name shown at the top of this page, *Barbus 'odessa'*, is, technically, invalid; it is merely included here for ease of identification.

The fact is that although there are several species of barb which look – to a greater or lesser extent – similar to the Odessa Barb, no Odessas appear to have ever been found in the wild. Inevitably, therefore, this has led to the belief that the Odessa Barb is not a true species at all, but is more likely to have somehow arisen, by accident or design, from one or other of the following potential ancestral candidates: the Ticto Barb (*B. ticto* – regarded by some as a subspecies: *B. ticto ticto*), Stoliczk's Barb (*B. stoliczkanus* – also referred to as *B. ticto stoliczkanus* or *B. stoliczkae*), Cuming's Barb (*B. cumingi*) and/or the Rosy Barb (*B. conchonius*).

Some people believe the Odessa Barb to be a colour variety of either the Ticto Barb or Stoliczk's Barb, while others believe it to be the result of crosses between some of its presumed ancestral species.

Natural Range: Not known in the wild (see main text for details).

Size: About 6cm (2.4in).

Food: All foods accepted.

Tank Conditions: Water chemistry not critical, but a pH value around neutral and softish water suit Odessas well. This is a lively fish which likes vegetated areas and open swimming spaces. Although bright lights do not appear to affect its behaviour, subdued lighting shows off the intense colours of the males particularly well.

Temperature: Wide-ranging, from 21–30°C (70–86°F) with midway between both extremes probably being best.

Breeding: Can be a little erratic, with some pairs breeding with great ease and others with reluctance, if at all. This is a typical egg-scattering, egg-eating fish whose eggs hatch after 1$\frac{1}{2}$ days or so, depending on temperature.

Barbus oligolepis
(Checker/Island Barb)

THE CHECKER or Island Barb (*Barbus oligolepis*) is much prettier than it often seems. This may appear a strange statement to make, but it is absolutely true. The fact is that this species only shows off its best colours when the water in the aquarium is soft and relatively mature.

Achieving the first of these requirements is easy, whether we are talking about home or shop aquaria. However, establishing and maintaining mature water conditions is much more easily achieved in home systems than in shop ones, where tank water (albeit good-quality water) is constantly being topped up to replace the water that is taken out every time a fish is bought and bagged.

As a result, Checker Barb males, which are more colourful than the females, often do not exhibit their most attractive features until they have settled into an established home aquarium. Once they do, though, they are transformed into creatures of great beauty, particularly since healthy males will constantly display to, and spar with, each other – although they will rarely, if ever, become involved in outright violence.

Barbus oligolepis (Checker or Island Barb).

Natural Range: Wide range of waters in Indonesia and Sumatra.

Size: Reported to reach 15cm (6in), but usually considerably smaller than this.

Food: Will accept a wide range of foods, which should include a vegetable component.

Tank Conditions: This species does best in good-quality, soft mature water kept slightly on the acid side of neutral, e.g., pH 6–6.5. Under such conditions, the males show off their colours well. As for most other barbs, the aquarium should have thickly planted areas around the sides, corners and back, with open swimming space along the front.

Temperature: 20–24°C (68–75°F); slightly higher for breeding.

Breeding: Eggs are laid among fine-leaved vegetation, predominantly near the surface of the water. Although this is an egg-scattering/egg-eating species, the scattering involves numerous small batches of eggs (often one at a time). Owing to the 'sparring' tendency of males, it is best to spawn this species in single pairs, rather than as a group. Eggs hatch in $1^{1}/_{2}$–2 days, depending on temperature.

Barbus schwanenfeldi
(Tinfoil Barb)

THE TINFOIL Barb (*Barbus schwanenfeldi*) – also known as the Goldfoil or Schwanenfeld's Barb – is one of the giants of the aquarium hobby.

Given sufficient room, good water quality and an appropriate diet, the small specimens which we usually see offered for sale in shops will, very quickly, attain a size of around 15cm (6in) in a few months. If aquarium conditions (including tank size) are then modified in tune with the fishes' 'expanding' requirements, a full size of around 35cm (14in) can be attained in due course.

However, in order to achieve this, the aquarium in question needs to be considerably larger than most aquarists can normally provide, particularly if the species' requirements are to be fully catered for, including its distinct preference to be kept in a shoal.

The Tinfoil Barb is one of those relatively few 'aquarium' species that retains much of its attraction as it grows. Therefore, large specimens will exhibit a great deal of the colour usually associated with juvenile fish. In addition, golden-bodied and 'redder-than-normal' finned varieties developed by commercial breeders have made this species even more keenly sought after.

Natural Range: Widely distributed in southeast Asia.

Size: At around 35cm (14in), this is the largest of the barbs regularly found in aquaria, where the full size is usually not achieved (see main text for further details).

Food: Wide-ranging diet accepted, but with a distinct preference for soft, succulent vegetation.

Tank Conditions: Plenty of open swimming space surrounded by thickly planted areas consisting of robust types need to be provided. Minimum tank length should be around 1 metre (39in) for this active shoaling species. Tinfoil Barbs are excellent jumpers, so a tight-fitting aquarium cover is essential. Although soft water appears to be preferred and raw water should be avoided, other conditions are not critical.

Temperature: 22–25°C (72–77°F).

Breeding: This egg-scattering species has not yet been bred in home aquaria, although commercial spawnings are frequent.

A shoal of Barbus schwanenfeldi (Tinfoil Barb). Although adults also like to swim in shoals, most home aquaria are too small for this.

Barbus semifasciolatus
(Green/Half-striped/Golden/Schubert's Barb)

*B*ARBUS SEMIFASCIOLATUS is usually found in the hobby in what is presumed to be its golden form: the Golden or Schubert's Barb. These beautiful golden-scaled fish are often referred to as *Barbus schuberti* or *Barbus 'schuberti'* (in single quotes) but these names are, scientifically speaking, invalid, since such labels only apply to true species and not to artificially or commercially produced varieties (see entry for *Barbus 'odessa'* for details of another similar example).

The ancestry of the Golden Barb appears to be more or less agreed, while that of the Odessa Barb is still shrouded in mystery. The reasons for the greater confidence regarding the Golden Barb centre on two main criteria:

• Its close physical resemblance to the wild type *B. semifasciolatus*.

• The ease with which both types interbreed. Although the type which dominates the hobby is the golden one, it is well worth making the effort to track down some true wild type specimens of the species which, in the eyes of many experienced hobbyists, are even more beautiful than the cultured equivalent.

Natural Range: The wild type is found in southeast China. The golden form is not found in the wild.

Size: Up to 10cm (4in), but usually smaller.

Food: All types of food accepted.

Tank Conditions: The corners of the tank should be thickly planted, but the front should provide an ample open swimming area. Unlike some other barbs, *B. semifasciolatus* is comfortable (and looks good) in well illuminated aquaria. The water should be soft and slightly acid, but this is not too critical, as long as raw water is avoided. Good-quality aged water suits this species well.

Temperature: Coming from southeast China, it prefers the lower end of the tropical temperature range: 18–24°C (64–75°F) with slightly higher temperatures for breeding.

Breeding: This is a prolific egg-scatterer with a distinct appetite for its own eggs. Spawning usually occurs in the morning and hatching takes about 1 1/2 days.

Barbus semifasciolatus (Golden Barb) is a prolific egg-scatterer with an unfortunate appetite for its own eggs.

Barbus tetrazona
(Tiger Barb)

THE TIGER or Sumatra Barb (*Barbus tetrazona*) is one of the most popular of all barbs. Over the years, several colour varieties have been developed, and although most of these lack the distinct black vertical bands of the wild type, they still retain most of its behavioural characteristics.

Among these is a tendency towards fin-nipping, particularly when Tiger Barbs are kept, either singly or in very small numbers, in a community aquarium. If kept in a sizeable shoal (as they should), individuals appear to become so engrossed with one another's antics, that they seem to forget their fin-nipping habits to a greater or lesser extent. To be on the safe side, though, it is best to keep Tiger Barbs either in a special tank specifically set up for them, perhaps in the company of a few robust, preferably bottom-dwelling species, or in a community tank stocked with species that do not possess either long flowing fins, e.g., Fancy Guppies (*Poecilia reticulata*), or filamentous fin extensions as found in gouramis.

Of the commercial varieties developed over the years, the most popular are the Green/Moss Tiger Barb and the Albino Tiger Barb. Newer types like the Champagne Tiger Barb are, however, making significant progress as well.

Natural Range: Indonesia, particularly Sumatra; the island of Borneo (including Kalimantan). This species has also been reported from Thailand, but the validity of the claim is in doubt.

Size: Up to around 7cm (2.75in) but generally smaller.

Food: All types of food accepted.

Tank Conditions: Soft, acid water is preferred, particularly for breeding purposes (hard, alkaline conditions generally result in low fertilization rates). The tank should provide ample open swimming areas for this active shoaling species.

Temperature range: 20–26°C (68–79°F), with slightly higher temperatures for breeding purposes.

Breeding: Tiger Barbs are typical egg scatterers with a distinct liking for their eggs. Best results are often obtained by selecting fish which have paired up naturally within the shoal. Hatching takes about 1¹/₂ days.

Above: Barbus tetrazona (Tiger Barb) wild type is one of the most popular barbs. Top: Barbus tetrazona green type.

Barbus titteya
(Cherry Barb)

UNLIKE MOST other barbs, the Cherry Barb (*Barbus titteya*) is not a typical shoaler. Indeed, if a shoal is kept within the same aquarium, individuals tend to create their own space, generally seeking to maintain some distance between one another.

This does not, however, mean that Cherries should be kept as single specimens, but rather that adequate room should be allowed for a few individuals to space themselves out within their own 'comfort zones'.

During breeding, males develop intense red coloration and become particularly active as they display in front of the plumper and less colourful females. These colours are especially brilliant if the surface of the tank has a covering of vegetation that filters out some of the light.

In addition to the wild type, there is also an albino form of this species which is occasionally available.

Natural Range: Sri Lanka.
Size: 5cm (2in).
Food: Most foods accepted; vegetable component should be included.

Tank Conditions: This species tends to be somewhat more timid than most other barbs. Therefore, while still providing an open swimming area, the tank should also contain thickets of vegetation. Soft, slightly acid water is preferred.
Temperature: 22–24°C (72–75°F); a little higher for breeding purposes.
Breeding: This species scatters its eggs among fine-leaved vegetation. Breeding pairs show a distinct appetite for their own eggs. Hatching takes about 1 day.

OTHER COMMONLY AVAILABLE BARBS

There are many other species of barb available within the hobby. Most require similar general conditions to those described above. Some species well worth considering are:

B. arulius (Arulius Barb); *B. bimaculatus* (Two-spot Barb); *B. callipterus* (Clipper Barb); *B. everetti* (Clown Barb); *B. fasciatus* (Banded Barb); *B. gelius* (Dwarf Barb); *B. lineatus* (Lined/Zebra Barb); *B. pentazona* (Five-banded Barb); *B. rhomboocellatus* (Ocellated Barb).

During breeding the male Barbus titteya (Cherry Barb) develops an intense red coloration.

Brachydanio albolineatus
(Pearl Danio)

THE PEARL Danio (*Brachydanio albolineatus*) is a truly beautiful fish which regrettably is often not seen at its best in aquaria. To show off its most brilliant colours, this species should be kept in a shoal, in soft, acid water conditions, in a well-planted aquarium with plenty of open swimming spaces. Kept in this fashion, the males in particular (which are more colourful and smaller than the females) become resplendent.

Netting Danios always presents a challenge due to their agility and quick acceleration. However, despite this, fish that need to be netted should never be chased to the point of exhaustion. This creates unnecessary, and potentially damaging, stress which can be avoided with a little patience, the use of two nets (rather than one) and by switching the aquarium and room lights off during the exercise.

In addition to the wild type, a yellower form, usually referred to as the Yellow Danio, is also occasionally available (this should not be confused with the golden form of the Giant Danio, *Danio aequipinnatus*).

Natural Range: Burma (Myanmar), Thailand, Sumatra and Peninsular Malaysia.

Size: 6cm (2.4in).

Food: Most foods accepted.

Tank Conditions: This is an active shoaling species which requires plenty of swimming room. Long aquaria with open spaces are particularly suitable for this (and all the other) Danio species. Water chemistry is not too critical, but soft, slightly acid conditions are preferred.

Temperature: 20–25°C (68–77°F), but a little higher for breeding purposes. This species is an excellent jumper, so a tight-fitting aquarium cover is essential.

Breeding: This is best achieved by using a female (introduced into the tank prior to the males) and two males. Eggs are scattered among fine-leaved vegetation in relatively shallow water and are actively sought by the trio who should therefore be removed as soon as possible after spawning. Hatching takes between $1^{1}/_{2}$–2 days.

The lively Brachydanio albolineatus (Pearl Danio).

Brachydanio rerio
(Zebra Danio)

A long-finned Brachydanio rerio (Zebra Danio), one of several commercially produced varieties.

THE ZEBRA Danio (*Brachydanio rerio*) is an old favourite which remains as popular today as it has always been.

Several commercially produced varieties of this species are widely available, most notably, the Long-finned (wild-type coloration), Golden and Long-finned Golden Zebras.

Another fish traditionally regarded as a totally separate species, the Leopard Danio (*B. 'frankei'*) – also available in different fin and colour configurations – has now been shown, beyond reasonable doubt, to be a genetic mutant form of the Zebra.

Natural Range: Eastern India.

Size: 6cm (2.4in).

Food: Most foods accepted.

Tank Conditions: This is another active shoaling species which requires open spaces and plant thickets. Water chemistry is not too critical, but soft, slightly acid conditions are recommended.

Temperature: 18–24°C (64–75°F), but slightly higher for spawning.

Breeding: Although *B. rerio* is a shoaler, breeding is achieved using paired fishes, rather than a group. Eggs are scattered among fine-leaved vegetation (usually in the morning) and the parents must be removed immediately to prevent them from eating their own eggs. Hatching takes about 2 days.

OTHER COMMONLY AVAILABLE DANIOS

In addition to the above, there are a few other species of Danio widely available, all requiring the same basic conditions: *B. kerri* (Blue/Kerr's Danio); *B. nigrofasciatus* (Spotted Danio); *Danio aequipinnatus** (Giant Danio – also available in a golden form); *D. devario** (Bengal Danio).

*Both these species are larger than their *Brachydanio* counterparts, *D. aequipinnatus* attaining 10cm (4in) and *D. devario* growing to 15cm (6in).

Epalzeorhynchus bicolor
(Red-tailed Black Shark)

THE RED-TAILED Black Shark (*Epalzeorhynchus bicolor*) was formerly known as *Labeo bicolor* and is still widely referred to as such in aquarium literature. However, in line with modern thinking, I am using the latest nomenclature here.

Red-tailed Black Sharks (which are not true sharks, of course) are striking fish when in peak condition. If the water conditions, diet, or tank layout are deficient in any way, however, the deep velvety black of the body becomes grey and the normally brilliant red of the tail loses much of its brilliance.

Despite being very popular as community aquarium fish, *E. bicolor* is far from being an ideal choice for such set-ups. It is often (though not invariably) quarrelsome, sometimes to the point of being over-aggressive towards its tankmates, particularly if they are members of its own species.

A closely related species, the Ruby, Red-finned or Rainbow Shark (*E. frenatus*) is also widely available, both in the wild type form and as an albino. In this species, the body colour is considerably lighter than in *E. bicolor* and all the fins, rather than just the caudal, are red.

Below: Epalzeorhynchus bicolor (Red-tailed Black Shark). Right: Red-finned Shark, Albino form.

Natural Range: Thailand.

Size: Around 12cm (4.7in).

Food: Most foods accepted, particularly bottom-dwelling livefoods. A vegetable component should be included in the diet.

Tank Conditions: This is a territorial species which likes to base its home patch in and around selected hiding places. Caves and/or lumps of bogwood (or equivalent) should therefore be provided. There should also be open swimming spaces and plenty of vegetation. Mature soft to medium-hard water suits this species well.

Temperature: 22–26°C (72–79°F); higher for breeding (but see below).

Breeding: Only very occasionally achieved in home aquaria. Hormone-induced spawnings have resulted in eggs being scattered, while, in more natural spawnings, mating has been reported to have taken place in a depression on the bottom of the tank. Hatching takes about 2 days.

Epalzeorhynchus kallopterus
(Flying Fox)

THE FLYING Fox (*Epalzeorhynchus kallopterus*) spends much of its time resting on the bottom or, preferably, on a broad-leaved plant or piece of bogwood. However, when it moves, it can be lightning-fast. When resting, it tends to do so by extending its pectoral (chest) fins downwards and allowing the tips of these fins to take the weight of the front half of its body.

The Flying Fox is not a particularly colourful fish, but is, nevertheless, very popular, largely because of its wide availability and its reputation as an algae eater. In addition, it is one of the relatively few aquarium species to have a liking for flatworms (planarians) which can, occasionally, become a nuisance in aquaria.

Impressive though its appetite for algae may be, the Flying Fox is outdone in this department by a related species, the Siamese Flying Fox or Siamese Algae Eater (*Crossocheilus siamensis*) which takes algae eating to a higher plane by consuming thread algae, as well as the other types.

C. siamensis looks superficially like *E. kallopterus* but possesses clear (as opposed to pigmented) fins, a single upper lip barbel (as opposed to two) and a different arrangement of nasal (rhynal) lobes.

Natural Range: Northern India, Borneo, Indonesia, Thailand.

Size: Up to 15cm (6in), but usually smaller than this.

Food: Most foods accepted, particularly vegetable-based ones – including many species of algae (but not 'thread' types).

Tank Conditions: As this species likes to graze on encrusting algae, broad-leaved plants should be included in the aquarium. Hiding places should also be provided. An inhabitant of flowing waters in its natural habitat, this species benefits from frequent partial water changes (the new water should be treated with a suitable dechlorinator/dechloraminator). Although soft, slightly acid water is ideal, this species will tolerate some deviation from this.

Temperature: 24–26°C (75–79°F).

Breeding: No reports of successful aquarium breeding are, as yet, available.

Epalzeorhynchus kallopterus (Flying Fox) spends most of its time resting on bogwood or on the bottom of the tank.

Rasbora heteromorpha
(Harlequin Rasbora)

Rasbora heteromorpha (Harlequin Rasbora).

THE HARLEQUIN Rasbora (*Rasbora heteromorpha*) is a peaceful shoaling fish which should be kept in sizeable numbers for best effect. If this is not possible, then every effort should be made to keep it in a small shoal consisting of no fewer than six to eight individuals.

This basic requirement is one of the main reasons why the Harlequin, despite its enormous popularity, is not often seen at its best in home aquaria. A second factor is that the majority of such set-ups are, generally speaking, intensely illuminated, whereas the Harlequin prefers subdued lighting. This can be easily and attractively achieved by choosing plants, including some of the *Cryptocoryne* species from its native range, whose leaves are allowed to extend over the surface of the water.

Two other species closely resembling the Harlequin (but with a narrower-based body cone) are also available: the Narrow-wedged or Espes' Rasbora (*R. espei*) from Thailand and Hengel's Harlequin (*R. hengeli*), which is smaller and comes from Sumatra.

There is also a relatively new blue variety of *R. heteromorpha* which, while becoming quite popular in recent years, is not generally deemed to be as beautiful as the original wild type.

Natural Range: Southeast Asia, Malaysia, Singapore (though populations are now restricted to some small streams in the central catchment forest area of the island), Sumatra and Thailand.

Size: 4.5cm (1.75in).

Food: Most foods accepted, but bottom-dwelling livefoods are usually only taken with reluctance.

Tank Conditions: This species looks best when kept in shoals in subdued light and in a densely planted aquarium. The water should be mature (but of good quality) and maintained soft and slightly acid, although some deviation from this will be tolerated.

Temperature: 22–27°C (72–81°F),with the top end being suitable for breeding purposes.

Breeding: This is not an easy species to breed. To optimize one's chances of success, the water should be well-aged, very soft and shallow (around 15cm/6in deep) and the aquarium located in a sunny spot. Eggs are laid on the underside of a broad leaf and take about 1 day to hatch.

R. hengeli (Hengel's Harlequin).

Rasbora kalochroma
(Two-/Three-spot/Big-spot/Clown Rasbora)

THE VARIOUS common names given to *Rasbora kalochroma* illustrate beautifully the potential confusion which such nomenclature can create, as well as one of the main reasons why correct scientific Latin names are so important (see Species Introduction for fuller treatment of this subject). If we were to rely on common names only for identification purposes, we could easily be led to believe that we are dealing with four, rather than a single species.

When we use the name Two-spot Rasbora, we are using the two body spots as a means of identification, but are excluding the eye. When we use the Three-spot 'label', we are including the eye, while when we refer to this fish as the Clown Rasbora, we are adopting the widely used (and abused) approach of calling a fish a 'clown' if it has large spots or bands on its body.

Irrespective of which label we apply, *R. kalochroma* is an interesting aquarium subject and a bit of an exception among members of its genus in that it does not exhibit a strong shoaling tendency. Individual fish appear to create their own, small 'personal space' which they defend.

Nevertheless, the species seems to do better as a loose shoal than when kept singly or in pairs.

Natural Range: Southeast Asia, Borneo, Malaysia and Sumatra. The Two-spot Rasbora sometimes reported from Singapore is not *R. kalochroma*, but *R. elegans*.

Size: Up to 10cm (4in), but usually smaller.

Food: All foods accepted, particularly 'surface' livefoods.

Tank Conditions: Good-quality water is preferred. Since this is an active species, plenty of open swimming space should be provided, along with thickets of vegetation. As with *R. heteromorpha*, subdued lighting shows off this fish at its best. Some aquarists add about one teaspoonful of salt per 10 litres (2.2 Imp. gal/2.6 US gal) of aquarium water. However, this is not absolutely necessary and I, and many others, have kept this species successfully (but without breeding) in soft, acid conditions.

Temperature: 25–28°C (77–82°F).

Breeding: No details are currently available regarding breeding in aquaria.

Rasbora kalachroma (Clown Rasbora) does not exhibit strong shoaling tendencies.

Rasbora pauciperforata
(Glowlight/Red-line/Red-striped Rasbora)

THE GLOWLIGHT (*Rasbora pauciperforata*) is yet another species which does not always exhibit its best colours in shop or home aquaria where conditions are often too bright for its liking. However, when kept in a shoal in tannin-stained water under subdued lighting, it is a sparklingly attractive fish.

Despite its preferences, the Glowlight will tolerate the conditions which generally exist in community aquaria and this, added to its peaceful nature with regard to other species, plus its wide availability, makes it a very popular community choice with aquarists the world over.

An interesting aspect of the Glowlight's behaviour is that, while it is an active fish that likes to swim around in shoals, it also frequently spends some time quite motionless in mid-water, just lightly flicking its pectoral fins to maintain its position and holding all other fins erect.

At such times, the slight differences between the sexes (outside the breeding season) are quite easily detectable, with the males being slimmer than the females. When the latter are full of eggs, the differences are much more pronounced.

Natural Range: Southeast Asia, including the island of Belitung (Billiton), western Malaysia and Sumatra.

Size: Up to 7cm (2.75in), but usually smaller.

Food: Most foods accepted, but small livefoods preferred.

Tank Conditions: Open swimming spaces and thickly planted areas should be provided. Although this can sometimes be a relatively timid species, it is active and does well in the company of other species of similar size. Soft, slightly acid water is preferred, but some deviation from this will be tolerated. Glowlights look particularly good (as do some other *Rasbora* species) when the water is slightly stained with tannic acids from, e.g., bogwood or peat. Frequent partial water changes are recommended.

Temperature: 23–26°C (73–79°F).

Breeding: This is an egg scatterer which can be difficult to induce to spawn. Chances of success are enhanced when pairs are allowed to establish naturally from a shoal. Hatching takes about $1^1/_2$–2 days.

Rasbora pauciperforata (Glowlight/Red-line Rasbora) is seen at its best when kept in subdued lighting conditions.

Rasbora trilineata
(Scissortail/Three-lined Rasbora)

WHAT THE Scissortail or Three-lined Rasbora (*Rasbora trilineata*) may lack in body coloration, it more than makes up for in the striking black and yellow pattern of its caudal fin. This is especially evident when a sizeable shoal of this active swimmer is kept in soft, slightly acid water. Under other, less favourable, environmental conditions, or when specimens are kept singly or in pairs, the tail pattern often loses much of its brilliance.

When at rest in midwater, individual fish tend to line up beside each other, facing in the same direction and leaving a space of a few centimetres between them.

A similar species, the Giant or Greater Scissortail (*Rasbora caudimaculata*) – also from southeast Asia – is also widely available. Despite its common name, Giant Scissortails are not really much larger than fully mature 'normal' Scissortails.

Natural Range: Borneo, Sumatra, western Malaysia.
Size: Reported up to 15cm (6in), but usually considerably smaller.
Food: Most foods accepted, particularly 'surface' livefoods.
Tank Conditions: This is an active shoaling species which requires open swimming spaces surrounded by plant thickets. Although a range of water conditions is accepted, soft, acid water is preferred.

Rasbora trilineata (Scissortail).

Temperature: 22–25°C (72–77°F); slightly higher for breeding.
Breeding: This is one of the more difficult *Rasbora* species to breed. Shallow, soft, warm water with slightly acid pH, dense patches of fine-leaved vegetation and a dark substratum have sometimes proved successful. Hatching takes about 1 day.

OTHER COMMONLY AVAILABLE RASBORAS

There are other *Rasbora* species which are generally suitable for community aquaria, although there are a few exceptions (indicated by an asterisk in the following list). Well worth considering are, at least, the following:

R. borapetensis (Red-tailed Rasbora); *R. daniconius* (Golden-striped Rasbora); *R. dorsiocellata* (Hi-spot Rasbora); *R. elegans* (Elegant/Two-spot Rasbora – see also *R. kalochroma*); *R. maculata* (Dwarf/Pygmy/Spotted Rasbora*); *R. urophthalma* (Glass Rasbora*); *R. vaterifloris* (Orange-finned Rasbora – also known as the Orange-finned/Singhalese Fire Barb, although it is not a barb).

*Note: These two species are very small: *R. maculata* – 2.5cm (1in) and *R. urophthalma* – 3.5cm (1.4in) and should not be kept with large or boisterous species.

Rasbora maculata (Spotted/Dwarf Rasbora).

67

Tanichthys albonubes
(White Cloud Mountain Minnow)

THE WHITE Cloud Mountain Minnow (*Tanichthys albonubes*) is an old aquarium favourite which has never lost is popularity. Yet, despite its long history in the hobby, there still exists a certain amount of confusion regarding its identity.

This has arisen, largely, because the populations found in its original homeland around the White Cloud Mountain, near Canton in China, have white edges on the dorsal (back) and anal (belly) fins, while those from around Hong Kong have red edges. Most ichthyologists believe these to be merely two colour variants of the same species, although some believe that the two types should constitute separate subspecies.

A long-finned variety, which appeared to have lost favour during the 1980s is now, once more, widely available.

The White Cloud Mountain Minnow is more temperate in its requirements than most other community aquarium species. It is what I would term a 'coldwater tropical' species (see also – among others – the entries for the Paradise Fish (*Macropodus opercularis*), Mosquito Fish (*Gambusia holbrooki*) and Golden Medaka (*Oryzias latipes*) for other 'coldwater tropicals').

Natural Range: China: around the White Cloud Mountain near Canton. Wild populations are also found around Hong Kong, but these may have arisen from former aquarium-raised stocks.

Size: Around 4cm (1.6in).

Food: All foods, especially small-sized ones.

Tank Conditions: This is a peaceful shoaling species which does well in community aquaria that do not contain large, boisterous fish. While open swimming space should be provided, White Clouds also like to swim among fine-leaved vegetation. They are also tolerant of a wide range of water conditions, as long as the quality is good.

Temperature: From below 15°C (59°F) to around 22°C (72°F). Temperatures below and above both ends of this range will also be tolerated, but should be avoided over long periods.

Breeding: Single pairs should be introduced into a heavily planted small aquarium containing water maintained around the top end of the temperature range. Eggs are scattered among the plants and will hatch in about 1¹/₂ days. The parents should be removed immediately after spawning.

Tanichthys albonubes (White Cloud Mountain Minnow) remains a very popular species.

CHARACINS

Nematobrycon lacortei (Rainbow Emperor Tetra).

STRICTLY SPEAKING, the term 'characin' should only be applied to species and genera belonging to the family Characidae. However, common usage has led to the term also being applied to other families of characin-like (characoid) fish, which, together, form the order Characiformes.

At least, this is the case if one accepts the view held by many ichthyologists that these fish – while sharing several important characteristics – can be grouped into 'sub-units' (families and subfamilies). Others are of the opinion that all characoids should be grouped within a single family, the Characidae.

Either way, it is clear that the classification of the fish we usually refer to as characins is in dire need of close attention. In the meantime, the approach which I am adopting here is that which appears in *Fishes of the World* (3rd Edition) – see page 48 for full reference details.

Following this classification, the order Characiformes consists of ten families (some containing subfamilies), with around 237 genera and some 1,350 species. Around 208 of these are found in Africa, with the remainder distributed from the southwest United States, through Mexico, to Central and South America.

In the pages that follow, representatives of six families are featured: Anostomidae (headstanders), Characidae (characins, including the tetras and piranhas)

Citharinidae (e.g., *Distichodus*), Gasteropelecidae (hatchetfishes), Hemiodontidae (e.g., *Hemiodus*) and Lebiasinidae (pencilfishes and relatives).

Despite their wide diversity of form and habits (the Characidae, for example, includes fish as different from one another as the Cardinal Tetra, *Paracheirodon axelrodi*, and the Red-bellied Piranha, *Serrasalmus (Pygocentrus) nattereri*), the vast majority of characoids share, at least, the following characteristics: well-developed teeth, an adipose (small, 'second dorsal') fin, fully scaled bodies, a lateral line which is often decurved (i.e., it curves downwards), an anal fin with fewer than 45 rays and several other skeletal features. Among the characteristics that they lack are mouth barbels and (in most species) a protractile, or extendible, upper jaw.

Young black piranha – showing teeth.
Photo © John Dawes.

Anostomus anostomus
(Striped Anostomus/Headstander)

THE STRIPED Headstander (*Anostomus anostomus*) is a strikingly patterned fish which is widely available, but is probably best avoided by aquarists setting up their first community aquarium.

If kept as a single specimen with other sizeable fish, the Striped Headstander is generally peaceful. However, if a small number – say, between two and five or six – are kept together, they will scrap almost continually. Interestingly, though, above this number, the level of overt aggression decreases significantly.

Its preference for vertical hiding places and strong water flow, plus its relatively large size and need for spacious quarters and plentiful vegetable matter, are all additional factors that warrant serious consideration before deciding to buy Striped Headstanders. Having said this, if you can cater adequately for these needs, you would be strongly advised to obtain some specimens of this long-established and highly desirable species.

Other members of the genus, such as *A. taeniatus* (the Lisa or Lápis), *A. ternetzi* (Ternetz's Headstander) and *A. trimaculatus* (Three-spot Headstander), have more or less similar requirements, but are altogether more peaceful towards members of their own species.

Natural Range: Upper part of the Amazon, Orinoco River (Venezuela), Colombia, Guyana.

Size: Up to 18cm (7in) reported, but usually smaller (unless kept in large aquaria).

Food: Most foods accepted, which must include a vegetable component; small livefoods will also be readily consumed.

Tank Conditions: A well-planted aquarium layout should be provided for this species, which also benefits (because of its potentially large size) from roomy accommodation. Soft, slightly acid water suits *A. anostomus* best, but it will also tolerate some deviation from this. Lighting conditions should be bright and the water circulation strong (e.g., as generated by a power filter). Provide vertical fissures between pieces of rock or synthetic aquarium 'rockwork' for the fish to hide in.

Temperature: 22–28°C (72–82°F) with 25°C (77°F) being perfectly adequate.

Breeding: Although this has been achieved (but only rarely) in aquaria, no details are readily available.

Anostomus anostomus (Striped Anostomus) is large and requires a spacious aquarium.

Aphyocharax anisisti
(Bloodfin)

Apyocharax anisisti (Bloodfin) is a peaceful fish which will add a very special touch to any community aquarium.

THE BLOODFIN (*Aphyocharax anisisti*) is still referred to as *A. affinis* or *A. rubripinnis* in some books. These are, however, names of later origin which, in due course, were found to have been given to the same species. As *A. anisisti* is the earliest of the three, these newer names are now regarded as invalid 'junior' synonyms.

With the exception of the pectoral (chest) fins, which are colourless, all the other fins, particularly the anal (belly) and caudal (tail), carry varying amounts of red. Add to this the characteristic silvery/bluish coloration of the body, and we end up with a little gem of a fish, which will add a very special touch to any community aquarium.

The Bloodfin can be kept in unheated (so-called coldwater) aquaria, where it will survive without any undue hardship, as long as the temperature is not allowed to drop significantly below the lower end of the recommended range for a prolonged period of time. However, under such conditions, much of the brilliance which makes this species so attractive will be lost during the winter months.

Other superficially similar species from South America,

among them *Aphyocharax alburnus* (False Flame-tailed Tetra), *A. erythrurus* (Flame-tailed Tetra) and *A. rathbuni* (Rathbun's Bloodfin) are also occasionally available.

Natural Range: Panama River, Argentina.

Size: 5cm (2in).

Food: Most foods accepted, particularly small livefoods.

Tank Conditions: This is a peaceful shoaler which should be kept in a tank that provides both open swimming space at the front and vegetation along the sides and back. Water chemistry, in terms of pH and hardness, is not critical, but abrupt fluctuations in conditions should be avoided.

Temperature: Coming from a more temperate region than most other tropical species, the Bloodfin can tolerate a wide temperature range, from around 18°C (64°F) to 28°C (82°F).

Breeding: Spawning can be relatively easily achieved in temperatures near the top end of the range. This is an egg-scattering species with a distinct liking for its own eggs, so remove the parents immediately after spawning.

Astyanax fasciatus
(Blind Cave Fish Characin/Tetra)

EVEN THE briefest of surveys of aquarium books will reveal the Blind Cave Fish listed under a variety of names, ranging from *Arnoldichthys jordani*, through *Astyanax fasciatus mexicanus*, to *Astyanax mexicanus* and *Astyanax fasciatus*. The reason is that this interesting fish has been variously regarded as a species in its own right, a subspecies of the Mexican or Silvery Tetra (*A. fasciatus*) or – in line with current thinking – as a cave morph of *A. fasciatus*. A 'morph' is a naturally occuring 'form' which has developed as an eyeless, colourless, pinkish, blind form. A further factor contributing to the 'fluidity' of the name is that some authorities believe *A. fasciatus* to be a junior synonym of *A. mexicanus*.

Many authors (including myself) have 'evolved' with the changing scene and have, therefore, reflected this in our writing over the years. In this book, I am following the most widely accepted trend by referring to the Blind Cave Fish as *Astyanax fasciatus*... but 'watch this space' for further 'evolution' as new research brings us ever closer to the true identity of this hardy, active, fascinating fish.

Natural Range: The fully coloured, fully eyed form of the species is widespread through Texas, Mexico and Central America, through to Panama. The pink, blind morph is restricted to some limestone caves in San Luis Potosí, Mexico.

Size: Around 9cm (3.5in).

Food: All foods accepted.

Tank Conditions: The Blind Cave Fish does not, of course, require lighting of any kind, although it appears to be quite comfortable under normal community aquarium conditions. For a more natural look, a dimly lit aquarium, illuminated by one of the 'moonlight' fluorescent tubes which are sometimes used in tropical marine aquaria to simulate night conditions on a reef, and decorated with limestone rockwork or cave rocks (stalactites and/or stalagmites) will show off a shoal of these fish beautifully. Water chemistry is not critical (as long as the quality is good), but medium-hard, alkaline conditions are preferred.

Temperature: A wide range is tolerated – from as low as 15–18°C (59–64°F) to 28–30°C (82–86°F).

Breeding: This is a typical egg-scattering, egg-eating species which easily cross-breeds with the fully coloured, fully eyed members of the species. Hatching takes between 1–3 days, depending on temperature.

The Astyanax fasciatus (Blind Cave Tetra) is naturally found in limestone caves in San Luis Potosi, Mexico.

Copella arnoldi
(Splashing/Spraying/Jumping Tetra/Characin)

*C*OPELLA ARNOLDI derives its common names of Splashing/Spraying/Jumping Tetra from its unusual spawning habits. Instead of laying their eggs underwater as other fish do, these quite remarkable fish actually jump out of the water, stick for a few minutes to the underside of a broad leaf located a few centimetres above the water surface (owing to water surface tension adhesion), deposit a few eggs and then flop back into the water. This process is repeated many times until as many as 200 eggs have been laid.

Once spawning has been completed, the female plays no further part, but the male spends the next two to three days constantly splashing water onto the eggs with his pectoral fins, thus preventing them from drying out until they hatch. Interestingly, other species in the genus do not exhibit this type of behaviour, spawning, instead, in more 'traditional' fashion by laying their eggs on the underside of broad submerged leaves.

The remarkable Copella arnoldi (Splashing Tetra).

Natural Range: Lower Amazon basin.

Size: Up to 8cm (3in) – males; 6cm (2.4in) – females.

Food: Most foods accepted, particularly floating types.

Tank Conditions: On account of the jumping tendencies and capabilities of this species, the tank should be well covered. Surface vegetation with open swimming space beneath suits *C. arnoldi* well. It is a good community fish which does well either in pairs or shoals. Soft, slightly acid water is recommended, preferably tannin-stained by using a peat sandwich in the power filter, a piece of bogwood as part of the aquarium decor, or a commercial 'blackwater' additive.

Temperature: 25–29°C (77–84°F) with the higher end being suitable for breeding.

Breeding: Eggs are laid on the underside of broad leaves a few centimetres above water level. Therefore, the breeding tank must have a sufficiently deep aerial section between the water surface and the underside of the (essential!) aquarium cover. The eggs are kept moist for 2–3 days by the male until they hatch.

Distichodus lusosso
(Long-nosed Distichodus)

THE LONG-NOSED Distichodus (*Distichodus lusosso*) is an attractive fish, particularly during its juvenile stages. As they grow, though, specimens lose much of the bright coloration and this fact, coupled with the large eventual size that well-fed, well-housed individuals can attain, make the species an unsuitable long-term choice for most home aquaria.

The main reason why it is featured here is that it is the most commonly seen *Distichodus* in many countries, although a similar, but shorter-nosed, close relative, the Six-lined Distichodus (*D. sexfasciatus*) is also quite widespread. This latter species, while growing to a smaller size of around 25cm (10in), loses most of its colourful juvenile body markings as it grows, eventually becoming an overall dull greyish yellow.

Better choices (in terms of size) will be found among some of the other *Distichodus* species which can be found with varying degrees of regularity, such as *D. decemmaculatus* – Dwarf Distichodus, which only grows to around 6cm (2.4in) and the two following species, both of which grow to around 10–12cm (4–5in); *D. affinis* (Silver Distichodus) and *D. noboli* (Nobol's Distichodus).

All have requirements similar to *D. lusosso* and none appears to have been bred, as yet, in home aquaria.

Natural Range: Angola, Cameroon, Southern Congo (Katanga), Congo River basin.
Size: Up to 40cm (15.7in).
Food: Although this species will eat a range of foods, vegetation should comprise a major part of the diet.
Tank Conditions: Large aquaria are required for this peaceful species, although juveniles may be housed in smaller community set-ups. Its predilection for soft succulent plants will generally make it unsuitable for aquaria decorated with live plants, unless these are tough or of unpalatable composition, like Dwarf Anubias (*Anubias nana*), Congo Fern (*Bolbitis heudelotii*), Indian Fern (*Ceratopteris thalictroides*), Java Fern (*Microsorum pteropus*), or Java Moss (*Vesicularia dubyana*). Water chemistry should be around neutral pH and medium hardness.
Temperature: 22–26°C (72–79°F).
Breeding: No reports are available of successful spawnings in home aquaria.

The attractive Distichodus lusosso (Long-nosed Distichodus) may grow up to 40cm (15.7 inches) in length.

Gasteropelecus sternicla
(Common Hatchetfish)

THE COMMON Hatchetfish (*Gasteropelecus sternicla*) is one of several species of hatchetfishes which are widely available.

Hatchetfish – so-called because of their wedged-shaped bodies – are the only fish which are regarded as true fliers. While other 'flying fish', such as the marine species belonging to the genera *Cypsilurus*, *Danichthys* and *Exocoetus* are actually gliders which do not flap their 'wings' (pectoral fins) during flight, the freshwater hatchetfish actually do, using their powerful breast muscles (hence their deep chests) to do so.

Flights can measure up to 15m (50ft) in distance and are used as a means of escape from predators. Obviously, such behaviour cannot be observed in average-sized aquaria – especially since these are not supposed to house any species that will prey on hatchetfish (or any of the other tank occupants), but jumping out of the water can sometimes occur, particularly if the fish are startled.

In addition to *Gasteropelecus sternicla*, some of the other related species well worth considering are the similarly-sized *G. levis* (Silver Hatchetfish), the slightly larger *G. maculatus* (Spotted Hatchetfish) and *Thoracocharax securis* (another Silver Hatchetfish), along with the smaller *Carnegiella marthae* (Black-winged Hatchetfish) and *C. strigata* (Marbled Hatchetfish). All require similar conditions to those described for the Common Hatchetfish.

Natural Range: Brazil, Guyana, Surinam.

Size: Around 6cm (2.5in).

Food: Most foods, particularly 'surface' livefoods. Being predominantly surface to midwater species, hatchetfish will tend to ignore food lying on the bottom of the aquarium.

Tank Conditions: Areas of water surface free from vegetation should be provided. However, as hatchetfish also like surface cover, either some floating plants over part of the available surface, or submerged plants with leaves that will spread over the surface should also be provided. A good aquarium cover is also required for this excellent jumper (see main text for further details). Softish, slightly acid water is recommended.

Temperature: 23–28°C (73–82°F).

Breeding: Has, apparently, not yet been bred in aquaria.

Gasteropelecus sternicla (Common Hatchetfish) is an excellent jumper and 'flies' to escape predators in the wild.

Gymnocorymbus ternetzi
(Black/White/Red Tetra/Black Widow)

WITH THE passage of time, the number of common names given to *Gymnocorymbus ternetzi* increases in accordance with the new varieties of this popular species that are being produced in fish farms around the world.

Elegant and popular though some of these newer varieties undoubtedly are, the short-finned wild type of the Black Widow or Black Tetra still remains a firm favourite, particularly among established aquarists.

This is a peaceful fish which should be kept in shoals for maximum effect and for their long-term well-being. The shorter-finned types can be safely kept with all types of other community species, but the longer-finned varieties are likely to suffer if kept with fin-nipping species such as Tiger Barbs (*Barbus tetrazona*).

One of the main production and development centres of the fancier varieties of *G. ternetzi* is Florida, where some of the long-finned varieties that have been created are also quite large-bodied when compared with the original wild type of the species. All types have similar requirements in terms of diet and aquarium conditions, but the larger types should not be housed in small aquaria.

Because of its undemanding nature, the Black Widow (in all its various forms) is frequently recommended as a good species for beginners.

Natural Range: Paraguay River, Bolivian portion of the Guaporé River and Mato Grosso in Brazil.

Size: Around 5.5cm (2.2in); some cultivated varieties may be larger.

Food: Most foods accepted.

Tank Conditions: This species does well in aquaria that have open spaces, planted areas and tannin-stained water. Soft, acid water is preferred, but, being a hardy species, Black Widows will tolerate a range of conditions, as long as raw tapwater is avoided and the overall water quality is good.

Temperature: 20–28°C (68–82°F), with the top temperature (or even slightly higher ones) being suitable for breeding.

Breeding: This is a typical egg-scattering, egg-eating species, with the eggs being laid among fine-leaved vegetation. Hatching takes about 1 day.

The peaceful Gymnocorymbus ternetzi (Black Widow Tetra) is a firm favourite with aquarists. This is the wild type.

Hasemania nana
(Silver-tipped/Copper Tetra)

Hasemania nana (Silver-tipped/Copper Tetra) is a peaceful shoaler which does well in community aquaria.

THE SILVER-tipped Tetra appears in aquarium literature under several names: *Hasemania marginata, Hasemania melanura, Hemigrammus nanus* and, as in this book and the majority of other modern-day equivalents, as *Hasemania nana*. All refer to the same fish, as do the two most frequently used common names, both of which are quite appropriate in their respective ways.

As the accompanying photograph shows, the dorsal (back), anal (belly) and caudal (tail) fins are all tipped with white, hence the Silver-tipped name tag. In males, the tip of the anal fin is much whiter than in females (in which it is yellowish) and this may be used as a distinguishing factor between the sexes whether the fish are in breeding condition or not.

The second common name, Copper Tetra, is derived from the colour which males develop during the spawning season, at which time they become territorial and their basic light copper body colour becomes very intense.

Hasemania nana is a peaceful shoaler which does well in community aquaria, particularly if the light level is subdued to allow it to show off its colours to best effect. Unlike the vast majority of other characins, the Silver-tipped Tetra lacks an adipose ('second dorsal') fin.

Natural Range: Eastern Brazil (Rio São Francisco basin) and western Brazil (tributaries of the Rio Purus).

Size: Up to 5cm (2in), but often a little smaller than this.

Food: Most foods accepted.

Tank Conditions: This species comes from flowing waters and is therefore an active swimmer which requires open areas, as well as shelter in the form of clumps of vegetation. Soft, slightly acid water, preferably tannin-stained and well-oxygenated, is recommended, although some deviation from this will also be tolerated.

Temperature: 22–28°C (72–82°F).

Breeding: Very soft, acid, tannin-stained water maintained at the higher end of the temperature range, plus thickets of fine-leaved vegetation should be provided for this egg-scattering species. Hatching takes about 1 day.

Hemigrammus caudovittatus
(Buenos Aires Tetra)

Hemigrammus caudovittatus (Buenos Aires Tetra) is a really beautiful fish when fully coloured up.

THE BUENOS Aires Tetra (*Hemigrammus caudovittatus*) – so-called because of its (partly) Argentinian origins – has been around in the hobby since the early 1920s and is often recommended as an excellent fish for beginners.

In some ways, such as its undoubted hardiness in terms of water chemistry and temperature, plus its wide-ranging dietary preferences, such advice is totally justified. However, Buenos Aires Tetras and delicate plants do not make compatible tankmates and this characteristic, allied to the aggression that larger individuals sometimes exhibit towards smaller, less robust/more timid species, means that the 'good community aquarium species' recommendation should not be taken as being 100 percent applicable to all situations.

When fully coloured up, this is a really beautiful fish. The coloration is more vivid in the (slimmer) males, but both sexes are attractive, particularly when forming part of a sizeable shoal. A colour variant in which the caudal (tail) fin is predominantly yellow, as opposed to the more normal red, is also occasionally encountered.

Unhealthy or stressed fish lose much of their red coloration, at which time they closely resemble the Mexican Tetra (*Astyanax fasciatus*) and could easily be confused with this species.

Natural Range: Argentina (mainly around La Plata), southern Brazil and Paraguay.

Size: Sizes up to 12cm (4.7in) are reported, but 7–8cm (2.8–3.2in) are more usual.

Food: All foods accepted.

Tank Conditions: As an active shoaling species – and a little larger than many other tetras – *H. caudovittatus* benefits from a slightly larger-than-normal tank with ample swimming space and plant thickets. These plants should consist of robust or unpalatable types (see entry for *Distichodus lusosso* for some suggestions), since this species has a distinct liking for soft succulent vegetation. Water chemistry is not critical, but water should be well oxygenated and of good quality.

Temperature: Wide range is tolerated, from 18°C (64°F) to 28°C (82°F).

Breeding: This is a prolific species which has a distinct liking for its own eggs. Hatching takes about 1 day.

Hemigrammus erythrozonus
(Glowlight Tetra)

THE GLOWLIGHT Tetra (*Hemigrammus erythrozonus*) is often referred to as one of the most beautiful of all the tetras. This is perfectly true, but the comment only applies to healthy fish kept in the water and tank conditions recommended for the species. At other times, the glowing reds that stretch from the top half of the eye all the way to the caudal peduncle (base of the caudal or tail fin), can become somewhat 'washed out' and pale.

As so often happens with small tetras, Glowlights will shoal with other similarly sized species quite regularly, particularly if kept with few members of its own kind. It is a peaceful fish that tolerates all others but it can, itself, suffer from the attentions of more robust, boisterous tankmates.

Although there is some doubt regarding the true scientific identity of the Glowlight Tetra – with at least one authority suggesting that it might belong to the genus *Cheirodon* instead of *Hemigrammus* – I am retaining the more traditional assignation (*Hemigrammus*) for the species in this book, but may – of course – have to revise this in later editions if research findings dictate otherwise.

Natural Range: Guyana (Essequibo River basin).

Size: 4cm (1.6in).

Food: Most commercial foods and small livefoods.

Tank Conditions: This is a shoaling species which likes both open swimming space and thickly vegetated areas. Soft, slightly acid water is preferred, but some deviation from this will also be tolerated (but not for breeding). Changes in water chemistry should, however, be carried out gradually. The addition of natural bogwood, a peat 'sandwich' in the power filter, or the use of a commercial 'blackwater' preparation, will produce tannin-stained water which shows off the 'glowlight' nature of the species beautifully.

Temperature: From around 22°C (72°F) up to 28°C (82°F), the latter being suitable for breeding purposes.

Breeding: Soft, acid, tannin-stained water at around 28°C (82°F) is suitable for this eggscatterer. The breeders can be introduced either in a shoal, or as pairs. Hatching takes about 1 day.

Hemigrammus erythozonus (Glowlight Tetra).

Hemigrammus rhodostomus
(Rummy-nosed Tetra)

I N ADDITION to *Hemigrammus rhodostomus*, the 'true' Rummy-nosed Tetra, there are two other superficially similar species widely available: *Hemigrammus bleheri* and *Petitella georgiae*.

All require similar conditions and make good community fish, because of their peaceful nature, modest size and attractive coloration. Being predominantly soft water fish that prefer acid conditions, these species can also be used in Discus aquaria, or as part of a typical 'blackwater' selection incorporating Cardinal Tetras (*Paracheirodon axelrodi*), small cichlids like the Checkerboard (*Dicrossus filamentosus*) or Rio Negro *Apistogramma* species, pencilfishes, e.g., *Nannostomus eques*, and associated species.

Natural Range: Lower Amazon.

Size: 4.5cm (1.8in).

Food: Most foods accepted.

Tank Conditions: As this is a shoaling species, it requires open swimming space and plant thickets. It also likes tannin-stained water produced either via a peat 'sandwich' in a filter or a piece of natural bogwood being used as tank decor. There are also some commercial

'blackwater' preparations which can be used to good effect. Soft, acid water suits this species well, although it will tolerate some deviation from this.

Temperature: 22–26°C (72–79°F)

Breeding: Very soft, acid water will enhance the chances of success. Eggs will be scattered either among vegetation or over the substratum. Hatching takes about 1¹/₂ days.

OTHER COMMONLY AVAILABLE HEMIGRAMMUS SPECIES

Selecting *Hemigrammus* species to feature in detail in a book is always a difficult task because – no matter what choices one makes – there are others which one could just as easily choose, just as there are numerous desirable *Hyphessobrycon* species (see pages 82 and following). Among my personal *Hemigrammus* favourites are the following, all of which are small and have similar basic requirements to the three main species profiled above:

H. leulingi (Leuling's Tetra – only rarely found in shops), *H. ocellifer* (Head-and-Tail-Light Tetra/Beacon Fish), *H. pulcher* (Pretty Tetra), *H. rodwayi* (Golden Tetra), *H. ulreyi* (Ulrey's Tetra) and *H. unilineatus* (Featherfin).

Hemigrammus rhodostomus (Rummy-nosed Tetra) is a shoaling fish requiring open swimming space.

Hemiodopsis gracilis
(Slender Hemiodus)

THE SLENDER Hemiodus (*Hemiodopsis gracilis*) is also referred to as *Hemiodus gracilis* in aquarium literature, a feature that is reflected in the second part of its common name.

H. *gracilis* is perhaps the most attractive member of the genus and is one of two species that are commonly available, the other one being *H. semitaeniatus*, the Half-lined/Black-and-white-tailed/Silver Hemiodus.

Hemiodids are usually available as juveniles or half-grown fish, which, when seen in a shoal, appear very tempting indeed. They do, however, develop into relatively large fish and, although they are unlikely to pose a major problem in terms of temperament, their eventual size makes them – in due course – unsuitable for small community aquaria.

An additional factor that may count against these otherwise desirable fish is their tendency to nibble plants, particularly tender fine-leaved types. This does not, however, constitute a major hurdle, since most robust or unpalatable species, such as some of the aquatic ferns, will stand up to their attention. It is therefore quite possible to set up an attractive and appropriate display incorporating these plants and intermingling them with some of today's excellent artificial equivalents.

The effort is well worth it, since hemiodids are interesting, active and attractive fish which every aquarist should keep at least once in their 'career'.

Natural Range: Amazon and Guyana.

Size: Around 15cm (6in).

Food: Most foods accepted.

Tank Conditions: Owing to their relatively large size, all hemiodids require roomy aquaria. They are not therefore ideal fish for many community set-ups, especially since – as shoaling species – they should not be kept as single specimens or pairs. Ample open swimming space should be provided and, as all species are very active and have high metabolic rates, the water should be well-oxygenated at all times. While water chemistry is not too critical, soft, acid conditions should, if possible, be provided.

Temperature: 23–27°C (74–81°F).

Breeding: No details of successful aquarium spawnings are available.

Hemiodopsis gracilis (Slender Hemiodus) can grow to a relatively large size.

Hyphessobrycon bentosi
(Bentos/Rosy Tetra)

Hyphessobrycon bentosi (Rosy Tetra).

THE BENTOS or Rosy Tetra (*Hyphessobrycon bentosi*) is one of several similarly coloured and shaped fish over which there has been (and still is) considerable debate.

The matter is not helped by the fact that the species involved (or subspecies, depending on what literature is consulted) can vary in the intensity of their red pigmentation, that some may be able to interbreed and that most have been cultured commercially for many years, resulting in heightened coloration and fin extensions. Add to this a proliferation of synonyms, and you have the makings of a thoroughly confusing situation.

All types are, basically, rosy-red coloured fish with varying amounts of pigmentation on their bodies and fins. The red may be complemented by black and white in most fins; the pectoral (chest) fins are generally the least-coloured ones. In addition, there may be one or two black spots behind the head and these, too, may vary in intensity and size.

Not surprisingly, 'Rosy' Tetras may be found under a number of common and scientific names, among them: Bentos/Rosy/Rosaceous Tetra (*H. bentosi, callistus, ornatus, rosaceous*, the last two of which are gradually disappearing from aquarium literature) and Serpae Tetra (*H. serpae* – a name that also appears to be on the way

out), while Robert's Tetra, which is often labelled as *H. 'robertsi'*, may be a hybrid.

In addition, superficially similar fish which are regularly on offer include the Flame Tetra (*H. flammeus*) and Griem's Tetra (*H. griemi*).

Natural Range: Lower Amazon and Guyana for the 'true' Bentos/Rosy Tetra sometimes referred to as *Hyphessobrycon bentosi bentosi* (but see main text for further details of this and other closely related fish).

Size: Around 4cm (1.6in).

Food: All foods accepted.

Tank Conditions: This species, and all its close relations, are shoalers which tend to look at their best in slightly tannin-stained, soft, acid conditions. The aquarium should provide open swimming space and shelter in the form of plant thickets.

Temperature: 24–28°C (75–82°F).

Breeding: All the 'Rosy' Tetras are egg scatterers and eaters which spawn among fine-leaved vegetation. Hatching takes about 1 day.

Hyphessobrycon serpae (Serpae Tetra).

Hyphessobrycon erythrostigma
(Bleeding Heart Tetra)

THE BLEEDING Heart Tetra (*Hyphessobrycon erythrostigma*) – famous for its blood-red 'heart' spot – is also frequently referred to as *Hyphessobrycon rubrostigma*, both in aquarium books and shops. Both species names refer to the spot, with *'erythro'* and *'rubro'* meaning 'red', and *'stigma'* meaning 'spot'. Of the two names, the former, *H. erythrostigma*, is the one which is currently regarded as being the valid one.

Although Bleeding Hearts can grow to a relatively large size given appropriate aquarium conditions and a good diet, they are, nevertheless, peaceful fish which are tolerant of their tankmates. At first sight, males appear to be somewhat less tolerant of other males in their shoal, but a closer look will reveal that physical contact and body/fin damage hardly ever occur.

Since this species also lives in shoals in the wild, we must conclude that this type of behaviour is quite normal among males. Indeed, it could even be one of several essential factors that keep them naturally 'fit for reproduction. There are, obviously, other factors involved, one or more of which – judging by our lack in success of breeding the species – we appear to be incapable of simulating in aquaria at the moment.

Natural Range: Upper Amazon basin.
Size: Reportedly up to 12cm (4.7in), but usually around 6cm (2.4in) or slightly smaller.
Food: All foods accepted.

Tank Conditions: The aquarium should include the open swimming spaces with bordering plant thickets that shoaling species, which also like a bit of cover prefer. If particularly large specimens are obtained, these should be provided with a roomy aquarium. The use of a peat 'sandwich' in the power filter, a piece of natural bogwood as part of the decor, or the addition of a commercial 'blackwater' preparation will produce the brown-stained water that this species looks particularly resplendent in.
Temperature: 23–28°C (73–82°F).
Breeding: This is a difficult egg-scattering species which rarely breeds in aquaria.

Hyphessobrycon erythrostigma (Bleeding Heart Tetra) are peaceful fish.

Hyphessobrycon herbertaxelrodi
(Black Neon)

Hyphessobrycon herbertaxelrodi (Black Neon Tetra) has become one of the most popular species in the hobby.

ALTHOUGH REFERRED to as a 'Neon', the Black Neon (*Hyphessobrycon herbertaxelrodi*) is very different in coloration to the Neon Tetra (*Paracheirodon innesi*). In its own way, though, it is every bit as beautiful, especially if kept in a shoal under the conditions recommended below.

The attractive appearance of the species, allied to the ease with which it will breed in captivity, has resulted in an unlimited supply of commercially bred, modestly priced specimens which have made the Black Neon one of the most popular community fish in the hobby. Other contributing factors are its peaceful nature and its adaptability to a range of water chemistry conditions, provided changes are carried out gradually and the overall quality of the water is good.

While being adaptable and, therefore, a good beginner's fish, Black Neons (especially small specimens) should not be housed with large or boisterous species which might either attack them or stress them unduly.

Despite the large numbers produced commercially, no fancy-finned or colour varieties of this species have been developed to date.

Natural Range: Restricted to the Rio Taquari, Mato Grosso region of Brazil.

Size: Up to 5cm (2in), but often a little smaller than this.

Food: Wide range of commercial and livefoods accepted.

Tank Conditions: This is a species with strong shoaling tendencies which should be provided with open swimming areas bordered by clumps of vegetation. Water chemistry is not too critical, but softish, tannin-stained water, produced via a peat 'sandwich' in the power filter, the use of a piece of natural bogwood as part of the aquarium decor, or the addition of a commercial 'blackwater' preparation, allied to subdued lighting and a dark substratum, all help to enhance the coloration of the fish.

Temperature: 23–28°C (73–82°F).

Breeding: Soft, acid water is recommended for this egg-scattering species. Hatching takes about 1¹/₂ days.

Hyphessobrycon pulchripinnis
(Lemon Tetra)

THE LEMON Tetra (*Hyphessobrycon pulchripinnis*) can be either a beautiful fish, or a rather drab one; it all depends on what conditions are provided for it.

For example, the best-looking and longest-lived Lemon Tetras I have ever kept were in a large shoal in an aquarium which was thickly planted around the sides and back with Cryptocorynes whose leaves extended over the water surface, thus providing deep shade for the fish. The swimming space at the front of the aquarium measured some 60cm (24in) in length and some 30cm (12in) from front to back. The water was heavily stained from tannins leaching out of a large lump of bogwood...and the water hardness was very high: 300mg/l (ppm). Filtration was via a small, air-operated box filter. Lemons which I have kept in brightly lit aquaria with crystal-clear water and strong, efficient power filtration have never been as beautiful.

Natural Range: Central Brazil.
Size: Up to 5cm (2in).
Food: Most commercial foods and livefoods accepted.
Tank Conditions: This is an active shoaling species which requires a roomy aquarium with plenty of open swimming spaces and thickets of vegetation. Tannin-stained water and subdued lighting show the colours off to brilliant effect. Water chemistry is not critical, with a wide pH and hardness range being tolerated. However, any changes which are carried out must be effected gradually and overall water quality must be good.
Temperature: 23–28°C (73–82°F).
Breeding: This species is only occasionally bred in aquaria. It is an egg scatterer/eater.

OTHER AVAILABLE HYPHESSOBRYCON SPECIES

Hyphessobrycon tetras are a must for any aquarium. However, there are so many desirable species available (some more regularly than others) that it is often hard to choose. In addition to the species featured above, the following are all worth considering:

H. amandae (Ember Tetra), *H. bifasciatus* (Yellow Tetra), *H. heterorhabdus* (Flag Tetra), *H. loretoensis* (Loreto Tetra), *H. metae* (Purple Tetra), *H. peruvianus* (Peruvian Tetra), *H. reticulatus* (Netted Tetra), *H. socolofi* (Lesser Bleeding Heart/Socolof's Tetra) and *H. vilmae* (Vilma's Tetra).

Hyphessobrycon pulchripinnis (Lemon Tetra).

Megalamphodus megalopterus
(Black Phantom Tetra)

THE BLACK Phantom Tetra (*Megalamphodus megalopterus*) is a lovely fish which endears itself to all aquarists who keep it, not just because of its attractive body markings, but also because of the tendency of both males and females to hold their dorsal (back) and anal (belly) fins erect. This is particularly evident among the males when kept in a sizeable shoal in conditions that suit the species.

The Red Phantom Tetra (*M. sweglesi*), a similar-looking close relative of the Black Phantom which is found in the Orinoco basin and parts of Colombia, is also regularly available. As its name indicates, the overall coloration is red, although the body spot is black and (particularly) the dorsal fin carries a pronounced black patch with a distinct white mark near the tip of the front rays.

The Red Phantom is not as hardy as its black cousin, preferring soft, acid conditions and considerably lower temperatures (around 20–23°C /68–73°F).

Long-finned varieties of both the Black and Red Phantoms have been developed commercially and are widely available. Some of these fancy types are slightly larger than their respective wild types.

Natural Range: Guaporé – region around the Bolivian/Brazilian border.

Size: Around 4cm (1.6in), but some cultivated varieties may be slightly larger.

Food: Most commercial and livefoods accepted.

Tank Conditions: This is a hardy species which is not demanding in terms of water chemistry, as long as the quality is good. It does, however, look at its best in a shoal kept in aquaria that provide open swimming space, and shelter in the form of plant thickets. Subdued light also shows off well the colours of this impressive little fish.

Temperature: 22–28°C (72–82°F).

Breeding: This is not one of the easiest tetras to breed in home aquaria, although large numbers are produced commercially. Soft, acid water and subdued lighting are recommended.

Above: Megalamphodus megalopterus (Black Phantom Tetra). Top: Megalamphodus sweglesi (Red Phantom Tetra).

Metynnis hypsauchen
(Silver Dollar/Plain Metynnis/Pacu)

DESPITE ITS appearance, the Silver Dollar (*Metynnis hypsauchen*) is not a piranha, but a peaceful, plant-eating characin which should be kept in shoals.

The genus *Metynnis* is easily distinguished from other similar-looking fish in that their adipose ('second dorsal') fin is very large in comparison with its closest relatives.

There is considerable confusion regarding the exact nomenclature of species within this genus with some synonyms of *M. hypsauchen*, e.g., *M. schreitmülleri*, being quoted as distinct species in a number of books, and the name Silver Dollar being applied to several species, including (perhaps most correctly of all) *M. argenteus*, and *M. lippincottianus*, otherwise known as the Spotted Metynnis, a name that is also attributed to *M. maculatus*!

Natural Range: Western region of the Amazon basin, Rio Paraguay basin, Orinoco and Guyana.
Size: Around 15cm (6in).
Food: The diet should be predominantly vegetable-based (fresh lettuce is avidly accepted). Will also take a range of other items, including flakes, pellets, livefoods and freeze-dried and deep-frozen foods.

Tank Conditions: On account of its relatively large size and shoaling tendencies, Silver Dollars should be kept in spacious aquaria with large open swimming areas. Since natural plants form an integral part of this fish's diet, unpalatable types or artificial substitutes need to be used if permanent greenery is desired. Alternatively, other types of decorations, such as rocks, driftwood, bogwood and/or their commercially produced equivalents, may be used to good effect. Water chemistry is not a critical factor, but soft, slightly acid conditions are preferred.
Temperature: 24–28°C (75–82°F).
Breeding: This can be achieved in roomy aquaria containing soft, acid water, preferably tannin-stained. It is recommended that the aquarium should, initially, be darkened and that the level of illumination be then increased gradually. Eggs (up to 2,000) will be laid among clumps of fine-leaved plants on the feathery roots of floating plants, but will drop to the bottom where the parents ignore them. Hatching can take around 3 days.

Metynnis hypsauchen (Silver Dollar) needs spacious aquaria with large open swimming areas.

Micralestes interruptus
(Congo Tetra)

THE CONGO Tetra (*Micralestes interruptus*) is also widely referred to as *Phenacogrammus interruptus* in aquarium literature. However, in keeping with recent trends, *Micralestes* is preferred here.

The Congo is one of relatively few species of 'aquarium' tetras to come from Africa. It is also one of the most beautiful, with the iridescent colours of the males showing up particularly well under the tank conditions recommended below, the extended flowing finnage of males further adding to the overall effect. Females, while being drabber and smaller than males – and lacking the fin extensions – are, nevertheless, also very attractive in their own right.

Despite its relatively large size when compared with some of the smaller tetras, *M. interruptus* is a peaceful, tolerant species. It is, therefore, a good choice for a community aquarium, as long as this is large enough to provide adequately for, at least, a small shoal.

Natural Range: Republic of the Congo (formerly Zaire).
Size: Up to 9cm (3.5in) for large males; females somewhat smaller at around 6cm (2.4in).

Food: Most foods accepted. This species – which can be a timid feeder – may also nibble fine-leaved, or otherwise succulent, plants.
Tank Conditions: This is an active shoaler which should therefore be kept in groups of at least six fish or more. This, allied to the size attained by mature males, dictates that a spacious aquarium be provided for this species, with an ample swimming area at the front. Since Congo Tetras can also be timid or easily frightened, dense clumps of vegetation should be planted along the sides and back of the aquarium, thus offering them shelter as and when required. Soft, slightly acid, 'black' water is preferred, along with subdued lighting and a dark aquarium bottom.
Temperature: 24–27°C (75–81°F).
Breeding: This is possible, but not common, in home aquaria. Well-conditioned pairs or shoals may spawn in the morning, scattering eggs over the substratum. Hatching takes about 6 days.

An attractive Micralestes interruptus (Congo Tetra).

Moenkhausia pittieri
(Diamond Tetra)

THE DIAMOND Tetra (*Moenkhausia pittieri*), while being a generally undemanding fish, dislikes hard, alkaline water. It does not, therefore, always adapt to such conditions as readily as some other tetras can.

Males of this species are more impressive than females, because of their fuller dorsal (back) and anal (belly) fins and higher concentration of sparkling ('diamond') scales on their bodies.

Juvenile specimens lack much of this splendour and so are not as attractive, a factor than can result in them being overlooked by potential buyers in aquarium shops. A second factor counting against juveniles is that, while lacking much of the iridescence of the adults, they still exhibit the silver/grey base body colour which also extends onto the fins, making them rather drab-looking fish overall.

However, astute aquarists who know just how these rather uninspiring fish will develop, given a little time and appropriate rearing conditions, will often take the opportunity of buying a shoal of these modestly priced fish, soon ending up with a magnificent display at a fraction of the price of adults.

Despite their high level of activity, Diamond Tetras are peaceful towards other fish and so make good community aquarium subjects. They tend to occupy the middle and lower reaches of the tank.

Natural Range: Area around Lake Valencia in Venezuela.
Size: 6cm (2.4in).
Food: Most commercial and livefoods accepted.
Tank Conditions: This is an active shoaling species that demands plenty of open swimming space, but not necessarily the heavily planted aquarium sides and back that many other tetras prefer. Tasteful aquascaping will, nevertheless, enhance the appearance of this attractively scaled fish. The water should be soft and acid, preferably tannin-stained, i.e., 'black' water, and the aquarium lighting should be subdued.
Temperature: 24–28°C (75–82°F).
Breeding: Soft, acid water should be provided for this egg-scattering, egg-eating species. Darkening the tank at first and then gradually increasing the level of illumination is recommended. Hatching takes 2–3 days.

Moenkhausia pittieri (Diamond Tetra) are lively fish which develop into magnificently coloured adults.

Moenkhausia sanctaefilomenae
(Red-eyed Tetra / Yellow-banded Moenkhausia)

WITHOUT DOUBT, the common name Red-eyed Tetra is a far more appropriate one for *Moenkhausia sanctaefilomenae* than Yellow-banded Moenkhausia, as the accompanying photograph demonstrates.

Although, at first sight, the Red-eye looks quite different to the Diamond Tetra (*M. pittieri*) featured in the previous entry, skull, dental and lateral line characteristics, allied to the possession of scales on the caudal (tail) fin, place them both within the genus *Moenkhausia* and separate them from the other tetra genera.

Without being spectacularly coloured, *M. sanctaefilomenae* is quite a splendid fish when kept in a large shoal. Under such conditions, the dark-edged scales on the upper half of the body, the overall silvery scalation, the brilliant red of the eye, the jet-black spot in the front half of the tail and the shiny yellow band on the caudal peduncle (the bit that links the body to the tail and which is responsible for the 'Yellow-banded' common name) combine to create a moving picture of great beauty that has made the Red-eyed Tetra a firm favourite within the aquarium hobby. In addition, the species is an active swimmer, but is peaceful towards other fish, two other commendable qualities in a good community fish.

Natural Range: Eastern Bolivia, western Brazil, Paraguay and eastern Peru.

Size: Up to 7cm (2.8in); often a little smaller than this.

Food: All foods accepted.

Tank Conditions: This is a hardy species that is not too demanding with regard to water quality, either in terms of pH or hardness. Being a shoaler, it requires open swimming areas bordered by plant thickets into which it can retreat.

Temperature: 23–26°C (72–79°F) recommended, but will also tolerate slightly lower and higher temperatures.

Breeding: Pairs or shoals will spawn among fine-leaved vegetation or the feathery roots of some floating plants. Soft, acid water tends to produce best results in this egg-scattering, egg-eating species. Hatching takes 1–2 days.

Moenkhausia sanctaefilomenae (Red-eyed Tetra).

Nannostomus beckfordi
(Golden Pencilfish)

PENCILFISH CLASSIFICATION is in a state of some confusion with regard not just to the number of genera in the family (Lebiasinidae), but also the species or subspecies in each genus.

Three genera are often referred to in aquarium literature: *Nannobrycon*, *Nannostomus* and *Poecilobrycon*. However, there is no universal agreement regarding distinguishing characteristics. In view of this – and awaiting firm scientific evidence – I am grouping all the 'aquarium' species of pencilfish within the genus *Nannostomus*. I am also, for the same reason, subsuming the following species (or subspecies – depending on what literature one consults) within *Nannostomus beckfordi*: *N. anomalus* (*N. beckfordi anomalus*) and *N. aripirangensis* (*N. b. aripirangensis*).

All pencilfishes are timid fish which should not be kept with aggressive or boisterous species. Of those available, the Golden Pencilfish (*N. beckfordi*) is the most adaptable and, consequently, the easiest to keep, as long as a little commonsense is exercised in the choice of tankmates and recommended environmental conditions are adhered to.

The more demanding species which are fairly regularly available include: *N. bifasciatus* (Two-lined Pencilfish), *N. eques* (Tube-mouthed / Three-striped / Hockey Stick Pencilfish), *N. espei* (Espe's / Barred / Common Pencilfish), *N. harrisoni* (Harrison's Pencilfish), *N. marginatus* (Dwarf Pencilfish), *N. trifasciatus* (Three-lined / Banded Pencilfish) and *N. unifasciatus* (One-lined Pencilfish).

Nannostomus beckfordi (Golden Pencilfish).

Nannostomus harrisoni (Harrison's Pencilfish).

Natural Range: Central Amazon, lower reaches of the Rio Negro and Guyana.

Size: Up to 6.5cm (2.6in) reported, but usually grows to around 5cm (2in).

Food: Most small-sized foods, particularly small swimming livefoods.

Tank Conditions: *Nannostomus beckfordi* is a bit of an exception among the pencilfishes in that it is bolder and does not require the dense planting that its close relatives demand for their long-term well-being. Nevertheless, soft, acid water – preferably tannin-stained – and subdued lighting are preferred.

Temperature: 24–28°C (75–82°F).

Breeding: In general, pencilfishes are not the easiest egglayers to get to spawn in home aquaria. Subdued light, soft, acid water, fine-leaved clumps or 'bushes' of vegetation, e.g., Java Moss (*Vesicularia dubyana*) and elevated temperatures, e.g., around 30°C (86°F) are all recommended for this egg scatterer which has a distinct appetite for its own eggs. Hatching takes from 1–3 days.

Nannostomus unifasciatus (One-Lined Pencilfish).

Nematobrycon palmeri
(Emperor Tetra)

Nematobrycon palmeri (Emperor Tetra).

THE EMPEROR Tetra (*Nematobrycon palmeri*) is a peaceful, sometimes timid, species which makes a good community aquarium fish. It will not bother its tankmates, although older males may spar with one another, but without causing physical damage, either to themselves or the (smaller) females. In their turn, though, Emperor Tetras can be upset by more aggressive, boisterous fish, so bear this in mind when choosing a community that includes these tetras.

Emperors are among the longest-lived tetras and can survive upwards of five years if they receive a good diet and are kept in appropriate water conditions in a well maintained, stress-free (or relatively stress-free) aquarium.

A closely related species – also from western Colombia – the Rainbow Emperor Tetra (*N. lacortei*) is also occasionally available. The requirements of this red-eyed 'sparkling' fish are similar to those recommended for *N. palmeri* (which is blue/green-eyed). A third 'species' – generally referred to as *N. 'amphiloxus'* – is believed to be a smoky-coloured, darker variant form of *N. palmeri* and is just as easy to keep.

Natural Range: Western Colombia.

Size: Up to 6cm (2.4in), usually a little smaller.

Food: Most foods accepted.

Tank Conditions: While it is not necessary to keep the Emperor Tetra in shoals, at least a pair or two should be kept together. Open swimming space bordered by ample clumps of vegetation should be provided. Tannin-stained soft, acid water is preferred, but is not essential, as slightly alkaline, medium-hard conditions will also be tolerated comfortably, as long as any changes are carried out gradually.

Temperature: 23–27°C (73–81°F).

Breeding: This is not an easy species to breed. Good results are sometimes obtained in soft, acid water at the higher end of the recommended temperature range, or even a little higher still, in a small, darkened aquarium supplied with fine-leaved vegetation. The eggs are laid singly and will be eaten by the parents, given the chance. Hatching takes 1–2 days.

Paracheirodon axelrodi and Paracheirodon innesi
(Cardinal Tetra and Neon Tetra)

THESE TWO delightful tetras are among the most popular of all aquarium fish. They are featured together here, because new aquarists in particular sometimes find it difficult to distinguish between the two.

The easiest way of doing this is by examining the red body stripe that both fish possess. In the Cardinal, this extends all the way from the tail forwards to the head. In the Neon, it extends only halfway up the body, giving the fish a distinctly silvery belly.

Both species are excellent community fish, as long as they are not kept in the company of large fish which may regard them as a tasty mouthful. A golden form of the Neon Tetra is occasionally available and requires the same conditions as its wild type counterpart.

Natural Range: Cardinal Tetra: From the Orinoco (Venezuela), through the northern tributaries of the Rio Negro (Brazil), and on to western Colombia.
Neon Tetra: Eastern Peru.
Size: Cardinal Tetra: 5cm (2in).
Neon Tetra: 4cm (1.6in).
Food: All small commercial and livefoods.
Tank Conditions: Both species are shoalers and must not be kept either singly or in pairs. While the Neon is

Paracheirodon innesi (Neon Tetra).

reported to be highly adaptable, both in terms of pH and hardness, the Cardinal is generally reported to be less so. Despite these reports, I have kept Cardinals in hard water 300mg/l (ppm) for around five years under subdued lighting, gentle filtration and in tannin-stained water. No breeding occurred under these conditions, but the health of the fish was beyond doubt. Both Neons and Cardinals should be provided with open swimming areas and thick clumps of vegetation.
Temperature: Usually kept between 22–25°C (72–77°F), but slightly lower temperatures are accepted, primarily by Neons, and slightly higher ones by Cardinals.
Breeding: Neither species is easy to breed in home aquaria. Very soft, acid, tannin-stained water at the higher end of the temperature range, plus subdued lighting, should be provided. These are egg-scattering, egg-eating species. Hatching takes about 1 day.

Paracheirodon axelrodi (Cardinal Tetras) shoaling.

Pristella maxillaris
(X-ray Tetra/X-ray Fish/Water Goldfinch)

THE X-RAY Tetra (*Pristella maxillaris*) – its common name reflecting its transparent/translucent musculature – is an old and well-loved favourite which still appears in aquarium literature under its former name, *Pristella riddlei*.

Although, like its avian counterpart, its body has white, black, yellow and red coloration, the use of the common name, Water Goldfinch, seems rather fanciful and is probably a relict of the days when the Goldfinch was more popular among bird keepers than it appears to be today.

To be at its best, the X-ray Tetra needs to be kept in a shoal, and while it will tolerate both alkaline, hard water conditions and bright aquarium lights, it is only at its most beautiful under the conditions recommended below.

In the wild, this species is sometimes found in brackish water areas, but unless the other tankmates chosen for this peaceful community aquarium fish are also comfortable in such an environment, it is wiser (and easier!) to stick to freshwater.

The translucent Pristella maxillaris (X-Ray Tetra).

Natural Range: Lower Amazon (Brazil), Guyana, Venezuela.

Size: 4.5cm (1.8in).

Food: Will accept a wide range of commercial and livefoods.

Tank Conditions: The X-ray Tetra is a small undemanding shoaling species which will tolerate a range of water chemistry conditions, as long as the overall quality is good. Nevertheless, it prefers soft, slightly acid water. Subdued lighting and a dark substrate help to show off this subtly-coloured species to best effect. As a shoaler, it also requires open swimming space bordered by vegetation.

Temperature: As low as 21°C (70°F) and as high as 28°C (82°F) will be tolerated, with the higher end of the range recommended for breeding. The lower end should be avoided over any length of time.

Breeding: Once compatible pairs have formed, breeding is not particularly difficult. Failing this, spawning success is often elusive. This is an egg-scattering species whose eggs hatch in about 1 day.

Pyrrhulina vittata
(Striped / Banded Pyrrhulina)

THE STRIPED or Banded Pyrrhulina (*Pyrrhulina vittata*) looks superficially (in terms of body shape, rather than colour) like its family relative, the Splashing Tetra (*Copella arnoldi*). However, unlike its 'cousin', the Striped Pyrrhulina lays its eggs on a submerged leaf or stone, rather than on aerial vegetation.

This slim-bodied, beautifully marked fish is peaceful towards other species and can therefore be kept in a community aquarium with similarly sized tankmates (but see below for further details regarding its own species).

Several red-spotted species of *Pyrrhulina* (some species of the genus are difficult to differentiate from one another) are also available with varying degrees of regularity. Among these are *P. rachoviana* (Red-spotted Pyrrhulina), *P. laeta* (Half-banded Pyrrhulina) and *P. eleanora* (Eleanor's Pyrrhulina), which are similarly-sized to *P. vittata* and require the same basic conditions.

Although *Pyrrhulina* can be distinguished from its closest relatives by dental features, considerable confusion still exists between the various genera and (particularly) species.

Natural Range: Amazon Basin.

Size: Up to 7cm (2.8in) reported; usually slightly smaller than this.

Food: This species shows a strong preference for livefoods, but will also accept deep-frozen and freeze-dried food. Flakes and other dry foods are only accepted reluctantly.

Tank Conditions: Although males can be somewhat aggressive towards their own kind, Striped / Banded Pyrrhulina should not be kept either as single specimens or a pair. It is better, instead to provide a suitably large aquarium with open and sheltered areas for a small shoal, offering them the opportunity to retreat under cover when circumstances so dictate, while, at the same time, having sufficient 'breathing space' not to be under constant stress. Subdued lighting and a dark substrate are also recommended for this species, along with a sufficiently vigorous filter outlet spray / flow to create a current.

Temperature: 24–27°C (75–81°F)

Breeding: Breeding is not easy. Eggs are laid on broad-leaved plants or a stone and guarded by the male until they hatch after about 2 days.

Pyrrhulina vittata (Striped Pyrrhulina) is a slim fish which is peaceful towards other species.

Serrasalmus (Pygocentrus) nattereri
(Red/Red-Bellied/Natterer's Piranha)

THE RED-BELLIED Piranha (*Serrasalmus (Pygocentrus) nattereri*) has a formidable reputation as a vicious killer. It can certainly be this...and has the perfect equipment to do so...but its reputation as a predator that will attack anything that it encounters, is somewhat exaggerated.

Without a doubt, extreme care needs to be exercised when carrying out maintenance duties in a piranha tank, just as caution and commonsense are prudent when working in piranha-populated waters. It is not, for example, wise to enter piranha waters, or to immerse one's hands in a piranha aquarium, if one has an open wound.

Surprisingly, piranha can be timid and easily frightened if they are kept in bare, brightly lit aquaria.

Export of piranha from certain countries is either restricted or banned. Equally, some countries or regions have restrictions on the keeping of piranha.

Natural Range: Amazon and Orinoco basins.
Size: Up to 30cm (12in).
Food: Flesh-based diet, including large livefoods, fish and meat chunks. Piranha will eat live fish (their main food in the wild). However, whether or not to feed a live vertebrate to another is an ethical question that every piranha keeper should consider well before making a decision.

Tank Conditions: Large, well-filtered aquaria are essential for this substantial carnivore, which – owing to its flesh-based diet – is a notorious water polluter. Soft, slightly acid water is preferred, but is not absolutely essential. Only very robust plants are likely to survive for any length of time; artificial counterparts may therefore be a better bet. Large pieces of bogwood (or equivalent) may be used as decor.

Temperature: 24–27°C (75–81°F).

Breeding: Can be achieved in large aquaria. Pairs have been known to spawn among the feathery roots of large floating plants. More commonly, though, eggs (numbering several thousand) are laid in a depression in the substratum and defended by both parents. The female will usually be chased away by the male after about one day. Hatching takes 2–3 days.

Large livefoods are the preferred diet for the formidable Serrasalmus nattereri (Red-Bellied Piranha).

Thayeria obliqua
(Penguin Fish)

THE PENGUIN FISH (*Thayeria obliqua*) has been in the hobby for nearly 50 years. Its close relative, Boehlke's Penguin Fish (*T. boehlkei*), from Peru and western Brazil, has been around even longer.

Although, at first sight, it may seem easy to confuse one species with the other, once you know what to look for, telling them apart poses no problem. Just as Neon and Cardinal Tetras (*Paracheirodon innesi* and *P. axelrodi*) can be identified by the extent of their red body stripes, the two Penguin Fish can be distinguished according to the length of their black stripes.

In *Thayeria obliqua*, the stripe begins at the tip of the lower lobe of the caudal (tail) fin and only extends into the posterior half (at most) of the body. In *T. boehlkei*, however, the black pigmentation extends all the way to the top corner of the operculum (gill cover).

Another difference between the two species is that, while *T. obliqua* has not, apparently, been bred in home aquaria, *T. boehlkei* is a prolific breeder, both in home aquaria and commercial premises.

Both species are peaceful and undemanding and are therefore good choices for community aquaria.

Natural Range: Several river systems in Brazil.
Size: Up to 8cm (3.1in) reported; usually a little smaller.
Food: Most foods accepted.
Tank Conditions: A thickly planted aquarium is recommended for this species. It will also swim in open water at the front of the aquarium, particularly if kept as a small shoal, a situation which gives individuals a greater sense of security than when they are kept either singly or in pairs. Softish, slightly acid water is preferred, but some deviation from these conditions is tolerated, provided any changes are carried out gradually, the overall quality is good and the oxygen concentration adequate.
Temperature: 22–28°C (72–82°F).
Breeding: No reports of home spawnings are available.

Thayeria boehlkei (Boehlke's Penguin Fish).

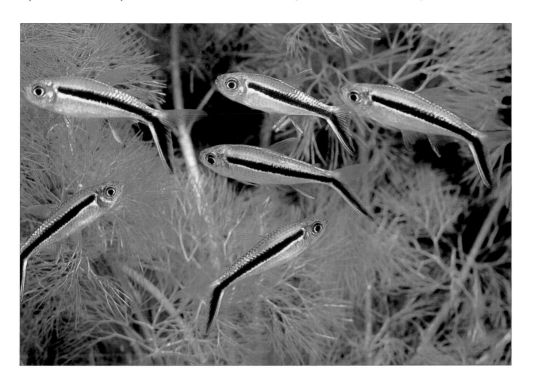

CATFISH

WHILE IT IS true to say that all catfishes possess mouth barbels ('whiskers'), it would be wrong to assume that all fish that possess barbels are catfish, as the barbs and many of their relatives belonging to Cyprinidae prove. There are other features – often occurring in combination – that, while not applying to every single species, distinguish catfishes (which belong to the order Siluriformes) from other fish.

In addition to the ubiquitous barbels, which are visible even to the casual observer, catfish possess a number of skull bone arrangements which can only be observed through detailed dissection (not, however, a great deal of help when you are trying to determine whether the fish you have swimming in front of you in an aquarium is a catfish or not!).

Nevertheless, some of these 'hidden' skull features are crucial in catfish classification. One of these can be observed in the development of the urohyal bones of the branchiocranium (the lower part of the skull associated with the support of the gills) which arise as 'unpaired' ossifications (bone formations) of a tendon in other fish, but as a 'paired' arrangement, which later fuses, in catfishes.

Much more easily detectable are features such as an adipose ('second dorsal') fin and the possession of one or more spines at the front of the dorsal (back) and pectoral (chest) fins, which can form 'locking' mechanisms that afford catfish considerable protection against predators. In addition, instead of having 'normal' scales, catfish either have a naked body or bony plates.

Pyjama Synodontis showing mouth barbles.

The little Corydoras habrosus (Dwarf Corydoras).

Catfish classification is currently in an unsettled state (a factor shared with other groups of fish) and, while estimates vary, there are reckoned to be about 34 families, containing some 412 genera and over 2,400 species. In the pages that follow, examples of the following families will be profiled: Aspredinidae (Banjo Catfishes), Callichthyidae (Armoured Catfishes), Loricariidae (Suckermouth Catfishes), Mochokidae (Squeakers/Upside-down Catfishes), Pimelodidae (Long-whiskered Catfishes) and Siluridae (Sheatfishes).

Corydorus paleatus (Peppered Catfish) male showing high dorsal fin.

Ancistrus hoplogenys
(Spotted Bristle-Nosed Catfish)

THE SPOTTED Bristle-nosed Catfish (*Ancistrus hoplogenys*) is a particularly attractive member of this genus, which is now imported with considerably greater regularity than it was in the past. A second species, the Bristle-nosed Catfish (*A. dolichopterus*), is also widely available and has similar requirements. Other species, while being less well known and sometimes incorrectly identified, are generally equally easy to keep as the two best-known representatives.

One of the main attractions of Bristle-nosed Catfish is the profusion of 'bristles' – which look more like fleshy tentacles – that males possess around the mouth, snout and forehead. Females either lack these adornments, or have weakly developed bristles.

All species are nocturnal and therefore spend most of the day out of sight in their selected hiding places, only coming to life as evening approaches.

Natural Range: Amazon basin.
Size: Quoted as ranging from 8cm (3.1in) to 15cm (6in). Most specimens are offered for sale at the smaller size and attain around 10cm (4in).

Food: This is a herbivorous (plant-eating) species with a distinct liking for encrusting algae, and should be provided with vegetable tablets, pellets and flakes, as well as fresh plant material, such as lettuce or raw potato slices. It will also take food of a less plant-based nature, such as general-formula pellets, etc.

Tank Conditions: Hiding places consisting preferably of natural bogwood/driftwood pieces should be provided for this predominantly nocturnal species. The use of a 'moonlight' fluorescent tube at night will allow you to appreciate this interesting species fully as it goes about its 'everynight' business. Delicate plants are often damaged or eaten, so broad-leaved, robust species should be selected. Fairly soft, acid water is preferred, but deviations from this will be accepted, as long as any changes that are carried out are introduced gradually.

Temperature: 21–26°C (70–79°F).

Breeding: Eggs are laid inside hollow logs (or equivalent) and are generally guarded by the larger, and more generously 'bristled', male, who will also protect the young for 2–3 weeks after hatching.

Ancistrus hoplogenys (Spotted Bristle-Nosed Catfish) male displaying impressive bristles around the mouth.

Brochis britskii
(Giant Brochis)

THE GIANT Brochis (*Brochis britskii*) – probably so-called because of the large size to which it is reported to grow, but which has not, as far as I am aware, been achieved in aquaria to date – is the most recent of the three species of *Brochis* known in the hobby. Despite this, it has quickly become extremely popular and widespread owing to its attractive iridescent coloration and peaceful nature.

Although *Brochis* catfish look similar to their *Corydoras* relatives, they can be easily distinguished from them by their longer snouts, deeper bodies and – most significantly – their higher number of dorsal (back) fin rays which gives them a sailfin-like appearance when held fully extended. In *Brochis*, there are more than 11 – and sometimes up to 18 – such rays, while *Corydoras* only possesses 7 or 8.

Brochis britskii itself is further distinguished by possessing a bony plate on the underside of the head. Within the species, males are distinguished from females by being a little slimmer and possessing a more concave snout profile.

Natural Range: Mato Grosso in Brazil.

Size: Up to 13cm (5.1in) quoted, but usually smaller than this at around 8–9cm (3.1–3.5in).

Food: Wide range of foods accepted, especially sinking formulae and bottom-dwelling livefoods.

Tank Conditions: Because the natural habit of this (and related) species is to root around the bottom and (frequently) under the surface of the substratum in search of food, aquaria housing *Brochis* and *Corydoras* catfish should not contain sharp-edged gravel or other potentially dangerous bottom material. Fine, rounded gravel or coarse sand suits these species best. Open grazing areas surrounded by vegetation should be provided for this peaceful species, which should be kept in a shoal. Water chemistry is not too critical, as long as the overall quality is good, but slightly acid, soft to medium-hard water is generally recommended.

Temperature: 22–26°C (72–79°F).

Breeding: Probably as for *Brochis splendens* (see next entry).

Brochis britskii (Giant Brochis) possesses a peaceful nature.

Brochis splendens
(Emerald Catfish/Brochis, Common Brochis, Short-Bodied Catfish, Sailfin Corydoras)

Brochis splendens (Emerald Catfish), first imported into Europe from Peru in the late 1930s, remains very popular.

OF THE VARIOUS common names used for *Brochis splendens*, the most appropriate (and most widely used) is the Emerald Catfish/Brochis, which is an accurate description of the colour of the body plates (scales) under reflected light. The name Sailfin Corydoras refers to the particularly large dorsal (back) fin of juvenile specimens and the superficial similarity of adults to the Bronze Corydoras (*Corydoras aeneus*). See, however, the previous entry for *B. britskii* for remarks on distinguishing features between the two genera.

B. splendens is the oldest member of the genus in terms of its availability to hobbyists, having been first imported into Europe in the late 1930s. The fact that it is still so popular today is a true reflection of the species' many commendable characteristics, including its tolerant nature, high level of activity and its undoubted adaptability.

The third known member of the genus, the Hog-nosed Brochis (*B. multiradiatus*) is occasionally available. It has a slightly longer snout than the other two species, and is somewhat more demanding in terms of water conditions.

Natural Range: Upper Amazon, Peru, Ecuador.

Size: Around 8cm (3.1in).

Food: Most foods accepted, particularly sinking types and bottom-dwelling livefoods.

Tank Conditions: This is an active shoaling species which should not be kept either singly or in pairs, but in a small group. Open swimming and grazing areas surrounded with thickets of vegetation should be provided. Sharp-edged decorations and substratum must be avoided, so reducing risks of injury to this bottom-hugging, foraging species. The water should be kept on the slightly acid side and should be soft to medium-hard, although some deviation from this will be accepted.

Temperature: 21–28°C (70–82°F).

Breeding: Eggs are generally laid on the underside of broad-leaved vegetation, although there are reports of them being laid among floating plants as well. No protection of either eggs or fry has been reported. Hatching takes about 4 days.

Bunocephalus coracoideus
(Banjo/Frying Pan Catfish)

THE BANJO or Frying Pan Catfish (*Bunocephalus coracoideus*) – so-named because of its overall banjo or pan shape – is probably the species that is most frequently available within the hobby.

It is, however, difficult to be absolutely certain about this, because most of the 20 species in the genus *Bunocephalus* are so similar to one another that they are easily confused. Three other names by which these unusual fish are also frequently known are *B. amaurus*, *B. bicolor* (believed to be a synonym of *B. coracoideus*) and *B. knerii*.

Whatever their correct name may be, Banjo Catfish make interesting additions to an aquarium, particularly one fitted with a 'moonlight' fluorescent tube that will allow them to be observed when they are most active during the hours of darkness.

Natural Range: Amazon region.

Size: Up to 15cm (6in).

Food: Will accept all sinking foods, particularly bottom-dwelling livefoods.

Tank Conditions: Banjo Catfish are mostly inactive during the daylight hours, hiding among bottom debris, e.g., leaves, in hollows, or buried, to a greater or lesser extent, in the substrate. A tank designed to house these fish should therefore provide, at least, one of these conditions. As exporters often include several large leaves in the bags in which Banjos and other secretive fish are transported, it is quite possible that your dealer will still have some leaves available and might be able to supply you with these. Alternatively, well-browned, dry oak leaves will soon become waterlogged and sink to the bottom, thus providing a safe (i.e., non-toxic) authentic-looking bottom covering. Bogwood (or equivalent) will provide hiding hollows, and a fine-grained (preferably dark) substratum will meet the third of this species' preferences. Water chemistry is not critical as long as the quality is good.

Temperature: 20–26°C (68–79°F) is recommended for this species.

Breeding: *B. coracoideus* is the only Banjo Catfish that appears to have been bred in captivity. Eggs were laid in a depression dug by the male and guarded by him. Two spawnings yielded between 4,000 and 5,000 fry.

Bunocephalus coracoideus (Banjo Catfish).

Corydoras aeneus
(Bronze Corydoras/Catfish)

Above: Corydoras aeneus (Bronze Corydoras)
Right: Albino Bronze Corydoras.

THE BRONZE Corydoras (*Corydoras aeneus*) is an old favourite which is every bit as popular today as it was some 30 years ago. It is a hardy, peaceful species which looks particularly impressive when kept in a shoal in a community aquarium.

It is sometimes said that one of the many endearing qualities of the Bronze Corydoras is that it 'winks' at you. However, since – as fish – *Corydoras aeneus* and its relatives within the genus do not possess eyelids, winking is a totally biological impossibility. Nevertheless, they do frequently roll their eyes as if to clean them of irritating debris and this can create the illusion that they are winking in an almost-human fashion.

Several naturally occurring colour forms of the species are known, including a very attractive one exhibiting a considerable amount of old gold-brass, almost-orange pigmentation. In addition, a widely bred albino form is also available.

Natural Range: Trinidad, Venezuela and southwards all the way down to the La Plata region of Argentina.
Size: Up to 7.6cm (3in).
Food: Wide range of foods accepted, particularly sinking formulations and bottom-dwelling livefoods (although swimming livefoods will also be taken).

Tank Conditions: A fine-grained substratum should be provided for this species, which likes to bury its snout and barbels as it forages for food under the surface. Open swimming spaces and sheltered, planted areas should also be provided. Water chemistry is not critical but excessively acid conditions should be avoided.

Temperature: 18–26°C (64–79°F), making it suitable for some unheated aquaria – but not on a permanent basis.

Breeding: In 1995, it was discovered that a female can actually drink sperm while facing the male at right angles and nuzzling his vent during spawning (this is the T-position). The sperm then pass undamaged through her alimentary canal and are ejected, via the anus, onto the female's cupped pelvic (hip) fins into which she releases a few eggs which are thus fertilised. She then deposits the eggs on rocks or plants. Hatching takes about 5 or 6 days, depending on temperature.

Corydoras barbatus
(Bearded Corydoras, Barbatus)

THE BEARDED Corydoras (*Corydoras barbatus*) is one of the few species in the genus in which the males are not only slimmer than the females (as in other species), but also exhibit morphological differences. One of the most characteristic is the anterior (front) edge of the pre-operculum (the bone that lies in front of the operculum – gill cover – proper) which contains bristles in fully mature males. These are the 'beards' that give rise to the common name for *C. barbatus* and for the species part of the scientific name. In females, the bristles are either weakly developed, or absent. Males also have a higher dorsal (back) fin and longer pectoral (chest) fin spines. Both sexes show variation in colour patterns throughout the natural range of the species.

Corydoras barbatus is one of the largest species in the genus; it is also one of the most streamlined. These factors, allied to others like the possession of bristles, has led to the suggestion that the species should be assigned to a separate subgenus, *Scleromystax*.

Corydoras barbatus (Bearded Corydoras).

Natural Range: Rio de Janeiro to São Paulo (both in Brazil).

Size: Up to around 8cm (3.1in).

Food: Most foods accepted, but, particularly, sinking formulations and bottom-dwelling livefoods.

Tank Conditions: Open swimming/feeding areas of fine-grained gravel or coarse (but rounded) sand, surrounded by pebbles and clumps of vegetation, suit this species well. Coming from areas where the water can flow fairly quickly (I measured surface flow at a rate of 1 metre per second at a collecting site on the Rio Aguinaldo, some 60 km [37 miles] from Rio de Janeiro), *C. barbatus* benefits from a current created by the outflow of a power filter. Water chemistry is not too critital, but excessively high (alkaline) pH should be avoided.

Temperature: 22–26°C (72–79°F), but considerably lower temperatures are also accepted.

Breeding: Basically, as in *Corydoras aeneus*, with hatching taking about 3–4 days. Excessively hard or alkaline water may inhibit hatching.

Corydoras habrosus
(Dainty/Dwarf Corydoras)

*C*ORYDORAS HABROSUS is one of several 'Dwarf Corydoras'. *C. cochui*, a similarly patterned species (but from the Rio Araguaia in Brazil), which some catfish specialists believe could turn out to be a variant of *C. habrosus*, is also occasionally available and has the same basic requirements. A third – even smaller – species, *C. hastatus*, which has the delightful habit of hovering in shoals in midwater, is also referred to as the Dwarf Corydoras, but should, perhaps, be more appropriately called the Pygmy Corydoras.

All three species represent good additions to a community aquarium, as long as their tankmates are chosen with due attention and potential aggressors or predators are excluded.

Although, like all *Corydoras* species, the Dwarf Corydoras and its closest relatives possess strong, protective fin spines, they should not be placed in a position where they need to use these in self-defence, since this can cause damage, both to them and their attackers, to say nothing of the unnecessary stress involved.

There are several colour variations of *C. habrosus* and *C. cochui*, which can cause confusion. However, knowledge of the place of origin of specimens should be sufficient to identify them with certainty.

Corydoras hastatus (Pygmy Corydoras).

Natural Range: A few rivers in Venezuela and Colombia.
Size: Up to 3.5cm (1.4in) reported.
Food: Most foods accepted, particularly small-sized sinking types and small bottom-dwelling livefoods.
Tank Conditions: Fine gravel or coarse sand areas surrounded by clumps of vegetation and bogwood (or equivalent) should be provided for this small shoaling species. On account of its small size, *C. habrosus* should not be kept with large, boisterous species, especially those – like some of the cichlids – which like to root around the bottom of the aquarium in search of food. Water chemistry is not critical, but extremes of pH and hardness should be avoided, particularly for breeding purposes.
Temperature: 22–26°C (72–79°F) is quite suitable, although lower temperatures can be tolerated for short periods.
Breeding: Spawning follows the typical *Corydoras* pattern, including the adoption of the T-position (see *C. aeneus*).

Corydoras habrosus (Dwarf Corydoras).

Corydoras julii
(Leopard Corydoras)

THE JULII OR Leopard Corydoras (*Corydoras julii*) is one of three very similarly patterned species, which are difficult to tell apart...until you know exactly what to look for.

All three species (*C. julii, C. leopardus* and *C. trilineatus*) are, basically, silvery fish with black dots/blotches/streaks on the head, body and caudal (tail) fins and a prominent black spot on the dorsal (back) fin. *C. leopardus* has the longest snout of the three. The spotting on *C. leopardus* also tends to be stronger than in *C. julii*, as is (generally speaking) the central horizontal black body line. Both these species can be distinguished from *C. trilineatus* (the Three-lined Corydoras) in that the black marks on the head appear as dots in *C. julii* and *C. leopardus* and as irregular streaks or a reticulated pattern in *C. trilineatus*.

Establishing the origin of the specimens can also prove helpful, since *C. trilineatus* comes from Peru, Colombia and Ecuador (but not Brazil), while *C. leopardus* is found both in Brazil and Peru, and *C. julii* only in Brazil.

Not surprisingly, the close physical resemblance between the three species, has led to some confusion within the hobby, to the extent that many of the fish that have appeared as *C. julii* over the years have actually been *C. trilineatus*. *C. leopardus*, because of its easily distinguishable more-pointed snout, has, generally, been identified more accurately.

Natural Range: Brazilian part of the Amazon.

Size: Around 6cm (2.4in).

Food: Most foods accepted, particularly sinking formulations and bottom-dwelling livefoods, although some swimming livefoods will also be taken.

Tank Conditions: As with other *Corydoras* species. *C. julii* should be provided with open swimming and feeding spaces and surrounding cover. The substratum should be of fine gravel or coarse sand. Water chemistry is not too critical, but extremely low or high pH and hardness levels should be avoided, particularly if an attempt is to be made to breed the species.

Temperature: 22–26°C (72–79°F).

Breeding: This species spawns in typical *Corydoras* fashion (see *C. aeneus* above), but getting it to breed in aquaria can be difficult.

Corydoras julii (Leopard Corydoras).

Corydoras metae
(Bandit/Masked Corydoras)

THERE ARE several 'fleshy-coloured' *Corydoras* species which have a black 'mask' stretching vertically from the top of the head, down through the eye and on to the bottom edge of the cheek. In addition, many of these have a black band along or across the body, ending at the caudal peduncle (the base of the tail fin), plus a black spot or patch on the dorsal (back) fin. In some species, the body band is replaced by a larger or smaller black patch on the caudal peduncle, while in others, the peduncular spot is missing altogether.

The Bandit or Masked Corydoras (*Corydoras metae*) is about the most regularly encountered of these species which include: *C. adolfoi* (Adolf's Corydoras), *C. arcuatus* (Skunk Corydoras), *C. burgessi* (Burgess' Corydoras), *C. melini* (Diagonal Stripe Corydoras), *C. narcissus* (Narcissus Corydoras), *C. panda* (Panda Corydoras) and *C. rabauti* (Rabaut's Corydoras). *C. myersi* (Myer's Corydoras) is now accepted as a synonym of *C. rabauti*.

All these species have basically similar requirements and all should be kept in shoals. If at all possible, a dozen or so specimens should be obtained, since the larger the shoal of these strikingly masked fish, the more impressive the spectacle they present.

Natural Range: Several rivers in Colombia, including the Rio Meta from which the species' name is derived.

Size: Up to 6cm (2.4in) reported, but usually smaller.

Food: Most foods accepted, especially sinking commercial preparations and bottom-dwelling livefoods.

Tank Conditions: Open areas consisting of fine gravel or coarse sand surrounded by vegetation should be provided for this species, as for other *Corydoras*. Pebbles, rocks and other decorations may also be used in designing the aquascape, but these must not have sharp or jagged edges which could cause injury as the fish scuttle along the bottom in search of food. Water chemistry is not critical, but extremes of pH and hardness should be avoided.

Temperature: 22–26°C (72–79°F).

Breeding: Spawning occurs in typical *Corydoras* fashion and hatching takes about 4 days.

Corydoras metae (Bandit or Masked corydoras) are an impressive sight when kept in a large shoal.

Corydoras paleatus
(Peppered Corydoras)

THE PEPPERED Corydoras (*Corydoras paleatus*) is one of the most widely kept tropical community aquarium species. It is hardy, peaceful, gregarious, and beautiful, making it an ideal choice for new aquarists. It is also widely available in an albino form.

The vast majority of specimens available today are commercially bred in farms in all fish-producing areas of the world. Interestingly, most of these fish, while retaining the majority of the characteristics of their wild counterparts, have lost the exceptionally long dorsal (back) fin that makes wild males such spectacular fish.

Natural Range: Argentina, southern Brazil and around Montevideo in Uruguay.
Size: Around 7.5cm (3in).
Food: All foods accepted, particularly sinking formulations and bottom-dwelling livefoods.
Tank Conditions: Although this is an undemanding species, due care should be paid to its preferences, such as a soft substratum and both open and sheltered areas. Water chemistry is not critical, as long as the overall quality is good.
Temperature: 18–26°C (64–79°F), but the top end of the temperature

range should not be maintained on a permanent basis.
Breeding: This is a widely bred species which spawns in typical *Corydoras* fashion.

OTHER COMMONLY AVAILABLE CORYDORAS

With over 120 species of *Corydoras* so far described, this genus offers aquarists a wide range of sizes and colours to choose from. All the basic details relating to the aquarium care of popular shoaling catfish, which are provided in the above entries, generally apply to other members of the genus. Among these species, some of the more or less widely available include: *C. acutus* (Black-top Corydoras), *C. axelrodi* (Banded Corydoras), *C. caudimaculatus* (Tail-spot Corydoras), *C. delphax* (Delphax Corydoras), *C. elegans* (Elegant Corydoras), *C. haraldschultzi* (Harald Schultze's Corydoras), *C. latus* (Iridescent Corydoras), *C. leucomelas* (Black-finned Corydoras), *C. melanistius* (Black-spot Corydoras), *C. reticulatus* (Reticulated/ Network Corydoras), *C. robinae* (Robina's Corydoras) and *C. sterbai* (Sterba's Corydoras).

Below: Corydoras paleatus (Peppered Corydoras).
Left: Albino form.

Dianema urostriata
(Flag-/Stripe-Tailed Catfish)

The nocturnal Dianema urostriata (Flag-tailed Catfish) spends most of its daylight hours resting or hiding.

THE FLAG-TAILED Catfish (*Dianema urostriata*) and its closest relatives from a small group of 'armoured' catfishes (subfamily Callichthyinae) within the family Callichthyidae, which includes their slightly more distant relations like the *Corydoras* species dealt with in the preceding pages.

Within their subfamily, the Flag-tailed Catfish and the Porthole Catfish (*Dianema longibarbis*) can be easily identified by their long, pointed snouts and somewhat lighter 'armour' when compared to the other members of the subfamily.

For their part, the Flag-tailed Catfish and the Porthole can be distinguished from one another at a glance, the beautifully striped caudal (tail) fin of the Flag-tail identifying it without any difficulty. The Porthole Catfish possesses somewhat variable caudal fin pigmentation, ranging from virtual total transparency to heavy spotting, but lacks the distinctive stripes of *D. urostriata*.

Both *Dianema* species are predominantly crepuscular (twilight)/nocturnal fish which spend a large part of the day either resting or hiding. They do, however, also become active during the daylight hours, particularly at feeding time for the other 'daytime' species. Despite this, food should be provided shortly before the main aquarium lights are swithced off in the evening for these and other fish with similar habits. They can be observed during their nocutral activities through the use of a 'moonlight' fluorescent tube.

Natural Range: Lower Rio Negro, Brazil.

Size: Around 10cm (4in).

Food: Wide range of commercial and livefoods accepted.

Tank Conditions: This shoaling species likes both to hover in midwater and rest on top of logs (bogwood) or rocks. The tank layout must therefore make allowances for this, providing open spaces, suitable resting surfaces and clumps of vegetation. Owing to its relatively large size, *D. urostriata* needs roomy accommodation. Water chemistry is not critical, but slightly acid, soft to medium hard water is recommended.

Temperature: 22–26°C (72–79°F).

Breeding: Only very occasionally achieved in aquaria. Eggs are laid in a floating nest of bubbles in warm-water conditions (around 28°C/82°F).

Farlowella acus
(Twig/Stick Catfish)

The herbivorous Farlowella acus (Twig/Stick Catfish) may not be the obvious choice for newcomers to the hobby.

THE TWIG/STICK Catfish (*Farlowella acus*), so-called because of its excellent resemblance – both in terms of its colour and shape – to a submerged thin twig or small stick, is a fish that is more popular among established aquarists than among newcomers to the hobby.

New aquarists sometimes consider its lack of striking coloration and activity as a little boring, but, of course, there is no such thing as a boring fish...whether or not we rate a species as such is merely a reflection of what we seek in our choice of species.

For those aquarists who welcome owning a fish that has evolved and survived through time by the strategy of looking like something else, few choices can be better than the Twig Catfish or its closest relatives like the Whiptailed or Mottled Twig Catfish (*Farlowella gracilis*). In addition, few fish can present us with such a great opportunity of gaining a really close-up view of their reproductive behaviour as *Farlowella* species do when they choose (as they sometimes do) to lay their eggs and brood them on the front glass of an aquarium right in front of our eyes.

Natural Range: Southern regions of the Amazon.

Size: Up to 17cm (6.7in) reported, but usually a little smaller.

Food: This is a predominantly algae-grazing (herbivorous) species which will take sinking types of vegetable-based commercial foods, e.g., vegetable flakes, granules and tablets, as well as fresh plant material like lettuce and spinach leaves, green peas and slices of potato.

Tank Conditions: Plenty of resting and hiding places should be provided for this species, which spends most of its time clinging on to, and feeding from, suitable surfaces, e.g., a broad-leaved plant, bogwood, rocks or, even, the panes of the aquarium. The water should be soft and on the acid side.

Temperature: 21–26°C (70–79°F).

Breeding: If conditions are to their liking, pairs will breed in aquaria, laying adhesive eggs on a suitable substrate. For the next 7–10 days, they are protected by one or both parents (reports vary on this).

Glyptoperichthys gibbiceps
(Spotted Pleco/Sailfin Suckermouth Catfish)

NUMEROUS AQUARIUM books still list this species as *Pterygoplichthys gibbiceps*. However, recent research has resulted in the disappearance of *Pterygoplichthys* and its replacement with *Glyptoperichthys*, which includes species like the Spotted Pleco (or Plec), and *Liposarchus*, which includes some of the other Plecos, e.g., *L. anisisti* (the Snow King Pleco).

Other Plecos, such as the very dark 'original' Pleco (*Hypostomus plecostomus*) and the Spotted Hypostomus (*H. punctatus*) remain in their original genus, *Hypostomus*. These are easily distinguished from their related genera by their lower number of dorsal (back) fin spines and rays (one spine and seven rays in *Hypostomus* and one spine plus more than ten rays in the other two genera).

All are commonly available as small (10cm/4in) specimens – or even smaller – and all grow to a substantial size, given appropriate conditions. Therefore, unless provision can be made to accommodate specimens as they grow, Plecos are best given a miss until one is in a position to cater adequately for their needs.

Glyptoperichthys gibbiceps (Spotted Pleco).

Natural Range: Peru.

Size: Up to 50–60cm (20–24in).

Food: Plant-based sinking foods (particularly granules and tablets) are recommended for this algae-eating species. Offer the food late in the evening or just prior to switching off the aquarium lights.

Tank Conditions: Beacause of the large size that this species attains, only roomy aquaria with adequate open and sheltered areas can offer suitable longterm accommodation for it and the other various Plecos. *G. gibbiceps* and its relatives are nocturnal fish which only really come alive when the main aquarium lights are switched off. Therefore, in order to appreciate these nighttime feeders at their most active, a 'moonlight' fluorescent tube should form part of the aquarium lighting system. Water chemistry is not critical, but the quality must be good.

Temperature: 22–27°C (68–81°F), but the lower end of the range should not be maintained over an extended period.

Breeding: Breeding in aquaria has not been achieved, largely because *Glyptoperichthys* naturally spawns in long burrows which are excavated below water level in river banks.

Lepthoplosternum pectorale
(Spotted Hoplo)

Lepthoplosternum pectorale (Spotted Hoplo) is a tough, hardy species.

THE SPOTTED HOPLO (*Lepthoplosternum pectorale*) appears in virtually every aquarium book published to date as *Hoplosternum pectorale*. However, in 1997, a major revision of the genus was carried out by Roberto Reis, based at the University of Rio Grande do Sul in Brazil, and the genus was split up according to skeletal structures, caudal (tail) fin shape and other criteria.

As a result, the three former *Hoplosternum* species, which have been popular aquarium fishes for many years, are now assigned to separate genera: *Hoplosternum littorale* – the Cascudo Hoplo – retains its name; *Hoplosternum pectorale* becomes *Lepthoplosternum pectorale*; *Hoplosternum thoracatum* – the Port Hoplo – becomes *Megalechis thoracata*. The other closely related species generally known as the Armoured Catfish, *Callichthys callichthys*, also retains its name.

All these species can be found in large shoals in the wild and, in at least some countries, they are collected in considerable quantities as food fish. In aquaria, they are best kept singly or, if in larger numbers, in set-ups that offer retreats for any individuals that may feel harassed.

Males, in particular, can become very aggressive during the breeding season and are, therefore, not the best choices for a community aquarium.

Natural Range: Paraguay.

Size: Around 15cm (6in) reported, but usually considerably smaller than this.

Food: All commercial and livefoods accepted.

Tank Conditions: Although this is a tough species that can withstand poor water conditions, this must not be used as an excuse for laziness on the part of the aquarist. A wide range of pH and hardness is tolerated, making this species appear as a good candidate for a community aquarium. However, even though these are generally not aggressive fish (but see text above), they should not be housed with fish that are small enough to be considered as 'livefood'. These armoured catfishes prefer a dark aquarium with numerous hiding places.

Temperature: 20–28°C (68–82°F).

Breeding: This is not an easy species to breed. Eggs are laid in a floating bubblenest and are guarded.

Kryptopterus bicirrhis
(Glass/Ghost Catfish, Ghostfish)

THE GLASS CATFISH (*Kryptopterus bicirrhis*) is a 'once-seen-never-forgotten' fish. Its body is virtually transparent, so much so that its backbone is perfectly visible through the crystal-clear body musculature. Overlaying this is an iridescent sheen the colours of which vary depending on the quality and angle of the light. In addition, the body organs are compressed inside a small, spherical, silvery body cavity which lies directly behind the large eyes. Finally, there are the long, fine barbels which the fish constantly waves as it senses its environment.

Put all these features together and then multiply them several times over (for a shoal), and it is easy to see why so many aquarists have found this species so irresistible over the years.

It must be emphasised, though, that the Glass Catfish is not always the easiest of species to feed and that it must be kept in, at least, a small shoal, since single specimens invariably deteriorate sooner or later.

The beautiful Kryptopterus bicirrhis (Glass Catfish) is virtually transparent and thrives in a small shoal.

Natural Range: Eastern India and widely distributed through southeast Asia.

Size: Up to 15cm (6in) reported, but usually considerably smaller than this.

Food: The diet should consist predominantly of swimming livefoods, although deep-frozen, freeze-dried and even dried foods may be taken if they are distributed around the aquarium by a current, such as the outflow of a power filter.

Tank Conditions: Unusually for a catfish, *Kryptopterus bicirrhis* is a midwater species that hovers in shoals with its head pointing slightly upwards. A suitably large open space should, therefore, be provided, preferably at the centre front of the aquarium, to be able to appreciate the full beauty of a shoal of these lovely fish. Clumps of vegetation along the sides and back of the aquarium should also be provided. Water chemistry is not too critical but soft, slightly acid conditions seem best.

Temperature: 21–26°C (70–79°F).

Breeding: No documented accounts of successful breeding in aquaria are available, but fry have been reported on, at least, one occasion.

Otocinclus affinis
(Dwarf/Golden Otocinclus, Midget Sucker Catfish)

THE DWARF OTOCINCLUS (*Otocinclus affinis*) is no tinier than the other most commonly encountered *Otocinclus* in the hobby, the Marbled Otocinclus (*O. paulinus*), and only marginally smaller than its largest relatives in the genus, such as the Ampiyacu Dwarf Sucker Catfish (*O. vestitus*). Despite this, it is still generally known as the Dwarf Otocinclus. Its other common names are no more accurate either, since it is neither the smallest of the 20 or so species in the genus, nor is its light body stripe particularly golden in colour!

During the day, *O. affinis* tends to be a shy, retiring species. During the evening and night, it is, however, as active as most of its suckermouthed cousins within the family Loricariidae.

Although individuals can be territorial, their displays do not result in physical injury and, since the species is found in groups in the wild, this should be replicated within the aquarium, as long as a sufficient number of hiding places or retreats are provided.

Otocinclus affinis (Dwarf Otocinclus).

Natural Range: Southeastern Brazil.

Size: Up to 5cm (2in) reported, but nearly always smaller than this.

Food: Predominantly algae-based. Sinking vegetable granules, sticks and tablets are perfectly acceptable commercial alternatives.

Tank Conditions: This small species is a good candidate for the community aquarium, because of its small size and peaceful nature. It can, however, sometimes prove a little demanding at first in terms of water quality. Initial recommended conditions include soft water with an acid pH value (as low as pH 5) which can be raised gradually to neutral or even slightly above (pH 7–7.5). Hardness, too, can be raised gradually. Once fully acclimatised, no water chemistry problems should arise, as long as the overall quality is good. Dense vegetation and numerous resting/hiding places should also be provided.

Temperature: 20–26°C (68–79°F).

Breeding: Adhesive eggs are laid on leaves. Hatching takes about 3 days and the fry require the smallest foods at first, e.g., rotifers or micro-encapsulated food or suspension- type liquid foods.

Panaque nigrolineatus
(Royal/Pin-striped Panaque, Emperor Pleco)

THE ROYAL PANAQUE (*Panaque nigrolineatus*) is a truly impressive fish, especially when a reasonably sized specimen is kept in a well-maintained and decorated aquarium that will cater for its needs.

Although juveniles with their beautifully marked body stripes appear to be ideal choices as shoaling community aquarium fish, the temptation to buy more than one specimen should be resisted. Panaques (both *P. nigrolineatus* and the other commonly available species, the Blue-eyed Plec or Pleco, *P. suttoni*), are territorial fish which do not take kindly to other members of their own kind. Fights between individuals can result not just in a completely destroyed planting arrangement, but – far more importantly – in serious injury to the combatants, which possess powerful opercular (gill) and pectoral (chest) fin spines.

The pattern of stripes which give rise to the species name varies from specimen to specimen and may be indicative of the locality from which it was collected. They are not, however, generally believed to be significant enough (at least, at present) to warrant separation of the types into separate species.

Natural Range: Southern Colombia.

Size: Up to 30cm (12in), but usually smaller.

Food: Predominantly algae-based. Suitable commercial alternatives include sinking vegetable granules and tablets. It will also take vegetable flakes and some non-vegetable formulations.

Tank Conditions: This species, like many of its family relatives, likes flowing water that is well filtered. It also requires hiding places and large flat or rounded stones or pieces of bogwood (or artificial equivalent). Despite its size, *P. nigrolineatus* is quite peaceful towards other large fish, but not towards members of its own species. Being territorial, fights are likely to occur within the confines of an aquarium, so it is best to keep this species as single specimens in sufficiently large aquaria to cater for their needs. Softish, slightly acid to neutral water is generally recommended, although it will tolerate some deviation from this.

Temperature: 22–26°C (72–79°F).

Breeding: No aquarium spawnings have, as yet, been reported for this species.

Panaque nigrolineatus (Pin-striped Panaque) is very territorial and will not tolerate other members of its own kind.

Pimelodus pictus
(Angelicus Pim/Pimelodella)

THE ANGELICUS PIM (*Pimelodus pictus*) is a very striking fish, particularly when not fully grown, since – during this stage – its black body spots are at their most prominent.

Several species are sold under the name of Angelicus Pim, which can be quite confusing for the would-be purchaser. If there is any consolation to be derived from this situation, it is that aquarists are not alone in their confusion. The whole classification of not just species of *Pimelodus*, but also the genus itself, along with the closely related *Pimelodella*, is in a very uncertain state.

So, until the taxonomy of these genera and their constituent species is sorted out, we will continue to find various closely related fish available under a number of names. Besides *P. pictus*, other species which are fairly commonly available and well worth considering (despite their predatory habits) are the Graceful Pimelodella (*Pimelodella/Pimelodus gracilis*) and the White-striped Pim (*Pimelodus albofasciatus*).

Pimelodus pictus (Pictus Catfish) is a predatory fish.

Natural Range: Colombia and Peru.

Size: Around 12cm (4.7in).

Food: Although this species will accept commercial foods, it is predominantly a carnivore/insectivore preferring livefoods above all else.

Tank Conditions: Although *P. pictus* is one of the less aggressive members of its genus, it is still predatory and should not be kept with fish that are small enough to be considered as food items. Pimelodids occur in shoals in the wild and will tend to hide if kept singly in aquaria, at least until they build up confidence. Kept in a group, they will also tend to be more active during the day than would otherwise be the case for this crepuscular/ nocturnal species. As with other such fish, the use of a 'moonlight' fluorescent tube will be found particularly useful for observing their nighttime activities. The aquarium – which should be roomy – should provide both open swimming spaces and suitable hiding places. Soft, slightly acid water which is well filtered is recommended.

Temperature: 22–25°C (72–77°F).

Breeding: No details of aquarium spawning are available.

Rineloricaria fallax
(Whip-tailed Catfish/Loricaria)

The behaviour of Rineloricaria fallax (Whip-tailed Catfish) makes it a particularly interesting fish to keep.

LIKE ALL THE other 40 or so species in the genus, the Whip-tailed Catfish (*Rineloricaria fallax*) comes from fast-flowing bodies of water. Being a suckermouthed catfish (family Loricariidae), it is perfectly suited for life in such environments, and it is largely the biological adaptations that allow it to attach itself to the substratum that make the Whip-tail such an interesting aquarium fish.

Since the lower margin of the head is wider than the upper part where the eyes are located (making it impossible for a Whip-tailed Catfish to see what's going on directly below its body), it is perfectly possible to observe a specimen at really close quarters when it is attached to the front pane of the aquarium with its mouth and underside in full view. It is even possible to examine the mouth and underbelly with a magnifying lens without even disturbing the fish. Should a specimen be disturbed, however, it is likely to move away at lightning speed to a safer spot.

Rineloricaria fallax is still widely available as *Rineloricaria parva* or *Loricaria parva*.

Natural Range: Fast-flowing streams in the La Plata region of Paraguay.

Size: Around 12cm (4.7in).

Food: Will take a variety of commercial foods and livefoods, but the diet must include a vegetable component.

Tank Conditions: Good-quality, well-oxygenated water is required by this species. A current of water (as produced by the outflow from a power filter) is also recommended. Despite its algae-grazing habits, plants – particularly broad-leaved types – are generally not damaged. This is a crepuscular/nocturnal species and should therefore be provided with suitable daytime retreats. The use of a 'moonlight' fluorescent tube will permit the night-time activities of this interesting fish to be observed at close quarters. Soft, acid water is recommended.

Temperature: 15–28°C (59–82°F), but temperatures at the higher end of the scale should not be maintained on a long-term basis.

Breeding: Spawning caves or hollows and soft, acid water are recommended. The eggs are adhesive and are guarded by the male. Hatching can take as long as 12 days, depending on temperature.

Sturisoma panamense
(Royal/Hi-fin Whiptail, Royal Farlowella, Sturgeon Catfish)

CONSIDERING ITS length, the Royal Whiptail (*Sturisoma panamense*) is not a bulky fish. It is, in fact, very slim-bodied, though not quite as slim as the Twig Catfish (*Farlowella acus* – see page 110).

There are about 15 species in the genus, but very few are actually imported in any significant numbers. The most frequently encountered of these 'less-frequent' species is the Giant Whiptail (*S. aureum*) which – true to its popular name – can grow up to 30cm (12in) in length.

Despite its predominantly twilight/nighttime habits, the Royal Whiptail will spend much of its time resting on a leaf or rock, or other suitable perch, in full view and, often, close to the surface of the water.

On account of its peaceful, tolerant nature, this, and other related, species can be kept in a community aquarium, though considering the relatively large size that can eventually be attained, the accommodation should be roomy.

Natural Range: Panama.

Size: Up to 25cm (10in), but often considerably smaller than this.

Food: Although it will eat a number of foods, the Royal Whiptail is – like other Loricariids (Suckermouthed Catfish) – predominantly a herbivorous species which grazes on algae and the microscopic organisms that live among them. (This algae/micro-organism 'mixture' is generally referred to as 'aufwuchs', a term that is usually applied to the natural diet of grazing African Rift Lake cichlids – see entries for these in the cichlid section).

Tank Conditions: Clean (well-filtered), flowing water is recommended for this species, as are subdued lighting and plenty of resting/hiding places provided by rocks, bogwood or their equivalents. This is a peaceful, though potentially large, species which therefore requires a spacious aquarium. A 'moonlight' fluorescent tube is also recommended for this crepuscular/nocturnal fish. Water chemistry should be around neutral, or slightly acid and soft to moderately hard.

Temperature: 22–27°C (72–81°F).

Breeding: Males (which can be identified by their cheek bristles) guard the adhesive eggs, which are sometimes laid on the sides of the aquarium. Hatching can take up to 8–10 days, depending on water temperature.

Sturisoma panamense (Royal Whiptail) will spend much of its time resting on a leaf or a rock in full view.

Synodontis angelicus
(Angel Catfish/Synodontis, Polka Dot Synodontis)

THE ANGEL CATFISH (*Synodontis angelicus*) is perhaps the most beautiful member of its genus. Several forms of the characteristic dark background with light spots 'format' exist, ranging from a black/purplish base with whitish/yellowish spots, through chocolate brown with light orange spots, to a dark ground colour with the light spots interspersed with streaks. This last form is sometimes referred to as *Synodontis angelicus zonatus*, i.e., as a subspecies.

Like all other *Synodontis* species, the Angel Catfish possesses an armour-plated head, a powerful, serrated spine on the dorsal (back) fin and similar spines on the pectoral (chest) fins. These afford the fish protection against predators which find an Angel Catfish with extended spines and hard skull a less-than-appetising mouthful.

Although they are capable of swimming upside-down (a characteristic that gives the family – the Mochokidae – its common name of Upside-down Catfishes), the Angel Catfish will only do so very occasionally.

Synodontis angelicus (Angel Catfish).

Natural Range: Around the Stanley Pool area of Congo (formerly Zaire), Cameroon.

Size: Up to 20cm (8in) reported, but usually smaller.

Food: Although predominantly a livefood feeder, this species will also accept commercial foods.

Tank Conditions: Suitable daytime hiding places should be provided for this nocturnal species whose nighttime foraging activities are best viewed under the dim illumination of a 'moonlight' fluorescent tube. Despite its nocturnal habits, the Angel Synodontis will also be active (though to a considerably lesser degree) during the day. Since it likes to dig for hidden food, the substratum should be fine-grained to avoid damage to the species' delicate barbels (whiskers). In the wild, *Synodontis* catfish tend to be found in large groups. In aquaria, though, unless provision can be made for a shoal, specimens are generally best kept singly to avoid outbreaks of aggression (though not all specimens are aggressive). The water should be soft to moderately hard, with the pH ranging from slightly acid to slightly alkaline.

Temperature: 22–28°C (72–82°F).

Breeding: No details of aquarium spawning are available.

Synodontis nigriventris
(Upside-down Catfish/Synodontis)

THE UPSIDE-DOWN Catfish (*Synodontis nigriventris*) truly lives up to its name by tending to swim and rest in an inverted position most of the time. It is, however, quite capable of swimming in the more conventional manner and occasionally does so, particularly when hunting for small prey items among debris lying on the bottom.

Interestingly, the inverted swiming position is not exhibited by young fish until they begin to approach two months of age. At this time, they begin to turn upside-down occasionally, increasing the frequency of these inversions over succeeding weeks until they develop the adult upside-down orientation.

Natural Range: Congo basin.
Size: Up to 10cm (4in) reported for females, though they are usually a little smaller; around 8cm (3.1in) for males.
Food: In the wild, this species feeds mostly on floating insects by swimming upside-down and taking them from the surface. In aquaria, floating live or freeze-dried foods are, therefore, ideal. However, other foods will also be taken, albeit more reluctantly.
Tank Conditions: This is a crepuscular/nocturnal species which should be provided with suitable daytime hiding/resting places that will allow it to adopt its characteristic upside-down position. *S. nigriventris* is at its best when kept in a shoal in subdued light. For optimal viewing of its nighttime activities, use a 'moonlight' fluorescent tube once the main aquarium lights have been switched off in the evening. The pH of the water should range from slightly acid to slightly alkaline and the hardness from soft to moderate.
Temperature: 22–26°C (72–79°F).
Breeding: Spawning has been occasionally achieved in aquaria, with the eggs being laid in a depression or on the roof of a cave. Hatching takes about 7 days.

SOME OTHER SYNODONTIS SPECIES

Nowadays, there are quite a few of the 100 or so members of the Upside-down Catfish family (Mochokidae) available. Among these, some of the most popular are: the Clown Synodontis (*S. decorus*), the Feather-fin Synodontis

Synodontis nigriventris (Upside-down Catfish).

Synodontis Decorus (Clown Synodontis).

(*S. eupterus*), the Pyjama Synodontis (*S. flavitaeniatus*), the Cuckoo Synodontis (*S. multipunctatus*), the False Upside-down Synodontis (*S. nigrita*), the One-spot Synodontis (*S. notatus*), the Pgymy Synodontis (*S. petricolor*), and the Big-eyed Synodontis (*S. pleurops*).

All require the same basic conditions, and most grow between 15–30cm (6–12in) in length, an exception being *S. petricolor* which only attains 10cm (4in).

CICHLIDS

Above: Apistogramma cacatuoides (Cockatoo Cichlid), sunburst variety, shows extended finnage. Right: Juvenile Cockatoo Cichlid.

THE CICHLIDAE constitute the second largest family in the order Perciformes, the largest being the Gobiidae (Gobies) with more than 1,800 species. There are about 1,300 cichlid species grouped into approximately 100 genera, many of which have found their way into the hobby at one stage or another.

Cichlids are widely distributed, mainly in freshwater (although there are some brackish species, e.g., the Chromides, *Etroplus spp*), in Central and South America, the West Indies, Africa, Madagascar, Syria, the coastal areas of the southern half of the Indian subcontinent and Sri Lanka. The northernmost species is the Texas Cichlid, *Herichthys cyanoguttatum.*

Being so numerous and widely distributed, cichlids exhibit a wide range of body shape, colour, behaviour and size. The largest species is *Boulengerochromis microlepis* found in Lake Tanganyika. At a maximum length of 90cm (36in), it is, not surprisingly, rarely seen in aquaria. At the other extreme, some of the Dwarf Cichlids belonging to the genus *Apistogramma* grow no larger than 3.5 cm (1.4in).

Despite their size and other differences, all cichlids possess at least one characteristic in common: only a single nostril on each side of the head, rather than the usual two. In addition, cichlids usually have a 'split' lateral line, the front (longer) section being located higher up the body. Most species also have brown-tipped teeth. The dorsal (back) fin is divided into a spiny, unbranched (hard) anterior section and a branched (soft) posterior one supported by rays.

Spawning behaviour is varied, although parental care is characteristic. Typical spawning strategies among cichlids include substrate spawning, i.e., deposition of eggs on rocks, leaves, etc. as in Angelfish (*Pterophyllum spp*), and mouthbrooding, as in many African species such as the Golden Lake Malawi Cichlid (*Melanochromis auratus*). A few species, like Discus (*Symphysodon spp*), Angels,(*Pterophyllum spp*), Pike Cichlids (*Crenicichla spp*) and Uarus (*Uaru amphiacanthoides*), go a stage further by producing a body secretion on which the fry feed during the first few weeks of life.

Aequidens pulcher
(Blue Acara)

The large Aequidens pulcher (Blue Acara) requires a spacious aquarium and is generally a tolerant fish.

THE BLUE ACARA (*Aequidens pulcher*) has been in the hobby for nearly 100 years. It is, therefore, interesting to note that, even today, some debate exists regarding its identity. Some authorities, for example, believe that the Blue Acaras which originate from Colombia are not *A. pulcher* but a closely related species, *A. latifrons*. Others maintain that both, along with *A. coeruleopunctatus*, are merely geographical variants of the same species.

Irrespective of who turns out eventually to be correct or otherwise, all so-called Blue Acaras are magnificent fish, wherever they come from and whether they are wild-caught or captive-bred.

On account of their relatively large size and less-than-timid nature, Blue Acaras do not constitute good choices for community aquaria housing small or delicate species. They are, however, good candidates for communities consisting of larger, more robust, species, as long as the aquarium is large enough and provides an adequate number of retreats.

Generally speaking, Blue Acaras are peaceful fish, even towards members of their own species. Even so, older specimens can become intolerant, as do breeding pairs, particularly when they are guarding eggs and fry. Good pairs make excellent parents and, once they have spawned once, they will do so several times in a single season.

Natural Range: Colombia, Panama, Trinidad and northern Venezuela (but see main text for further details).
Size: Up to 20cm (8in), but usually considerably smaller than this.
Food: All commercial and livefoods accepted.
Tank Conditions: Since this is a robust species, delicate plants are likely to suffer. Tough plant species and/or their artificial equivalents are therefore recommended. Hiding places, as well as open areas, should be provided. Water chemistry is not too critical; as long as the overall quality is good, a wide range of pH and hardness is accepted.
Temperature: 18–25°C (64–77°F).
Breeding: Adhesive eggs are laid on a pre-cleaned stone and are guarded, along with the fry, by both parents.

Apistogramma agassizii
(Agassiz's Dwarf Cichlid)

AGASSIZ'S DWARF Cichlid (*Apistogramma agassizii*) and the other members of its genus are exceptionally spectacular fish, despite their modest size. They can be timid fish if the accommodation does not provide dense vegetation and other places where they can hide. However, when conditions are to their liking, the males (in particular) are truly impressive as they move around their territory in full colour and with extended fins.

Apistogramma cichlids are fish which every aquarist should keep at some stage, not only because of their colours, but also because of their interesting courtship and breeding behaviour and their tolerance of other species. They should not, however, be kept with boisterous or aggressive tankmates.

Natural Range: Widespread in the southern tributaries of the Amazon.

Size: Up to 8cm (3.1in), but often smaller.

Food: Most commercial foods accepted, although livefoods are preferred.

Tank Conditions: Good-quality water (with frequent partial changes) is preferred by this species. The tank should be thickly planted, offering numerous hiding places and easy-to-defend territories. Several females and a single male will offer good opportunities for observing the different territorial behaviours of the sexes (see below). The water should be soft and acid and the substratum should, ideally, be dark.

Temperature: 22–25°C (72–77°F), but slightly higher temperatures will also be tolerated.

Breeding: A single male (males are larger, more colourful and possess longer fins) will often spawn with several females, each of which will have its own territory based around a cave. The females will guard their own eggs, while the male will defend the overall territory.

Apistogramma agassizi (Agassiz's Dwarf Cichlid).

SOME OTHER APISTOGRAMMA SPECIES AVAILABLE

In addition to *Apistogramma agassizii*, there are several other species of the genus available. All are small and have, basically, similar requirements. Among the species worth considering are the following: *A. bitaeniata* (Banded Dwarf Cichlid), *A. borellii* (Borelli's/Umbrella Dwarf Cichlid), *A. cacatuoides* (Cockatoo/Crested Dwarf Cichlid) see page 121, *A. macmasteri* (Macmaster's Dwarf/Red-tailed Cichlid), *A. steindachneri* (Steindachner's Dwarf Cichlid), *A. trifasciata* (Three-striped/Blue Dwarf Cichlid) and *A. viejita* (Viejita Dwarf Cichlid).

Apistogramma borellii (Umbrella Dwarf Cichlid).

123

Archocentrus nigrofasciatus
(Convict/Zebra Cichlid)

CONVICT OR ZEBRA Cichlids (*Archocentrus nigrofasciatus*) – often referred to as *Heros nigrofasciatus* – have been popular since the mid-1930s, a remarkable achievement for a fish that can be so belligerent towards tankmates of its size – or even towards larger specimens during breeding, or when a new fish is introduced into its territory.

Only fish for which there is a demand are bred on a commercial basis, so the fact that most of the specimens available to hobbyists are captive-bred can be taken as a firm indication of the species' continuing popularity. Although this may appear a little surprising, bearing in mind the aggressive and territorial tendencies outlined above and below, the fact is that a well-matched pair of *A. nigrofasciatus* care for their eggs and fry with such vigour, that – as long as one is prepared to cater for their needs – the species is a delight to keep.

Natural Range: Most of Central America.
Size: Up to 15cm (6in) reported, but usually smaller. Males are considerably larger than females.

Food: All commercial and livefoods accepted. Diet should include a vegetable component.
Tank Conditions: The aquarium should be roomy, not just because of the size that can be attained by males, but also because of the intense territorial behaviour that most individuals and (particularly) pairs develop. The Convict Cichlid is not a good 'normal' community fish and should be kept either in a species tank, or in a community consisting of equally robust species. The layout should include open spaces, shelters and flat or rounded stones. Delicate plants will tend to be eaten. Therefore, only tough or unpalatable types and their artificial equivalents should be chosen. Water chemistry is not critical, as long as the quality is good.
Temperature: 20–25°C (68–77°F).
Breeding: The adhesive eggs are laid on a pre-cleaned site, which may be the roof of a cave or the top of a smooth stone. Both parents guard the eggs and fry.

Archocentrus nogrofasciatus (Convict or Zebra Cichlid).

Astronotus ocellatus
(Oscar, Peacock-Eye/Velvet Cichlid)

THE OSCAR (*Astronotus ocellatus*) is a large, rough, tough and very beautiful fish, which is widely available and enjoys an enthusiastic following among cichlid fanciers.

Frequently available as either strikingly marked wild-type juveniles, or less strikingly marked young specimens of one or other of a growing number of varieties, Oscars will quickly outgrow an 'average-sized' aquarium and wreak havoc among tankmates, if these are not chosen carefully.

Once they begin to put on any real size and weight, juveniles must be provided with a roomy aquarium of their own. Eventually, such an aquarium may only be able to accommodate a single pair, which should, preferably, have arisen naturally from a group of fast-growing young.

Clearly, this is not an ideal fish for a beginner. Nevertheless, it is well worth considering, once the basics of aquarium husbandry have been mastered.

Astronotus ocellatus (Oscar) may soon outgrow its tank.

Natural Range: Amazon region.

Size: Around 30cm (12in).

Food: This is a carnivorous/piscivorous (meat/fish-eating) fish which requires flesh-based foods. It will also take pellets and tablet food.

Tank Conditions: Oscars are large, boisterous fish which will destroy delicate plants and disrupt the aquarium decor virtually at will. Should tough natural plants be considered, they should be potted up and the surface of the soil covered with pebbles to protect the roots from the digging activities of the fish. Rockwork and bogwood pieces should be substantial and arranged in such a way that they cannot be knocked over by the fish. Oscars are hearty, messy eaters and prodigious water polluters, so a good power filter is essential. Water chemistry is not critical, as long as extremes of pH and hardness are avoided.

Temperature: 20–25°C (68–77°F).

Breeding: Once a pair bond has been formed (which can be a rough and, sometimes, prolonged affair), large numbers of eggs (1,000-2,000) will be laid on a pre-cleaned site. Both parents will guard the eggs and fry vigorously.

Aulonocara nyassae
(African Peacock Cichlid)

The strikingly coloured Aulonocara nyassae (African Peacock Cichlid) enjoys a large open swimming space.

ALTHOUGH THE African Peacock Cichlid is referred to as *Aulonocara nyassae* here, it is widely believed that the vast majority of Peacocks available within the hobby belong to a different, though closely related – and similar – species. It is, in fact, claimed that, at least until recently, the true *A. nyassae* had never been exported from Lake Malawi.

Three of the Peacocks which are most frequently available are the following species and their colour morphs: *A. baenschi* (Baensch's Peacock Cichlid or Yellow Regal Cichlid), *A. hansbaenschi* ('*Aulonocara nyassae*', Aulonocara Red Flush or Aulonocara Fort Maguire) and *A. jacobfreibergi* (Malawi Butterfly). In addition, there are numerous other Peacocks known from Lake Malawi, many of which have not yet been described scientifically, but which are available under a variety of trade names.

Natural Range: Lake Malawi, Africa.

Size: Around 18cm (7in), but often a little smaller.

Food: Although this is a predominantly carnivorous species in the wild, it will also accept many commercial foods in aquaria.

Tank Conditions: Being African Rift Lake cichlids, Peacocks should be housed in a large, well-filtered aquarium which provides numerous rock shelters best arranged in the form of a cliff running along the back of the aquarium. It is essential, however, to make the rockwork safe, e.g., by making it wider at the bottom than at the top, and sticking the individual rocks together with silicone sealant, which must be allowed to cure fully, i.e., disperse its caustic fumes, before any fish are introduced. Alternatively, some excellent synthetic rockwork designed specifically for 'African' aquaria is available. Open swimming space should be provided in front of the aquarium and the substratum should be light-coloured and fine-grained. The water should be moderately hard and alkaline (soft, acid conditions must be avoided).

Temperature: 24–26°C (75–79°F); slightly higher for breeding.

Breeding: All Peacocks are maternal mouthbrooding cichlids – the female carries the 60 or so eggs in her mouth until they hatch. For a time, she will also protect her young by taking them into her mouth whenever danger threatens.

Cichlasoma portalegrensis
(Port/Brown Acara)

THE PORT or Brown Acara (*Cichlasoma portalegrensis*) has been around for many years. It is, however, widely believed that many of the fish which have been available within the hobby during this time were not, in fact, *C. portalegrensis* at all, but look-alikes, such as the Two-spot or Black Acara (*C. bimaculatum*), *C. boliviense* and *C. dimerus*.

According to Sven Kullander, a leading cichlid expert, the true Port Acara is only found in the area of Lagoa dos Patos (Lake of Ducks) and Torres in Rio Grande do Sul in southern Brazil. If this is, indeed, the case, then the Ports reported from elsewhere must belong to one or other of its most closely related species.

Disagreement even surrounds the actual spellings of the names themselves, since, to be consistent with the rules of Latin grammar, *C. dimerus* should be *C. dimerum* and *C. portalegrensis* should be *C. portalegrense*.

All four fish, irrespective of their names or true identities, are generally peaceful towards their tankmates and can be kept in community aquaria. However, the nature of these communities should change in accordance with the progressively larger size that Port Acaras attain on their way to adulthood.

Natural Range: Bolivia, Brazil, the Guianas, Paraguay and Venezuela (but see main text).

Size: Up to 15cm (6in), but often smaller than this.

Food: All commercial and livefoods accepted.

Tank Conditions: During their juvenile and young adult stages, Port Acaras can be kept in a tank decorated with a mixture of plants. However, once they begin to attain their full aquarium size (even if this is smaller than the maximum reported size), only sturdy plants should be incorporated in the aquascape. Caves, pieces of bogwood (or equivalent) and flat or rounded stones should also form part of the decor. Water chemistry should be from soft and slightly acid, to neutral.

Temperature: 19–26°C (66–79°F).

Breeding: Port Acaras will spawn quite readily. Eggs are laid on a pre-cleaned flat or rounded stone and both they and the fry will be guarded by both parents.

Confusion still exists regarding the true identity of the Port or Brown Acara.

'Cichlasoma' Red Parrot
(Parrot/Red Parrot Cichlid)

'Cichlasoma' (Parrot Cichlid) are available in various shades, from yellow, through to pink, red, and finally blood red.

STORIES ABOUND about the origin of the Red Parrot but, as with other 'mystery' fish, such as the Odessa Barb (see page 54), no-one seems to understand the full picture.

There can be no doubt that the Red Parrot is a cichlid. Beyond that, it is currently difficult to pin down any hard facts about this spectacular fish which created a tremendous stir during the early to mid-1990s.

There is a strong case, it appears, to assign at least part of its ancestry to the Severum or Eye-Spot Cichlid (*Heros severus*). Some writers (a minority, at the moment) believe it to be merely a mutant form of this species; most, though, believe it to be a hybrid between *H. severus* and a closely related species (because of it being fertile). Suggestions regarding this second species vary from the reasonable (e.g., an *Amphilophus* or *Heros* species), to the 'most unlikely' (e.g., the Goldfish – *Carassius auratus*).

Parrots come in varying shades, from yellow, through pink, to red and, finally, blood red. Diet, genetics and several other factors contribute to the eventual coloration of the adults. All juveniles are, basically, greenish and change through a blotched stage, to achieve their adult coloration over a period of several months.

Natural Range: Not known in the wild (see main text for details).

Size: Up to 12cm (4.7in).

Food: All commercial and livefoods.

Tank Conditions: Because of the relatively large size that this fish attains, a roomy tank is recommended, with sufficient open space at the front to accommodate a small group of specimens. Caves, thickets of vegetation, bogwood (or equivalent) and flat or rounded stones should also be provided. The colours, particularly of the Blood Red type, are best appreciated under bright lights. Water chemistry is not too critical, but medium to hard, neutral to alkaline, conditions are recommended.

Temperature: 24–28°C (75–82°F).

Breeding: Although not always easy to breed, well matched pairs lay their adhesive eggs on a pre-cleaned site and will protect both their spawn and their fry.

Cleithracara maronii
(Keyhole Cichlid)

ALTHOUGH THE Keyhole Cichlid (*Cleithracara maronii*) is a substantial fish, it is one of the most peaceful of all cichlids. Indeed – unusually for a cichlid – it can be easily frightened, hence the need for adequate shelter. Keyholes make good choices for a spacious community aquarium housing medium-sized or large specimens. The peaceful nature of the species often extends to the fry which can usually be left with their parents for up to six months, after which time they begin to be seen as potential rivals.

The 'Keyhole' label refers to the body mark that is often (but not always) detectable two-thirds of the way down the body. The top bit of the 'hole', i.e., the rounded part below the dorsal (back) fin is always present as a black spot with golden edges, but the lower, and longer, part extending vertically downwards towards the anal (belly) fin, is often diffuse or absent.

Most books still list *Cleithracara maronii* as *Aequidens maronii*, but – since 1989 – it has had its own genus ascribed to it and the 'new' name is gradually finding its way into the literature.

Natural Range: Guyana, Surinam, French Guiana.
Size: Up to around 15cm (6in), but often a little smaller.
Food: All commercial and livefoods accepted.
Tank Conditions: As it will eventually grow large, a roomy aquarium is required for this peaceful cichlid. Thickets of vegetation, caves and/or other shelters, plus open swimming spaces and large flat or rounded stones, should also be provided. Water chemistry is not critical (as long as the overall quality is good), with a pH range between 6 and 8 being quite acceptable.
Temperature: 22–26°C (72–79°F).
Breeding: Despite their generally peaceful nature, Keyholes can become quite territorial at breeding time. Adhesive eggs are laid on a pre-cleaned flat or rounded stone and both they and the eventual fry are guarded by the parents.

Cleithracara maronii (Keyhole Cichlid) is a peaceful fish which is easily frightened and needs plenty of shelter.

Cyrtocara moorii
(Malawi Blue Dolphin, Blue Lumphead, Moorii)

Cyrtocara moorii (Blue Dolphin) will follow a sand-sifting fish of another species in order to discover livefoods.

IN THE WILD, the Blue Dolphin (*Cyrtocara moorii*) tends to follow sand-sifting species of cichlids as they scour the bottom in search of food, snapping up any small invertebrates that are disturbed by the sifters.

While a couple of juveniles may sometimes be allowed to accompany an adult *C. moorii* during these feeding sessions, other adults are not tolerated. This type of behaviour is clearly territorial, but with the unusual twist that the 'territory' is not a (static) rock or patch of substratum, but a (moving) fish! For breeding, though, males exhibit the more 'normal' type of territorial behaviour in which they defend their chosen spawning site against intruders.

Cyrtocara moorii males are polygamous, i.e., they will breed with a number of females, and should, therefore, be kept in groups that reflect this habit.

Natural Range: Lakes Malawi and Malombe, Africa.
Size: Maximum of around 23cm (9in) reported from the wild, but usually smaller than this.
Food: Mainly bottom-dwelling livefoods, but will also take some commercial preparations.

Tank Conditions: The decor should consist predominantly of rock shelters and/or safely arranged cliffs (see *Aulonocara nyassae* – page 126 – for further details) positioned along, at least, the back of a spacious aquarium. A fine-grained large open area should be provided at the front. Plants are not necessary but, if some are desired, then the larger, more robust species should be chosen and arranged in such a way – e.g., by placing pebbles around the roots or potting them up and covering the surface with pebbles – that the fish cannot uproot them during their foraging activities. The water should be slightly to moderately alkaline and medium-hard to hard. Good, efficient filtration and frequent water changes are essential.

Temperature: 20–26°C (68–79°F), but the lower temperature, while tolerated in the short term, should not be maintained for any length of time.
Breeding: This is a typical mouthbrooder in which spawning takes place on a rock or a sometimes barely discernible depression, following which the female incubates the eggs in her mouth.

Dicrossus filamentosus
(Checkerboard/Lyretail Checkerboard/Cheeseboard Cichlid)

THE Checkerboard Cichlid (*Dicrossus filamentosus*) is probably better known to most aquarists by its former name, *Crenicara filamentosa*, although it has been officially recognised as *Dicrossus* since 1990.

This peaceful, slender, small cichlid is rather timid if housed with larger, more robust, species and will tend to hide from view most of the time. When not feeling stressed, it likes to spend most of its time gliding gently in a small group, consisting of a single male and several females, along the bottom and middle layers of the water column. At such times, the sparkling colours of the males can be fully appreciated.

Although the distribution of *D. filamentosus* is said to stretch 'upwards' from the upper regions of the Rio Negro in Brazil, I have collected this species in the Lago São Joaquim (off the Rio Cuiuni), a little distance upriver from Barcelos, which is located in the middle reaches of the Rio Negro.

Natural Range: Upper Rio Negro (but see above) and Rio Orinoco regions.

Size: Up to 9cm (3.5in) for males; considerably smaller for females.

Food: Most commercial and livefoods are accepted by this predominantly carnivorous species.

Tank Conditions: This species, while not being difficult to keep, is a little more demanding than some with regard to water chemistry. This should be soft and on the acid side and – very importantly – clean. Regular partial water changes and good (though not turbulent) filtration are recommended, along with tannin-stained water (blackwater). A piece of natural bogwood will help achieve this, as will one or other of the excellent commercial 'blackwater' preparations currently available. The tank itself should be thickly planted with some of the larger specimens (or floating plants) offering surface cover. Tankmates should be relatively small and non-boisterous.

Temperature: 23–25°C (73–77°F); slightly higher for breeding.

Breeding: Very soft, acid water should be provided. The adhesive eggs are laid, either on plants or stones, and are guarded by the female.

Dicrossus filamentosus (Checkerboard Cichlid) is timid if housed with larger more robust species.

Etroplus maculatus
(Orange Chromide)

Etroplus maculatus (Orange Chromide) enjoys brackish water conditions.

THE ORANGE CHROMIDE (*Etroplus maculatus*) has been in the aquarium hobby for the best part of a century and is still, deservedly, extremely popular.

Its peaceful nature, modest size and the ease with which it spawns in aquaria have all been major contributing factors, to which must be added its availability in three colour forms. Of these, the wild type and the golden, orange-spotted types are the two most frequently seen. A third type, which is bluer than the wild type in overall coloration, is also seen from time to time, as is the Green Chromide (*E. suratensis*), a larger relative.

Natural Range: Western India and Sri Lanka.
Size: Up to 10cm (4in) reported, but usually less than 8cm (3in).
Food: All commercial and livefoods accepted. Diet should include a regular vegetable component.
Tank Conditions: The aquarium should contain thickets of vegetation along the sides and back, with an open area along the front (but the most delicate plants may suffer

as a result of the fishes' algae-grazing activities). Shelters and flat or rounded stones should also be provided. Orange Chromides are among the few cichlids that are regularly found in brackish water conditions in the wild. Adding a teaspoonful of salt – preferably a good-quality marine mixture – to every 4.5 litres (1 gallon) of aquarium water is, therefore, often recommended. However, this salt appears to be more important in preventing fungal infections affecting the fry, than for the long-term well-being of the adults. Neutral to alkaline, medium-hard water is preferred, along with good filtration.
Temperature: 20–26°C (68–79°F); slightly higher for breeding.
Breeding: Eggs are laid on a pre-cleaned spawning site and both they and the fry are guarded by both parents. The new-born fry often attach themselves to the sides of the body of the adults, probably thus obtaining nourishment from their parents' body mucus in the same way that Discus (*Symphysodon spp.*) fry and others are known to do.

Geophagus brasiliensis
(Pearl Cichlid)

DESPITE ITS relatively large size, the Pearl Cichlid (*Geophagus brasiliensis*) is quite tolerant of other similarly sized fish (at least, more so than the majority of 'earth eaters').

While the conditions recommended in the accompanying guidelines are best for the long-term well-being of this species, its range of tolerance is considerably wider than indicated. I have, for example, collected *G. brasiliensis* in Lagoa Rodrigo de Freitas not far from Copacabana beach in Rio de Janiero, Brazil, in polluted water of brackish content at a temperature of 36°C (97°F) which, consequently, was highly deficient in oxygen. Indeed, the lake has long been known locally as 'the lake of rotting fish' (!) and, while there were numerous fish corpses both in the water and lining the shore, *G. brasiliensis* specimens were beautifully coloured and actively feeding – as evidenced by the numbers that were being caught by local boys on hook and line.

Natural Range: Widely distributed along the Atlantic coastal strip of Brazil, down to Rio de la Plata in Argentina.

Size: Up to 28cm (11in) reported, but this is exceptional; most specimens are considerably smaller than this.

Food: All commercial and livefoods accepted.

Tank Conditions: Like all *Geophagus* species (the name means 'earth eater'), *G. brasiliensis* will burrow searching for food. Therefore, the substratum should allow for this activity by being fine-grained (fine gravel/coarse sand) in, at least, some parts of the spacious aquarium that is required by this fish. Such activity will uproot unprotected plants, so these may need to be potted with the soil surface covered in pebbles, or else planted directly into the substratum (but away from foraging areas, e.g., in the corners) and surrounded by protective rocks or large pebbles. Water chemistry is not critical, but slightly acid, soft to medium-hard conditions are recommended (but see above).

Temperature: 20–27°C (68–81°F), the top end being best for breeding.

Breeding: Adhesive eggs are laid on a pre-cleaned surface and both they and the fry are guarded by both parents.

The beautifully coloured Geophagus brasiliensis (Pearl Cichlid) burrows in its search for food.

Hemichromis bimaculatus
(Jewel Cichlid)

A S ITS NAME indicates, the Jewel Cichlid (*Hemichromis bimaculatus*) is a gorgeous fish with many desirable qualities. However, tolerance is not one of these, particularly during the breeding season. When in full reproductive 'mode', Jewels – which are territorial anyway – are especially aggressive towards tankmates. Indeed, if a pair is forced to share the same tank, but the selected specimens are not compatible with one another, violent fights will often result in the death of one or other of the potential mates.

Outside breeding time, Jewel Cichlids can share their aquarium with other similarly sized (or slightly larger) fish, but not with smaller, timid species or specimens.

Resplendent though *H. bimaculatus* undoubtedly is, there is an even more strikingly coloured 'Jewel' available: the Lifalili Cichlid (*H. lifalili*) from the Congo basin. Its requirements and habits are similar to those of *H. bimaculatus*, but its water requirements are a little more demanding.

Hemichromis bimaculatus (Jewel Cichlid).

Natural Range: Central Liberia to southern Guinea, Africa.

Size: Up to 15cm (6in) reported, but usually considerably smaller than this.

Food: This is a predominantly carnivorous species, which therefore prefers livefoods. It will, however, also accept commercial foods.

Tank Conditions: The layout should contain thick stands of stout vegetation, which should be protected against uprooting by means of strategically placed pebbles around the stems, or by being potted up and having the soil surface covered with pebbles. An open area should be left at the front of the aquarium and several flat or smoothly rounded stones provided as suitable spawning sites. Water chemistry is not critical, but, as these fish are energetic diggers, a good filter is essential to cope with the debris that is raised.

Temperature: 21–28°C (70–82°F) with the top end being reserved for breeding purposes.

Breeding: Eggs are laid on a stone and guarded by both parents who, subsequently, move them and the fry to temporary pits dug in the substratum.

Heros severus
(Severum/Eye-Spot/Banded Cichlid)

Heros severus (Severum) is usually a gentle giant but will defend its territory during breeding time.

THE SEVERUM (*Heros severus*) is one of the gentler giants of the hobby, being among the most peaceful of the large cichlids. It is, nevertheless, territorial in that it establishes its own 'home patch' in an aquarium. Despite this, it will not generally defend this territory in an over-aggressive manner that would be liable to cause injury to tankmates, except, perhaps, during breeding time.

The bands referred to in one of the common names for this species are most pronounced in juvenile specimens; although adults, at least from some areas, can also exhibit quite prominent banding. The species is so widespread in the wild, though, that differences in pigmentation and patterning occur naturally and this can make identification difficult. It could also mean that some, as yet unnamed, *Heros* species could turn out to be geographical varieties of Severum.

A few colour forms have been developed commercially, the most popular being a golden, red-spotted type and a lutino (similar to an albino, but with black, rather than pink/red eyes).

Natural Range: Widely distributed in tropical areas, from the northern regions of South America southwards into the Amazon basin.

Size: Up to 28cm (11in) reported for some wild-caught specimens and captive-bred ones raised in large aquaria, but usually around 20cm (8in) for most specimens.

Food: All commercial and livefoods accepted, though flakes are not ideal for the largest specimens.

Tank Conditions: This species requires a large aquarium provided with open areas, thickets of robust vegetation and a selection of flat or rounded stones and/or pieces of bogwood (or its equivalent). Water chemistry is not critical, but soft, acid conditions are preferred and overall quality must be good. An efficient filter is therefore essential.

Temperature: 23–25°C (73–77°F), with slightly higher temperatures being recommended for breeding purposes.

Breeding: Adhesive eggs (as many as 1,000) are laid on a pre-cleaned stone or piece of bogwood. Both the eggs and the fry are guarded by the parents.

Julidochromis regani
(Striped/Regan's Julie)

Above: Julidochromis regani (Regan's Julie).
Right: Julidochromis transcriptus (Masked Julie).

THE STRIPED JULIE (*Julidochromis regani*) is a beautifully marked fish, which, along with its closest relatives, forms a very distinctive-looking small group of cichlids. As Lake Tanganyika becomes more fully explored, further Julie species are likely to emerge, and if these turn out to be anywhere near as attractive as the known types, they are certain to enjoy great popularity in the hobby.

As things stand at the moment, the genus *Julidochromis* can be 'visually' split into two groups (some authorities believe that each should constitute a subgenus). There are two 'large' species, *J. regani* and Marlier's Julie (*J. marlieri*), varying from 10–30cm (4–12in) in reported length on the one hand, and then there is a distinct drop in size to the other Julies, the Brown or Dickfeld's Julie (*J. dickfeldi*), the Yellow or Ornate Julie (*J. ornatus*) and the Black-and-White or Masked Julie (*J. transcriptus*), all of which are around 7–8cm (2.8–3.1in) in length. In addition, there are various colour and pattern forms. All, though, require the same basic aquarium conditions.

Natural Range: Shallow rocky areas of Lake Tanganyika, Africa.

Size: Up to 30cm (12in) reported, but usually about half this size.

Food: Will accept most foods, but prefers livefoods. A vegetable supplement is recommended.

Tank Conditions: Being a rock dweller, *Julidochromis regani* must be provided with numerous shelters or caves in which to hide and spawn. Rock arrangements must, however, be safe, especially if individual pieces are stacked in the form of a cliff (see entry for *Aulonocara nyassae* on page 126 for further details). Some stout, alkaline-tolerant plants, such as *Vallisneria*, can be used as part of the decor. Water chemistry is very important for this and other Rift Lake species, which require alkaline, moderately hard water for their long-term well-being.

Temperature: 22–25°C (72–77°F).

Breeding: Adhesive eggs are laid in caves and both they and the fry are defended by the parents. The male can spawn with a number of females.

Labeotropheus trewavasae
(Trewavas'/Red-Finned Cichlid)

TREWAVAS' CICHLID (*Labeotropheus trewavasae*) is a territorial Rift Lake species in which males are quite aggressive towards each other. It is, therefore, best to keep just one male per aquarium; several females can, however, be kept together.

There are numerous colour morphs of this species, the best known being – in addition to the many 'traditional' blues – the O (orange) and OB (orange blotched) types.

L. trewavasae is virtually indistinguishable from Fuelleborn's Cichlid (*L. fuelleborni*) with which it co-exists in Lake Malawi. *L. trewavasae* is always a little slimmer and the maximum size attained by males is about 4cm (1.6in) less than that attained by their largest *L. fuelleborni* counterparts.

Interestingly, Ad Konings, a leading Rift Lake cichlid specialist, reports that, with only a few exceptions, O and OB morphs of *L. trewavasae* are found in locations where the equivalent *L. fuelleborni* morphs are absent. *L. trewavasae* is also generally assumed to be the species that occupies deeper water (down to 40 metres/130ft), while *L. fuelleborni* is believed to be restricted to the upper seven metres (23ft) or so.

Natural Range: Lake Malawi, Africa.

Size: Depending on race and diet, wild-caught males can be as large as 14cm (5.5in) or as small as 10cm (4in). Females are about 25 percent smaller.

Food: All commercial and livefoods accepted, including algae. In the lake, aufwuchs (algae and their resident micro-fauna) constitutes the main part of their diet.

Tank Conditions: Being a typical rocky habitat Rift Lake cichlid, *L. trewavasae* requires a tank arranged with numerous rock shelters, caves and cliffs (see *Aulonocara nyassae*, page 126, for details regarding safe rock arrangements). Some robust alkaline-tolerant plants can also be used as part of the decor. The water – which must be well filtered – should be alkaline and moderately hard.

Temperature: 21–25°C (70–77°F); slightly higher for breeding.

Breeding: Spawning usually occurs inside a cave. The eggs are incubated orally by the female who, later, also defends the fry.

Labeotropheus trewavasae (Trewavas' Cichlid) is a variable species.

Laetacara curviceps
(Flag Cichlid)

THE FLAG CICHLID (*Laetacara curviceps*) still appears frequently in aquarium literature under its old (pre-1986) name of *Aequidens curviceps*.

Throughout its extensive range, this variably coloured species is found in shallow, still or slow-moving bodies of water which are frequently littered with sodden (but not rotten) leaves, often over a sandy bottom.

Although the species has been in the hobby for nearly a century, it still continues to be popular and is, therefore, bred commercially in considerable quantities. Its non-belligerent nature, adaptability and attractive coloration are all contributing factors to its popularity. In addition, though, the ease with which well matched pairs will breed, and their readiness to do so in full view, has made the Flag Cichlid a firm favourite among both new and established aquarists.

The one thing *L. curviceps* dislikes is old water, tending to develop exophthalmia (Pop-eye disease) and other ailments if partial water changes are not carried out regularly. About 10–20 percent of the water changed every two weeks or so is perfectly adequate, as long as the overall quality is good between the changes.

Natural Range: Amazon basin.

Size: Up to 10cm (4in), but usually a little smaller.

Food: All commercial and livefoods accepted.

Tank Conditions: This is a peaceful, tolerant species which does well in community aquaria, except at breeding time when a pair will become territorial. When this happens, it is best to remove the pair to separate quarters. The aquarium should contain plant thickets – including some broad-leaved species – and open spaces, with a number of flat or rounded stones in the open areas. A bogwood (or equivalent) centrepiece can also be added. A fine-grained substratum is recommended, along with slightly acid to neutral water, which can range from soft to moderately hard.

Temperature: 22–26°C (72–79°F).

Breeding: Adhesive eggs are laid on a broad leaf, piece of bogwood or stone. Both the eggs and fry are protected by the parents.

Laetacara curviceps (Flag Cichlid) is a peaceful prolific species.

Melanochromis auratus
(Malawi Golden Cichlid, Auratus)

THE AURATUS or Malawi Golden Cichlid (*Melanochromis auratus*) – formerly referred to as the Golden Nyasa Cichlid – is a very distinctive-looking fish which was among the first Rift Lake cichlids to become popular in the aquarium hobby.

Unlike some of its co-inhabitants of the lake, this species is fairly consistently coloured throughout its range, with the only variations occurring in the intensity of the females' golden coloration and in the males' black bands.

Melanochromis auratus is known from the western lower half of Lake Malawi, but is unknown along the eastern coast, where another species, currently referred to as *Melanochromis* sp.'Dwarf Auratus', which only attains some 7cm (2.8in) in length, is found. Some authors believe this fish, the females of which, possess very attractive speckling, to be a race of *M. auratus*, while others (perhaps with greater justification) believe it to be a valid species in its own right.

Melanochromis auratus (Malawi Golden Cichlid).

Natural Range: Lake Malawi, Africa.

Size: Males around 10cm (4in); females slightly smaller (but see also main text).

Food: All commercial and livefoods accepted, with a vegetable component recommended.

Tank Conditions: As with the other Lake Malawi species so far mentioned in this book, the *M. auratus* aquarium should include plenty of rock shelters, caves and/or cliffs (see entry for *Aulonocara nyassae* on page 126 for details of how to arrange these safely). The water, which should be moderately hard and neutral to alkaline, should also be well-filtered. A small shoal consisting of a few females and a single male (males are aggressive towards one another during breeding) should be kept together, particularly for breeding purposes.

Temperature: 22–26°C (72–79°F); slightly higher for breeding.

Breeding: A single male will breed with several females, usually in a cave or near to a shelter. Females incubate the 20–30 eggs orally and will later protect the fry for a time.

Mesonauta festiva
(Festive Cichlid, Festivum)

THE FESTIVE CICHLID (*Mesonauta festiva*) is another long-standing aquarium favourite which has stood the test of time and, for many years, been bred in commercial quantities in most of the ornamental fish-producing areas of the world. The vast majority of Festives seen in shops today are, in fact, captive-bred specifically for the hobby, with a relatively low percentage coming from the wild.

Up to the early 1990s, *M. festiva* was the only species that could be assigned to the genus *Mesonauta* with any certainty, since some doubt existed (and still exists) regarding the validity of the very similar *M. insignis*. In recent years, several other species have been added to the genus, with yet others awaiting official description and with question marks regarding the true identity of a few Festive look-alikes.

The most likely species to be seen from time to time are: *M. acora, M. egregius* and *M. mirificus*. There is also the possibility that all the Festives from the Rio Negro may eventually be regarded as *M. insignis*, with those from Guyana and some of the Amazon regions away from the Rio Negro being the only 'true' *M. festiva*.

Natural Range: Widespread throughout the Amazon basin. Also reported from western Guyana.

Size: Up to 20cm (8in) reported for females and 15cm (6in) for males, but usually smaller.

Food: All commercial and livefoods accepted.

Tank Conditions: Festives can be rather timid, despite their size. The tank should, therefore, provide adequate shelter in the form of caves, rocks, bogwood (or equivalent) and dense plant thickets (but not delicate species, such as *Cabomba* or *Myriophyllum*). Flat or rounded stones should also be included. Water chemistry conditions are not critical, but soft, slightly acid conditions are recommended.

Temperature: 22–25°C (72–77°F); slightly higher for breeding purposes.

Breeding: Adhesive eggs are laid on a pre-cleaned broad leaf or flat or rounded stone. Both the eggs and fry are guarded by the parents.

The popular Mesonauta festiva (Festive Cichlid).

Microgeophagus ramirezi
(Ram, Butterfly / Ramirez's Dwarf Cichlid)

THE RAM (*Microgeophagus ramirezi*) often appears as *Papiliochromis ramirezi* in (mainly) European aquarium publications. *Microgeophagus* is the preferred name in the US and, with increasing regularity, elsewhere, although an official decision from the 'scientific nomenclature' authorities is still pending.

Rams have been around in the hobby for about 50 years and are widely bred in most ornamental fish-producing areas of the world. Several varieties are regularly available, including an Asian (Singaporean-developed) one in which specimens tend to be larger than normal, and an attractive golden one which is more delicate, in terms of water quality requirements, than the wild type.

While, at first sight, the sexes seem very similar to one another, closer examination will reveal an extended second ray in the dorsal (back) fin of the males and a more rounded body in females, which are also smaller than their mates.

Rams make excellent community fish, as long as their tankmates are not large or boisterous, and as long as water conditions are to their liking.

Natural Range: Colombia and western Venezuela.
Size: Around 7cm (2.75in) for wild-caught specimens; usually smaller for aquarium specimens.
Food: Most commercial and livefoods accepted.
Tank Conditions: Rams are peaceful, often timid, fish which require a thickly planted aquarium offering numerous hiding places. Bogwood (or its equivalent), rocks, etc., can be used to form shelters, but – at the same time – the aquarium layout should provide an open swimming area at the front. A number of flat or rounded stones should also be included to serve as possible spawning sites. The water should be soft and acid and the overall quality must be good for this somewhat sensitive species. Raw tapwater should be avoided during partial water changes, or it must be treated with a dechlorinator / dechloraminator / conditioner.
Temperature: 22–26°C (72–79°F); slightly higher for breeding purposes.
Breeding: Rams are typical substrate spawners who will guard their eggs and fry.

Microgeophagus ramirezi (Ram).

Nannacara anomala
(Golden Dwarf Acara, Golden-Eyed Dwarf Cichlid)

Nannacara anomala (Golden Dwarf Acara) exhibits varying coloration depending on its locality.

THE GOLDEN Dwarf Acara (*Nannacara anomala*) is a widely distributed species which exhibits varying coloration depending on locality. The reference, below, to the possible existence of the species in French Guiana may be the result of confusion regarding the significance of this varying pigmentation, since the French Guianan species, *N. aureocephalus*, may actually be a colour form of *N. anomala*.

Although spawning usually takes place in a cave, as stated below, eggs may also be laid on a flat or rounded stone, particularly if this is protected against attack from above by the leaves of a broad-leaved plant or some other form of cover. As in other cichlid species, females often move their new-born fry between a number of shallow pits or depressions in the substrate, hence the recommendation for a fine-grained substratum.

Outside the breeding season, *Nannacara anomala* is a good choice for a well-planted community aquarium.

Natural Range: Northern South America, particularly Surinam and Guyana (possibly also French Guiana).

Size: Males reported up to 9cm (3.5in); females just over half this size.

Food: Livefoods are preferred, but some commercial preparations are also accepted.

Tank Conditions: A heavily planted aquarium with numerous shelters and hiding places should be provided for this dwarf cichlid, which is peaceful towards its tankmates, except during breeding, at which time it becomes very territorial. If the aquarium is large, the male will guard the territory, with the female tending to the eggs and fry. In small aquaria, the male can become quite aggressive towards his mate and should be removed to separate quarters. A fine-grained bottom medium is recommended, consisting either of fine gravel or coarse sand. The water should be slightly acid and soft to moderately hard.

Temperature: 22–25°C (72–77°F) for general maintenance, but higher for breeding.

Breeding: Adhesive eggs are generally laid in caves and both they and the fry are guarded by the female.

Neolamprologus brichardi
(Fairy/Lyretail Lamprologus, Brichardi)

THE FAIRY or Lyretail Lamprologus (*Neolamprologus brichardi*) also appears quite frequently in aquarium literature under its other well-known name, *Lamprologus brichardi*. In this instance, it is not just a case of one name being older than the other, but of some authorities believing one name to be more 'correct' than the other. So, for the foreseeable future at least, both names will be quoted with equal conviction, depending on the views of the author.

The Lyretail Lamprologus was one of the first Rift Lake cichlid species to be exported in any quantity from Africa. Most specimens currently available have been captive-bred specifically for the aquarium hobby, with several colour varieties, including an albino, becoming widely available since the early to mid-1990s.

Natural Range: Lake Tanganyika, Africa.

Size: Around 10cm (4in).

Food: Although livefood is preferred, other foods will also be accepted.

Tank Conditions: This species occurs in large shoals in Lake Tanganyika, where it exhibits no aggression towards members of its own, or other, species. In the confines of an aquarium, however, especially if kept as a single specimen or a pair, older specimens can sometimes become intolerant. It is therefore best to keep Lyretails in a shoal and install numerous rock caves and shelters or a cliff to allow individuals to hide as and when necessary (see entry for *Aulonocara nyassae* – page 126 – for details on how to install safe rock arrangements). Well-filtered, alkaline, medium-hard to hard water is recommended.

Temperature: 22-25°C (72-77°F), but several degrees higher for breeding.

Breeding: Unlike the mouthbrooding cichlids of LakeMalawi, *N. brichardi* is a cave spawner in which the eggs are defended by the female. The young are not, however, defended with the same vigour that other cichlids demonstrate, but neither are they attacked. It is, therefore, usual for young of different ages to be found together, with the older ones offering their smaller siblings some degree of protection.

Neoamprologus brichardi (Lyretail Lamprologus) is available in several colour varieties.

Neolamprologus leleupi
(Lemon Cichlid / Lamprologus)

THE LEMON Lamprologus (*Neolamprologus leleupi*), like its relative, the Fairy/Lyretail Lamprologus (*N. brichardi*), is often referred to by its alternative scientific name of *Lamprologus leleupi*.

This is a remarkably coloured fish, the brilliant hues of which have made it a strong favourite among aquarists. Three forms (believed to be subspecies) of the species are known: *Neolamprologus leleupi leleupi*, which is bright yellow, *N. l. melas*, which is brown, and *L. l. longior*, which is orange-yellow and possesses more vertebrae (individual back bones) than either of its counterparts and is, therefore, longer.

The two yellow subspecies also differ in that *N. l. leleupi* can lose much of its brilliance in aquaria from one generation to the next, while *N. l. longior* retains much of its pigmentation.

Since these fish eat crustacea and other shelled creatures in the wild, the use of a commercial food containing natural pigments like canthaxanthin is therefore recommended, as are deep-frozen, freeze-dried and livefoods consisting of shelled organisms.

N.B. The similarly-named *N. leloupi* is a totally different species which must not be confused with *N. leleupi*.

Natural Range: Lake Tanganyika, Africa.

Size: Around 10cm (4in).

Food: Prefers livefoods, but will take commercial preparations as well (see main text).

Tank Conditions: *N. leleupi* likes an aquarium with an open swimming area consisting of a substratum, such as coarse sand or fine gravel, surrounded by rock shelters, or caves, or a cliff offering safe hiding places as and when required (see entry for *Aulonocara nyassae* – page 126 – for details on how to render rock arrangements safe). With this species – as with *N. brichardi* – plants are not required. If desired, stout alkaline-tolerant species like Tape Grass (*Vallisneria*) may be used as part of the decor, as these fish do not burrow. The water should be alkaline and medium-hard to hard.

Temperature: 22–26°C (72–79°F), but a few degrees higher for breeding.

Breeding: Adhesive, hard-shelled eggs are laid, usually in a cave, and are defended by the female. The male guards the overall territory established by the pair.

The brilliant Neolamprologus leleupi (Lemon Cichlid).

Pelvicachromis pulcher
(Krib, Kribensis, Purple Cichlid)

THE KRIB or Kribensis (*Pelvicachromis pulcher*), whose common name is a relic of its former scientific name, *Pelmatochromis kribensis*, is one of the most colourful dwarf cichlids available to aquarists.

Unusually for a cichlid, the females, while being smaller than their mates, can be more colourful than them during courtship and breeding; they also tend to be the more active partner during courtship.

As with its closest relatives, several colour forms of *P. pulcher* can be found in the wild, and although some of these are imported on a fairly regular basis, most specimens on offer in shops, including an albino morph, are captive-bred.

Other 'Krib' species which are available with varying frequency are: *P. humilis* (Yellow Kribensis), *P. roloffi* (Roloff's Kribensis), *P.* cf. *pulcher* (Giant or Dwarf Kribensis), *P. subocellatus* (Eye-spot or Ocellated Kribensis) and *P. taeniatus* (Striped Kribensis).

Natural Range: Lower Nigeria, often in brackish waters.
Size: Up to 10cm (4in) for males; females are considerably smaller.

Food: Most commercial and livefoods accepted.

Tank Conditions: Kribs like a heavily planted aquarium that also offers them shelter in the form of caves, rocks, etc. In addition, an open swimming area should be provided at the front to allow the fish to be viewed in all their splendour. Water chemistry is not critical, as long as the overall quality is good, but slightly acid, medium-hard water is generally recommended. So is the addition of a small amount of sea salt (one to two teaspoonfuls per 4.5 litres/1 Imperial gallon) on account of the species' brackish origins. However, this salt is not essential and can be dispensed with if the fish are being kept as part of a community set-up housing species from soft, acid regions.
Temperature: 24–28°C (75–82°F).
Breeding: Adhesive eggs are usually laid on the roof of a cave and are guarded, mostly by the female, while the male tends to defend the pair's territory. Once the fry are free-swimming, both parents undertake guard duties.

Pelvicachromis pulcher (Kribensis).
The top fish is the female.

Pseudocrenilabrus multicolor
(Egyptian/Nile Mouthbrooder)

THE Egyptian/Nile Mouthbrooder (*Pseudocrenilabrus multicolor*) is a dwarf African cichlid that has been known in the hobby for nearly 100 years. In that time, its popularity has waxed and waned with changing fashions and as 'newer' cichlids – most notably the Lake Malawi and Tanganyika species – have appeared on the scene.

Although generally recommended for a community aquarium, *P. multicolor* can prove intolerant, especially during courtship and breeding. At other times, a pair will tend to live in reasonable harmony with similarly sized fish. Since the female can suffer harassment from the male after spawning, it is advisable to separate the pair.

Two other species of *Pseudocrenilabrus* mouthbrooders are known: *P. philander* (South African/Mozambique/ Dwarf Copper Mouthbrooder) – several morphs or subspecies of which exist – and *P. nicholsi* (Dwarf Congo Mouthbrooder) the most beautiful, but least frequently seen, of the three species.

Pseudocrenilabrus multicolor (Egyptian/ Nile Mouthbrooder) has been known for over 100 years.

Natural Range: Widely distributed along the drainages of the River Nile in central east Africa. Also extends southwards as far as Lake Victoria.

Size: Up to 8cm (3.1in), with the males often being slightly larger than the females.

Food: Most commercial and livefoods accepted.

Tank Conditions: The aquarium should provide open swimming areas, as well as caves, rocks and/or bogwood (or its equivalent) as shelters for this tough little fish. Thick bunches of submerged plants, plus a covering of floating plants on the water surface, will help create the secluded habitat preferred by the species. Water chemistry is not critical, as long as the overall quality is good, but a neutral pH and medium-hard water are generally recommended.

Temperature: 20–26°C (68–79°F).

Breeding: Eggs are laid either in a shallow depression dug by the male, or on a pre-cleaned stone. They are picked up by the female who broods them orally until they hatch some ten days later. She will also offer the fry protection for a further week or so.

Pseudotropheus zebra
(Zebra/Nyasa Blue Cichlid)

THE ZEBRA CICHLID (*Pseudotropheus zebra*) is one of the most widely kept African Rift Lake cichlids. It is also the most varied of all such species, occurring in numerous colour morphs, depending on their home range within Lake Malawi.

Many of these variants, originally thought to constitute no more than colour varieties, were subsequently found to be sexually incompatible, giving rise to the belief that, at least, some were not morphs at all, but virtually identical, separate, species.

Most of these, along with a number of other Zebras which have not yet been exported from Malawi, are currently referred to as *Pseudotropheus* sp., followed by a descriptive name referring either to the colour, or the location where the fish occurs, as in *Pseudotropheus* sp. 'Zebra Red Dorsal' or *Pseudotropheus* sp. 'Zebra Metangula'.

All require the same basic aquarium conditions, as do the numerous other *Pseudotropheus* 'non-zebra' species regularly imported.

Natural Range: Lake Malawi, Africa.

Size: Up to 15cm (6in) reported, but usually remains smaller. The largest specimens collected at Makulawe Point, Likoma Island, in Lake Malawi, measured 13.5cm (5.3in).

Food: Will accept most commercial and livefoods; diet should include a regular vegetable component.

Tank Conditions: *P. zebra* is always found in close association with rocks in the wild and this must be maintained in aquaria. Brief details of how safe cave and cliff arrangements can be constructed are given on page 126, under Tank Conditions for *Aulonocara nyassae*. Robust alkaline-tolerant natural plants, or artificial equivalents, can be added, both as decor and as potential territory markers. Unless the aquarium is on the large size, e.g., around 120cm (48in) in length, the shoal of *P. zebra* should consist of a single male and several females, because of the aggressive, territorial behaviour of the males. The water needs to be moderately alkaline, medium-hard to hard, and be well filtered.

Temperature: 22–28°C (72–82°F).

Breeding: This is a typical maternal mouthbrooder – the female continues to protect the fry for a week or more after hatching.

Pseudotropheus zebra (Zebra Cichlid) is a species which is available in numerous colour forms.

Pterophyllum scalare
(Angelfish, Scalare)

THE ANGELFISH (*Pterophyllum scalare*) is one of the most frequently kept of all aquarium fish. It has been in the hobby since the early years of the 20th century and has been commercially developed into numerous fancy varieties with extended fins and colour variations which depart markedly from the original silver base with black vertical bands.

P. *scalare*, while being widely distributed in the Amazon region, has not been officially reported from one of its major rivers, the Rio Negro. Various authors have, however, reported the two other species of Angel, the elegant Altum Angel (*P. altum*) and Leopold's Angel (*P. leopoldi*) from this important tributary. In addition, I have collected some magnificent red-finned Angels, the largest specimens of which measured between 25–30cm (10–12in) from tip of dorsal fin to tip of anal fin, in a lake just off the Rio Negro. These fish did not appear to belong to any of the three known species, but what they were (or are), is, as yet, not known with any certainty.

Commercially developed or aquarium specimens do not attain such a large size. Even so, they are too large to be considered as ideal choices for a community aquarium that includes small species such as Neons (*Paracheirodon innesi*) or Cardinals (*P. axelrodi*) which will be considered merely as food items. Housed with larger fish, however, Angels are generally peaceful and sedate fish with a regal touch.

Natural Range: Central Amazon basin, but not reported in the Rio Negro (see main text).
Size: Up to 15cm (6in) reported for wild specimens, but usually smaller for aquarium specimens (see main text).
Food: All commercial and livefoods accepted.
Tank Conditions: Taking into account the considerable size that this species can attain, particularly from the tip of its dorsal (back) fin to the tip of its anal (belly) fin, the aquarium should not just be roomy lengthwise, but deep as well. Tall strap-leaved plants like *Vallisneria*, *Sagittaria* and *Crinum* species, along with other somewhat broader-leaved plants like Amazon Swords (*Echinodorus spp.*), go particularly well with Angels and should be planted along the sides and back of the aquarium. A bogwood (or equivalent) centrepiece should also be added, while, at the same time, a large open swimming area should be left along the front. Water chemistry is not critical, but soft, acid conditions are preferred, particularly by wild-caught specimens. Commercially bred Angels – which constitute the vast majority of aquarium stocks – are generally comfortable in a wider range of water conditions.
Temperature: 24–28°C (75–82°F).
Breeding: Adhesive eggs are laid on a pre-cleaned leaf. Both they and the fry are protected by the parents, who also secrete body mucus on which the fry will feed, just as they do in Discus (*Symphysodon spp.*), Uarus (*Uaru ampiacanthoides*) and some other species from similar habitats.

Koi Angelfish.

Main picture: Wild type Angelfish. Inset: Marble Angelfish.

Satanoperca jurupari
(Devil/Demon Fish, Earth Eater, Jurupari)

DESPITE ITS satanic or demonic names, the Demon Fish (*Satanoperca jurupari*) is one of the more peaceful and tolerant species of medium-sized to large cichlid. This, of course, changes when a pair decide to breed, at which time they become intensely territorial. Even so, large, robust tankmates are generally safe, as long as the aquarium is spacious and provides adequate hiding places.

The unusual breeding behaviour exhibited by this species, in which the eggs are neither left on the stone on which they are laid until they hatch, nor incubated orally from the outset (see Breeding below) is regarded by some as representing something of a halfway stage between strict substrate spawning and fully fledged mouthbrooding.

This species formerly used to be assigned to the genus *Geophagus*, a name which means 'Earth Eater' and, therefore, more clearly reflects its bottom-scouring tendencies.

Despite its rather fierce appearance, Satanoperca jurupari (Devil Fish) is a one of the more peaceful species.

Natural Range: Brazil and Guyana.

Size: Up to 25cm (10in), but usually smaller.

Food: Most commercial and livefoods accepted.

Tank Conditions: Earth Eaters, as their name implies, love rooting around the bottom of the aquarium seeking out buried food items. Plants must be protected from their attentions, either by being potted up and having the soil covered with pebbles, or – if they are rooted in the aquarium's substratum – by strategically arranging stones and pebbles around their stems. Again, because of the species' burrowing activities, the substratum must be fine-grained. Hiding places, plus an open swimming area, must also be provided. Although soft, acid water is preferred, other conditions are also tolerated, as long as these are not extreme and the overall quality is good.

Temperature: 22–28°C (72–82°F), with higher temperatures being recommended for breeding.

Breeding: Eggs are laid on a stone and guarded for around a day, after which they are picked up by the female for oral incubation. This duty, and the subsequent protection of the fry, is also shared by the male.

Steatocranus casuarius
(African Blockhead/Lumphead)

Staetocranus casuarius (African Blockhead) has an unusual appearance and exhibits unfishlike swimming movements.

THE AFRICAN Blockhead/Lumphead (*Steatocranus casuarius*) is a most unusual fish which is kept more for the pronounced forehead lump that fully mature males possess; than for the colour or behaviour of the species. Indeed, the basic coloration, while being subtly attractive, is not spectacular. In addition, behaviour often hovers between intolerance and aggression, especially during the breeding season. Blockheads do not, therefore, represent a good choice for a community aquarium containing small specimens or species.

What they lack in colour and social graces, though, they amply make up for in their unusual appearance and their somewhat unfishlike swimming movements. An added bonus is that when a pair spawns, the sight of a shoal of up to 150 small Blockheads hopping around the floor of an aquarium with their ever-watchful and intensely protective parents in close attendance provides a unique experience.

Wild-caught males, in particular, possess large frontal growths, but even commercially bred specimens of both sexes (which account for the vast majority of Blockheads available in shops) exhibit sizeable lumps.

Natural Range: Lower and central Democratic Republic of Congo.

Size: Up to 11cm (4.3in) for males and around 8cm (3.1in) for females.

Food: Most commercial and livefoods taken, except floating types.

Tank Conditions: Being strict bottom dwellers with poorly developed swim bladders, Blockheads require numerous caves, rocks and other forms of shelter. Rather than swim, they tend to hop or move jerkily along the bottom, maintaining almost continuous physical contact with the substratum. Rocks and other items of aquarium decor must not be sharp-edged. The water, which should be well filtered, should be slightly acid to neutral and medium-hard.

Temperature: 24–28°C (75–82°F).

Breeding: Small clutches of eggs are laid in caves and both they and the fry are protected by the parents, which, apparently, pair for life.

Symphysodon spp
(Discus, Pompadour)

The discus is a highly variable fish.

DISCUS (*Symphysodon spp.*) are often referred to as the kings or aristocrats of the hobby. They are, indeed, absolutely superb fish, the top specimens of which command very high prices. However, as technology has advanced – making their maintenance and breeding easier – large numbers produced in hatcheries, both in the East and the West, have led to more 'comfortably affordable' fish becoming widely available.

Traditionally, two species of Discus have been recognized: *Symphysodon aequifasciatia* (referred to as

aequifasciatus in some books) and *S. discus*. *S. aequifasciata* is usually subdivided into three subspecies:

S. aequifasciata aequifasciata – the Green Discus

S. aequifasciata axelrodi – the Brown Discus

S. aequifasciata haraldi – the Blue Discus

S. discus is sometimes subdivided into two subspecies:

S. discus discus – the Heckel Discus

S. discus willischwartzi – no common name

This apparently simple breakdown belies the underlying complexity of Discus classification, because, within each subspecies, numerous naturally occurring and naturally varying populations exist. These have been under scientific investigation for many years with, in recent times, DNA fingerprinting – a technique designed to demonstrate genetic relatedness – being brought into the research studies. As a result, there is now a school of thought that believes there to be just one species of Discus with, possibly, two subspecies.

Whatever the eventual outcome, '*discus*' specimens can be easily differentiated from '*aequifasciata*' fish in that the former always possess a very distinct central vertical band running down the body from the dorsal (back) fin, to the anal (belly) fin. '*Aequifasciata*' specimens, irrespective of variety, have several bands, but none is anywhere as wide or distinct as the '*discus*' central body band.

All the above characteristics and debate relate purely to wild type fish. To these, we must, of course, add all the myriad commercial varieties that have been developed over the years, along with those that are still being created at an ever-increasing rate, especially in the Far East. We are now at the stage where it is quite impossible to keep pace with every new variety that appears on the scene, particularly since some of these end up enjoying only a brief period of popularity (if at all), or else are further developed into newer creations.

Natural Range: Numerous tributaries of the Amazon basin.

Size: *Symphysodon aequifasciata* is generally reported as growing to 15cm (6in), but can grow larger than this. *S. discus* is usually quoted as growing to 20cm (8in).

Food: The diet should be predominantly live- or meat-based. Deep-frozen, freeze-dried and some commercial preparations, particularly those developed specifically for Discus, are also accepted.

Tank Conditions: Modern aquarium technology, and the ease with which it can be operated, has revolutionized Discus keeping from around the mid-1980s onwards. Discus require soft, acid water, preferably tannin-stained (although this is not essential). The aquarium must be large in every dimension, especially since these are sizeable fish which can be taller than they are long (at least, in some of the 'hi-body' varieties developed in Asia

from around the mid-1980's). There should be a large open swimming area at the front of the aquarium, bordered by plants along the sides and back. A centrepiece, consisting of a non-calcareous rock, or a large piece of bogwood, roots, 'safe' driftwood (or the equivalent) will add further character to the aquascape, as will a fine-grained dark substratum.

Temperature: 26–30°C (79–86°F), even slightly higher for breeding.

Breeding: Very soft, acid water is recommended. Adhesive eggs are laid on a pre-cleaned site, which can be a stone, leaf, or piece of bogwood. Both the eggs and the fry (which hatch after 2–3 days) are protected by the parents, who secrete body mucus (sometimes referred to as 'Discus Milk') on which the fry feed for a time. A commercial substitute which can be used instead of natural 'milk' is also available.

Turquoise Discus: one of the many 'aequifasciata' varieties.

Thorichthys meeki
(Firemouth)

ALTHOUGH wild-caught specimens of the Firemouth (*Thorichthys meeki*) are imported, the vast majority of aquarium stocks are captive-bred specifically for the hobby.

This is a species with two personalities. On the one hand, it is generally peaceful towards tankmates, except smaller individuals of the same species. Being territorial, males (in particular) will flare out their gill covers in a defensive display should any fish that is seen as a potential intruder enter their territory. However, this hardly ever ends up in outright violence.

Once a pair decides to spawn, though, a different facet of the Firemouth's character comes to the fore, with both breeders becoming exceedingly aggressive towards all their tankmates, often forcing them into the furthest corners of the aquarium. In common with other species that become pugnacious during the breeding season, Firemouths are excellent parents.

Natural Range: Guatemala and Yucatán region of Mexico.

Size: Up to 15cm (6in) reported for males; up to around 11cm (4.3in) for females.

Food: All commercial and livefoods accepted.

Tank Conditions: While this is a territorial species, it can be kept with other similarly sized fish if the aquarium is sufficiently large to provide suitable retreats when a pair of Firemouths decides to spawn. At other times, Firemouths can co-exist quite happily with other fish. The aquarium should have an open swimming area at the front, bordered by well-rooted, or suitably protected, plants along the sides and back. Flat or rounded stones, plus a few caves, should be provided and the substratum should, preferably, be fine-grained to cater for the species' burrowing habits. Neutral or alkaline, medium-hard water is often recommended, but other conditions will also be tolerated, as long as the overall quality is good.

Temperature: 21–25°C (70–77°F); slightly higher for breeding.

Breeding: Adhesive eggs (up to 500) are laid on a pre-cleaned stone and both they and the fry, are protected by the parents.

Thorichthys meeki (Firemouth) may be aggressive during breeding time but is an excellent parent.

Uaru amphiacanthoides
(Uaru, Waroo, Triangle Cichlid)

THE UARU (*Uaru amphiacanthoides*) is a large, generally peaceful, shoaling cichlid which – once past the spotted juvenile stage – develops a distinctive dark, elongated triangular shape on the side of its body, which gives rise to one of its other common names. The 'base' of this triangle is located just behind the gill covers, and the tip just in front of the black spot on the caudal peduncle. In some specimens the triangle's apex can actually merge with the spot, while in others it can fall quite a way short.

In the wild, Rummy-nosed Tetras (*Hemigrammus rhodostomus* and others) are reported to 'parasitize' Uarus, feeding off the body mucus that adults secrete for their own fry to feed on.

Natural Range: Northern Amazon region and Guyana.
Size: Up to around 30cm (12in), but usually smaller.
Food: This is a carnivorous species which will take livefoods, deep-frozen, freeze-dried foods and meat-based preparations, e.g., ground beefheart. It will also accept some commercial diets, like pellets, granules, etc.

Tank Conditions: On account of their considerable adult size, Uarus require a roomy tank with a large open swimming area (especially since, by nature, they are shoalers). In addition, there should be ample cover. Commonly found in the 'black waters' of the Amazon region, e.g., the Rio Negro, Uarus appreciate soft, acid water that is tannin-stained. Filtering the water through a 'peat sandwich' (a layer of peat held inside a power filter), using a large lump of natural bogwood as a centrepiece, and/or adding a commercial blackwater preparation to the aquarium, will all help provide such conditions. Lighting should be subdued, which excludes the use of many of the commonly available robust aquarium plants.

Temperature: 25–28°C (77–82°F), even slightly higher.
Breeding: This is a difficult species to breed in aquaria. Adhesive eggs are laid on a pre-cleaned surface, e.g., a flat or rounded stone or broad-leaved plant. Both they and the fry are protected by the parents who – like Discus (*Symphysodon spp.*) – produce body mucus on which the fry feed at first.

Uaru amphiacanthoides (Uaru) feeds its youngest fry on 'body milk', just as Discus do.

ANABANTOIDS/ LABYRINTHFISHES

ANABANTOIDS ARE frequently referred to as anabantids. Strictly speaking, though, anabantids constitute just one family (the Anabantidae) of anabantoids (suborder Anabantoidei). To avoid confusion, it might be better to use the other common name for the suborder: the labyrinthfishes.

This latter name is also more descriptive in that it makes direct reference to the labyrinth, an auxiliary respiratory organ that all the species possess. This labyrinth is a suprabranchial organ, i.e., it is situated above the gills, which contains a rich blood supply and is, as a result, perfectly equipped to act as part of the fishes' breathing apparatus.

While not totally replacing normal gills, either physically or functionally, the labyrinth permits anabantoids to take in atmospheric air at the water surface, channelling it through the labyrinth and, in the process, extracting some of the oxygen into the bloodstream. As fresh air enters the labyrinth chamber, it forces old air out, and this is expelled as bubbles via the gill covers.

Labyrinths have become so dependent on their auxiliary breathing apparatus that at least some of the species will actually drown if prevented from surfacing at intervals to take in atmospheric air.

Colisa sota (Honey Gourami).

The possession of the labyrinth also makes it possible for these fish to build nests consisting of tiny mucus-covered air bubbles, among which they lay their eggs. In this way, an organ that has evolved over aeons of time and which allows labyrinthfishes to survive in the seasonally oxygen-deficient waters of their natural habitat, also offers embryos an oxygen-rich environment in which to develop.

In the pages that follow, the following familes are represented: Anabantidae (anabantids/climbing perches/bushfish), Belontiidae (gouramis and their closest relatives), Helostomatidae (Kissing Gourami – *Helostoma*), Osphronemidae (Giant Gourami – *Osphronemus*). The family Belontiidae is split into three subfamilies: Belontiinae (combtail gouramis), Macropodinae (fighting and paradise fishes) and Trichogasterinae (gouramis such as the Dwarf, *Colisa lalia* and the Two/Three-spot, *Trichogaster trichopterus*).

Trichogaster microlepis (Moonlight Gourami).

Belontia signata
(Combtail, Ceylonese Paradise Fish)

THE COMBTAIL (*Belontia signata*) was first imported into the West in 1933 and, since then it has always been available to hobbyists, although never in very large quantities.

It is undoubtedly an impressive fish, particularly when fully mature and exhibiting the characteristic caudal (tail) fin extensions responsible for its common name. However, Combtails are quite aggressive, particularly as adults and during the breeding season, making them suitable only for communities housing equally boisterous species. Juveniles lack this aggression, however, and can form part of a more 'standard' community collection, albeit only on a temporary basis.

B. signata occurs in several natural forms in its native Sri Lanka, two of these being considered by many as constituting valid subspecies: *B. signata signata*, the reddish type that is most often available in shops, and *B. signata jonklaasi*, which is often bluer, carries a dark spot on the base of the pectoral (chest) fins and is often referred to as the Pectoral Spot Combtail. A further (larger) species, *B. hasselti* – the Java Combtail – is also occasionally available.

Natural Range: Sri Lanka.

Size: Up to 15cm (6in) reported, but usually smaller.

Food: All commercial and livefoods accepted.

Tank Conditions: Although it often likes to hide among dense vegetation, the Combtail should also be provided with open swimming areas and a centrepiece consisting of natural bogwood (or its equivalent). Good illumination and filtration are recommended. Water chemistry is not critical and can range from slightly acid to moderately alkaline, and relatively soft to medium-hard, to hard.

Temperature: 24–28°C (75–82°F).

Breeding: Males may or may not build a bubblenest. When they do, it is neither as large, nor as well constructed as in other 'aquarium' labyrinths. Eggs are deposited among the bubbles and are guarded by the male (although, on rare occasions, the female has also been reported as participating in brood care). Hatching takes about 1–1 1/2 days and the fry are guarded for a few days, usually by their father.

The impressive Belontia signata (Combtail).

Betta imbellis
(Crescent/Peaceful Betta)

Betta imbellis (Crescent, or Peaceful Betta) is a beautiful little fish.

deep-red patch that occupies the extended posterior half of the caudal fin.

Natural Range: Mostly still waters in Indonesia, Peninsular Malaysia and Thailand.

Size: Up to 5.5cm (2.2in).

Food: Most commercial and livefoods accepted.

Tank Conditions: As in other fighters, male *B. imbellis* are aggressive towards one another. Therefore, if the aquarium is on the small side, i.e., less than 60cm (24in) in length, only one male should be kept. In larger aquaria with good plant cover and other hiding places, it is

OF THE TWO common names in use for *Betta imbellis*, by far the more appropriate one is the Crescent Betta, on two counts. Firstly, it is an accurate reference to the beautiful crescent that the males exhibit along the posterior edge of the caudal (tail) fin. Secondly, *B. imbellis* males are nowhere as peaceful towards one another as the other common name implies, although several specimens can be kept together under certain conditions (see below).

There are several geographic races or morphs of this species within the distribution range, including one from Ko Samui Island in Thailand, which is believed to be endangered. There is also an aquarium-raised 'fan-tailed' variety in which the crescent has been replaced by a large

possible to keep more than one male, but a watchful eye must, nevertheless, be kept to remove any individual that is subjected to undue stress by his tankmates. Crescent Betta males are peaceful towards other fish and can be kept in community aquaria with other non-boisterous species. The water should be on the soft and slightly acid to neutral side, but some deviation from this will be tolerated.

Temperature: Although some specimens have been collected at temperatures as high as 34°C (93°F), a range of 22–25°C (72–77°F) is generally recommended.

Breeding: Pairs will spawn under a bubblenest constructed by the male, who is also responsible for caring for the fry.

Betta smaragdina
(Emerald Betta/Fighter/Smaragd Fighter)

THE EMERALD BETTA (*Betta smaragdina*) is a relative newcomer to the hobby, having first been imported into the West around 1970, about the same time as *B. imbellis* made its first appearance.

Its brilliant emerald body scales made it an immediate hit with *Betta* fanciers the world over, to the extent that it is still one of the few 'new-generation' Bettas to be found in aquarium shops with any regularity (though never in large numbers).

Although it is not a particularly productive species, *B. smaragdina* breeds quite readily in aquaria and a constant trickle of captive-bred specimens regularly finds its way into shops, largely as a result of spawnings carried out by members of aquarium societies dedicated to the study of Bettas and other labyrinthfishes.

While most specimens possess the typical emerald-green scales that give the species its common name, some localities yield males of a deeper blue hue. In all cases, though, the females are quite drab-coloured and exhibit two or three longitudinal brownish bands along the body.

Natural Range: Cambodia, Laos, northeastern and eastern Thailand.

Size: Up to 7cm (2.8in).

Food: The diet should consist predominantly of livefoods, although some commercial preparations will be accepted.

Tank Conditions: Coming from quiet waters, *B. smaragdina* likes a heavily planted aquarium with a good supply of hiding places. Males should not be kept together, unless the aquarium is large enough to provide adequate shelter as and when required. Several females can, however, be kept together. Despite their aggression towards conspecific males, i.e., males of the same species, Emerald Bettas are peaceful towards other species and can be kept in community aquaria, as long as their tankmates are neither large nor over-boisterous. There are no special water chemistry requirements, provided the overall quality is good and extremes of pH and hardness are avoided.

Temperature: 24–27°C (75–81°F).

Breeding: *B. smaragdina* is a bubblenester in which the male guards the eggs and fry.

Betta smaragdina (Emerald Betta) is much sought after.

Betta splendens
(Siamese Fighter)

THE SIAMESE FIGHTER (*Betta splendens*) is one of the most famous of all aquarium fish. Its fighting qualities are legendary and its popularity remains undiminished within the hobby, despite a history spanning more than 100 years.

Numerous colour and fin varieties have been developed over this period, to the extent that no-one really knows just how many established strains of Fighter actually exist. The popularity of this old favourite is such that there are even specialist aquarium societies dedicated solely to the study and breeding of the species.

Strictly speaking, *B. splendens* should no longer be known as the Siamese Fighter, since Siam is now called Thailand, but the name is so deeply ingrained in our psyche that it is most unlikely to be replaced by, say, the Thai Fighter.

Natural Range: Southeast Asia. Some wild populations, e.g., in Laos and Myanmar in Asia, and in Colombia, South America, have become established via releases or escapes.

Female Betta splendens (Siamese Fighter).

Size: Up to 6cm (2.4in).

Food: Most commercial and livefoods accepted.

Tank Conditions: Owing to the highly aggressive nature of males, only single specimens can be kept in an aquarium. Several females can, however, be kept together, especially in a heavily planted tank with numerous hiding places. Despite their belligerent nature with regard to rivals of their own species, *B. splendens* males are peaceful towards other fish and can, therefore, be kept in community aquaria. If anything, males with long flowing fins can themselves become the victims of fin-nipping species like Tiger Barbs (*Barbus tetrazona*). So it is always best to select alternative tankmates for an aquarium housing a *B. splendens* male. Water chemistry is not critical, as long as the overall quality is good and extremes of pH and hardness are avoided.

Temperature: 24–28°C (75–82°F), even a little higher for breeding purposes.

Breeding: This is a classic bubblenester in which males guard both the eggs and fry.

Male Betta splendens (Siamese Fighter).

Betta unimaculata
(One-spot Betta/Fighter)

THE ONE-SPOT Betta (*Betta unimaculata*) is a mouthbrooder which, typically, is not as brightly coloured as its bubblenesting relatives.

Up to the early 1980s, mouthbrooding species of *Betta* were rare in the hobby and while they have never become as widely available as the bubblenesters, numerous species are now known, thanks to a remarkable series of discoveries and to the enthusiasm and dedication of members of specialist labyrinthfish societes in several countries.

B. unimaculata and other mouthbrooding males are not as aggressive as their more territorial bubblenesting cousins. They are also peaceful towards other species and can be safely kept in community aquaria.

Natural Range: Kalimantan Timur and Sabah on the island of Borneo.
Size: Up to 12cm (4.7in).
Food: While livefoods are preferred, other foods are also taken.
Tank Conditions: The layout should include both open areas and plant thickets, plus hiding places provided by rocks, roots, natural bogwood (or its equivalent). Lighting should not be too bright. *B. unimaculata* is an agile species with good jumping ability; a tight-fitting aquarium cover

is therefore essential. Water chemistry is not critical, as long as the overall quality is good, with a pH around neutral and softish conditions being quite acceptable.
Temperature: 22–25°C (72–77°F).
Breeding: *B. unimaculata* is a mouthbrooding *Betta* and the eggs are incubated orally by the male. Hatching takes about 4 days and the fry are released some 5 days later.

SOME OTHER BETTA SPECIES

In addition to the above species, other Bettas are available with varying degrees of regularity. Before buying, it is well worth checking out their requirements with members of a specialist society. Here are a few of the species you are most likely to encounter.

Bubblenesters: *B. bellica* (Slender Betta), *B. brownorum* (Brown's Red Dwarf Betta), *B. coccina* (Vine Red Betta), *B. livida* (Selangor Red Betta), *B. persephone* (Black Betta), *B. tussyae* (Tussy's Betta).

Mouthbrooders: *B. anabatoides* (Unspotted Betta), *B. balunga* (Balunga Betta), *B. dimidiata* (Dwarf Betta), *B. edithae* (Edith's Betta), *B. foerschi* (Foersch's Betta), *B. macrostoma* (Peacock/Large-mouthed Betta), *B. picta* (Javan Betta), *B. pugnax* (Penang Betta), *B. taeniata* (Striped Betta).

Betta unimaculata (One-spot Betta) male. Photo © John Dawes.

Colisa fasciata
(Indian/Striped/Banded/Giant Gourami)

The peaceful Colisa fasciata (Indian Gourami) builds its bubblenest among floating vegetation.

THE INDIAN GOURAMI (*Colisa fasciata*) was first imported into the West some 100 years ago and has always maintained a steady following, particularly among those hobbyists who prefer their fish to be as close to the original wild type as possible.

Owing to the wide distribution of this species, several naturally occurring variations in both body shape and coloration are known to exist, some, for example, having a notably larger head than others. Indian Gouramis occur in such large numbers in certain parts of their range, that they are actually harvested as food fish, being sold either fresh or dried.

C. fasciata will hybridize with both *C. lalia* (Dwarf Gourami) and *C. labiosa* (Thick-lipped Gourami). Wild-caught hybrids between *C. fasciata* and *C. lalia* are known and while wild-caught hybrids between *C. fasciata* and *C. labiosa* are not possible (because their ranges do not overlap), they can be easily produced in aquaria and produce fertile hybrids.

Natural Range: Peninsular India, except south and southwest. Also reported from northern Burma (Myanmar).

Size: Up to 12cm (4.7in) is reported, but usually slightly smaller, even for 'sizeable' males.

Food: All commercial and livefoods accepted.

Tank Conditions: This species prefers a thickly planted aquarium (including some floating vegetation) with little water movement. Turbulent power filtration should therefore be avoided (this also applies to all the other small and medium-sized labyrinths featured in this book). Hiding places are also recommended. Water chemistry is not critical, as long as the quality is good and extremes of pH and hardness are avoided. While peaceful towards other species, except during breeding, males are not very tolerant of one another and are best kept singly (along with several females) or in groups which will deflect attention from any single individual.

Temperature: 22–28°C (72–82°F).

Breeding: *C. fasicata* is an energetic bubblenester which tends to build its nest among floating vegetation. The lighter-than-water eggs are released in a series of spawning embraces underneath the nest and are guarded by the male, who also cares for the brood once they hatch about 1 day after spawning.

Colisa labiosa
(Thick-lipped Gourami)

THE OVERALL coloration – which includes a deep chocolate-brown base and brilliant dark blue-green lines on the body of males during breeding – is one of several features that make the Thick-lipped Gourami (*Colisa labiosa*) easy to distinguish from the Indian Gourami (*C. fasciata*). Males also possess a long, full and pointed dorsal (back) fin tip, and both males and females have a smaller head than their *C. fasciata* counterparts.

Despite this, there have long been doubts regarding the true identity of the Thick-lipped Gourami. These appear to have first been expressed publicly as long ago as 1936, when it was noted that specimens which had been bred from stocks imported into Europe in 1911 were different to the single specimen that was originally imported in 1904. The fact that Thick-lipped and Indian Gouramis interbreed easily and produce fertile hybrids adds further to the doubts.

Although both species do not currently overlap geographically, it is possible that the headwaters of their respective river systems were confluent at one time, and that what we are are seeing in today's *C. labiosa* is a new species in the process of evolving, rather than a fully evolved one.

Golden and peach-coloured varieties of the Thick-lipped Gourami are widely available, in addition to the wild type.

Natural Range: Along the Irrawaddy River, in Burma (Myanmar).

Size: Up to 10cm (4in) is reported, but usually smaller.

Food: All commercial and livefoods accepted.

Tank Conditions: Thick-lipped Gouramis prefer heavily planted aquaria that are not too brightly lit, but they will also swim in open areas that are brightly illuminated. Filtration should be gentle. Water chemistry is not critical, as long as the overall quality is good, but a pH centring around neutral and soft to medium-hard water are usually recommended.

Temperature: 24–28°C (75–82°F), but will tolerate slightly lower and higher water temperatures.

Breeding: Spawning embraces occur under a bubblenest and the eggs (and subsequent fry) are cared for by the father for a few days. Hatching takes about 1 day.

Colisa labiosa (Thick-lipped Gourami).

Colisa lalia
(Dwarf Gourami)

THE DWARF GOURAMI (*Colisa lalia*) is, without doubt, the most widely kept gourami species. Despite this, few genuinely wild Dwarf Gouramis are seen in the hobby today, their place being almost entirely taken by commercially bred specimens exhibiting a wide range of colours; a few of these also incorporate extended finnage.

Where the natural range for the species overlaps that of *C. fasciata*, hybrids can occur. I do not, however, possess any details relating to the fertility or sterility of such wild crosses. Hybrids between *C. lalia* and *C. labiosa* which were at one time available, all apparently developed into males in the long term, while hybrids which I produced all turned out to be very vigorous, but sterile, nest-building males.

As far as I am aware, no hybrids have been produced between *C. lalia* and the fourth *Colisa* species, *C. sota* (see next entry).

Natural Range: Widely distributed in lowland areas in northern India.
Size: Up to 6cm (2.4in), but usually a little smaller than this.

Colisa lalia (Dwarf Gourami), blood red type.

Food: All commercial and livefoods accepted.
Tank Conditions: In the wild, Dwarf Gouramis like quiet, heavily vegetated areas with surface cover. These should be replicated as near as possible in aquaria, even though intensive commercial cultivation of the species has resulted in numerous hardy and adaptable varieties. Tankmates chosen for this peaceful community species should be selected with care, avoiding large or boisterous types. Despite being peaceful most of the time, males become intensely territorial during breeding, often forcing much larger tankmates to retreat into the furthest corners of the aquarium. Water chemistry is not critical, as long as the overall quality is good and extremes of pH and hardness are avoided.
Temperature: 22–28°C (72–82°F).

Breeding: Bubblenests tend to contain varying amounts of interwoven fine vegetation which provide considerable rigidity. Spawning embraces occur below the nest and the eggs and fry are guarded by the male for a few days. Hatching takes about 1 day.

Colisa lalia (Dwarf Gourami).

Colisa sota
(Honey/Honey Dwarf Gourami)

THE HONEY GOURAMI (*Colisa sota*) still regularly appears in aquarium literature under its former name, *C. chuna*.

Unlike the other members of the genus, this species lacks any sign of oblique body bands, but has, instead, a distinct longitudinal band running from behind the gill covers to the caudal peduncle (base of the tail fin), the intensity of which varies according to the mood of the fish and the breeding/non-breeding seasons. It also lacks much of the body sheen of its closest relatives. These factors, plus its apparent inability to hybridize with the other species in the genus, sets the Honey Gourami a little apart from the rest.

Males also exhibit a rather unusual form of display when trying to lead a female to the nest: they 'stand' on their tails, i.e., they position themselves vertically in front of the female, spread their fins and show off their most brilliant colours.

While the majority of Honey Gouramis on offer are of the wild type, golden, peach and mottled varieties have been produced and are fairly regularly available. Their requirements are identical in every respect.

Colisa sota (Honey Gourami), peach colour morph.

chemistry is not critical, but extremes of pH and hardness should be avoided.

Temperature: 22–28°C (72–82°F).

Breeding: If a good surface cover of floating plants is available, the male builds a deep bubblenest (shallower, but larger, where surface plants are lacking). Spawning takes place under the nest and the male guards the eggs, which take about 1 day to hatch, and the fry during their first few days.

Natural Range:
Northeastern India and Bangladesh.

Size: Up to 7cm (2.8in) reported, but usually smaller.

Food: Most commercial and small livefoods.

Tank Conditions: *C. sota* is a retiring species which likes a heavily planted aquarium with surface vegetation and gentle filtration. Being rather small and peaceful, this delightful species is a good community fish, as long as its tankmates are neither large nor boisterous. Water

Colisa sota (Honey Gourami) courting pair (female in front).

Ctenopoma acutirostre
(Leopard/Spotted Ctenopoma/Bushfish, Climbing Perch)

THE LEOPARD Ctenopoma (*Ctenopoma acutirostre*) is one of a growing number of species of this African genus that are beginning to appear with a little greater regularity in the hobby, thanks – largely – to the activities of some members of specialist labyrinthfish aquarium societies.

While species such as *C. acutirostre*, *C. kingsleyae* (Tail-spot Bushfish), *C. maculatum* (Single-spotted Bushfish), *C. ocellatum* (Eye-spot Bushfish) and some others attain sizes of 15cm (6in) and more, there is a second group of smaller species (around 8–10cm/3.2in–4in) which are easier to accommodate, at least, in terms of their size.

It must be borne in mind, though, that Bushfish, while being generally shy and retiring, are, nevertheless, predatory. With relatively few exceptions, therefore, they should not be regarded as community aquarium fish. Perhaps the best 'community' species is *C. fasciolatum* (Banded Bushfish), but others worth considering for a 'species' aquarium include *C. ansorgii* (Orange Bushfish), *C. congicum* (Congo Bushfish), *C. damasi* (Pearl Bushfish), *C. nanum* (Dwarf Bushfish) and *C. weeksii* (Mottled Bushfish – formerly *C. oxyrhynchum*).

Ctenopoma acutirostre (Spotted Ctenopoma).

The genus *Ctenopoma* is closely related to *Anabas* – the original Asian Climbing Perch, which was, quite wrongly, believed to climb trees – and to the genus *Sandelia*, known as the 'Rockies' in South Africa.

Natural Range: Lower and central Congo basin.

Size: Up to 20cm (8in), but usually considerably smaller than this.

Food: Most commercial preparations and livefoods accepted.

Tank Conditions: Despite its substantial size, this is often a retiring species which chooses to hide most of the day. Like many other predatory fish, however, it tends to become more active in the evening. The tank should, therefore, provide adequate cover, plus an open swimming area. In the company of equally large tankmates, *C. acutirostre* will become more active during the daylight hours. Lighting should be subdued; the use of a 'moonlight' fluorescent tube is recommended for nighttime observation. Water chemistry is not critical, but the overall quality must be good.

Temperature: 23–28°C (73–82°F).

Breeding: The male builds a bubblenest (of variable quality). Little brooding, if any, of the eggs occurs.

Helostoma temminckii
(Kissing Gourami)

ALTHOUGH THE Kissing Gourami (*Helostoma temminckii*) tends to grow too large for most 'average' aquaria, it remains popular, largely because of its thick, fleshy lips and unusual 'kissing' habit.

Kissing (in *Helostoma* terms) has nothing to do with feelings of tenderness. It is, rather, a form of mouth-to-mouth trial of strength between individuals, and while no damage is done during these bouts, they do perform a useful role in helping to establish who's boss in the aquarium.

The green morph of the species (the so-called wild type) is known to have originated in Thailand. The pink morph, which is the one that dominates the hobby, is said to have arisen in Java. However, Kissers have been introduced into so many regions as food fish, that the original range for the species can no longer be determined with any accuracy.

In addition to the two varieties named above, there is also a mottled or marbled one developed in Florida.

Helostoma temminckii (Kissing Gourami) pink type.

Natural Range: Widely distributed in southeast Asia.

Size: Although a maximum size of 30cm (12in) is reported, the vast majority of specimens only attain about half this size.

Food: All foods accepted; a regular vegetable component or supplement should be provided.

Tank Conditions: Owing to its large eventual size, the aquarium must be spacious with open swimming areas. Plants must either be tough and unpalatable, like some of the aquatic mosses (e.g., *Vesicularia dubyana*) and ferns (e.g., *Microsorum pteropus*), or artificial. Soft, succulent types will tend to be considered as food by this predominantly herbivorous species. The substratum should consist of gravel with a few scattered, larger, smooth stones. Water chemistry is not critical.

Temperature: 22–30°C (72–86°F), the top end being suitable for breeding.

Breeding: A token bubblenest may (or may not) be built and the characteristic brood care of labyrinth fishes does not occur. Hatching takes a little under 1 day at high temperatures.

Macropodus opercularis
(Paradise Fish)

The colourful Macropodus opercularis (Paradise Fish) is a hardy species first imported into Europe in 1869.

THE PARADISE FISH (*Macropodus opercularis*) has other claims to fame besides its gorgeous colours and finnage; it was the first tropical fish to be imported into Europe way back in 1869. It is also extremely hardy and may be kept in unheated aquaria in most temperate countries, i.e., it is a 'coldwater' tropical fish.

There are two other Paradise Fishes available, the Chinese Paradise Fish (*M. ocellatus* – formerly known as *M. chinensis*) and the Black Paradise Fish (*M. concolor*). All three species hybridize and produce at least partially viable offspring, thus raising some interesting questions regarding their closeness.

There is, for example, considerable doubt whether *M. concolor* is a species, or a clearly identifiable variant of *M. opercularis* which is on its way to evolving into a separate species. A somewhat similar situation exists as occurs with the Indian Gourami (*Colisa fasciata*) and the Thick-lipped Gourami (*C. labiosa*) – see pages 162–164.

Several colour forms of *M. opercularis*, particularly blue and albino, are available and are, generally, a little less aggressive than the wild type.

Natural Range: South China, Korea, Vietnam, Taiwan and other islands in the region. *M. concolor* is probably found in Cambodia and, possibly, Vietnam.

Size: Up to 12cm (4.7in), but usually smaller.

Food: All foods accepted.

Tank Conditions: Male Paradise Fish are intolerant of one another and should, therefore, be kept singly. Although many males may be considerably more tolerant towards other species, they cannot be regarded as totally 'risk-free' community fish. Several juveniles and females can, however, share the same aquarium with other species. A heavily planted tank incorporating open spaces is recommended. Water chemistry is not critical and can range from soft to hard, and acid to alkaline.

Temperature: from as low as 16°C (61°F) to around 28°C (82°F) for breeding.

Breeding: Beautiful bubblenests are built by males. After spawning, the eggs (which hatch in about 1 day) are usually guarded by the males, although females have also been known to assist with brood care.

Malpulutta kretseri
(Ornate Paradise Fish, Spotted Pointed Tail Gourami, Malpulutta)

ALTHOUGH THE Ornate Paradise Fish (*Malpulutta kretseri*) has been known in the aquarium hobby since around 1960, it has never been available in large numbers. Its small size and timid habits have, no doubt, contributed to this, but other significant factors include the fact that it is regarded as endangered in its native Sri Lanka.

Two distinct colour forms (generally regarded as subspecies) of the species are known. The form from the Bentota basin is referred to as *Malpulutta kretseri kretseri*, while a bluer form from the Kalu basin is known as *M. kretseri minor*. A third violet-coloured form has also been reported, but whether this is a variant of the blue subspecies, or a separate subspecies, is not clear.

Unusually for a labyrinthfish, *M. kretseri* does not depend as heavily as other species on its auxiliary respiratory organ for survival, being able to remain underwater for several hours without having to surface for air, as long as normal levels of oxygen saturation (as occurs in most aquaria) are maintained.

Natural Range: Sri Lanka.

Size: 9cm (3.5in) reported in at least one instance. Most references give a maximum size of around 6cm (2.4in), but even this is larger than the size attained by most aquarium and wild-caught specimens.

Food: Will accept a range of commercial preparations and small livefoods.

Tank Conditions: A quiet, heavily planted aquarium with surface cover suits this species best. Pieces of driftwood, roots or bogwood (or its equivalent) should also be added to the decor. A dark substrate and subdued illumination are advisable for this peaceful, retiring species. *Malpulutta* is an excellent jumper, particularly when startled, so a tight-fitting aquarium cover is essential. Ideally, the water should be soft and acid.

Temperature: 24–28°C (75–82°F).

Breeding: A bubblenest will be constructed by the male under an overhang or broad leaf. Although the female can approach the eggs after spawning, guard duties are the responsibility of the male. Hatching takes about 2 days.

Malpulutta kretseri (Ornate Paradise Fish) is a good jumper and requires a tight fitting cover on the aquarium.

Osphronemus goramy
(Giant/Common Gourami, Goramy)

Osphronemus goramy (Giant Gourami) is a true giant.

THE GIANT GOURAMI (*Osphronemus goramy*, or, in some books, *O. gorami*) is the true giant among the fish loosely termed 'gouramis'. Yet, despite the very large size that individuals can attain (see below), it is a popular fish, and not just among labyrinthfish specialists.

Specimens of different colour varieties are usually offered for sale at around 10cm (4in) or less, at which stage they possess a long pointed snout. They are hardy and tolerant of other species, thus making good community fish, at least for a time. They do, however, grow rather quickly, so make sure that you can cater for this, or that you can find a good home for your specimens once they outgrow their aquarium.

Natural Range: Difficult to determine, but probably originated in Borneo, Java and Sumatra. It is now widely distributed, mostly (but not exclusively) in tropical Asia.

Size: Generally reported as growing to 60cm (24in) but individuals have been known to grow even larger.

Food: Wide range of foods accepted, which should include plant material. I knew a specimen that even ate mint sweets as a treat!

Tank Conditions: Juvenile specimens grow quickly and while they may initially be kept with small to medium-sized species (up to around 10cm/4in) in length, they will soon become too large and will require roomier accommodation and larger tankmates. Ideally, the tank should be well planted, but bearing in mind the herbivorous tendencies of the species, only robust or unpalatable species are likely to survive. Artificial plants are, therefore, well worth considering for the Giant Gourami aquarium. Water chemistry is not critical, but efficient filtration is essential.

Temperature: A wide range is tolerated, from as low as 19°C (66°F) to 30°C (86°F).

Breeding: Bubblenests have been reported as being built, both at the water surface and below, with plant material incorporated into the structure. Both the eggs and the fry are guarded by the male. Hatching takes about 2 days.

Parosphromenus deissneri
(Liquorice/Licorice/Splendid Dwarf Gourami)

THE LIQUORICE Gourami (*Parosphromenus deissneri* – sometimes also referred to as *P. dreissneri*) is a beautiful little fish that was introduced into Europe during the early years of the 20th century. Despite this, it has never become widespread in the hobby, probably due to its small size, retiring nature and maintenance requirements.

This was the first of the Liquorice Gouramis described way back in 1859. Until the mid-1980s, only three other species were added to the genus: *P. paludicola* (the Swamp Liquorice Gourami), *P. parvulus* (the Small Liquorice Gourami) and *P. filamentosus* (the Filament-tailed Liquorice Gourami). Since then, though, the number of discoveries has gathered pace and several species have been described, with a number of others – or varieties/morphs – still awaiting scientific examination.

For the hobbyist with a love of small, beautiful, challenging fish, the genus *Parosphromenus* offers many exciting possibilities. The best sources of specimens are the members of specialist labyrinthfish societies.

Natural Range: Island of Banka (Indonesia), Sumatra and Peninsular Malaysia.

Size: Up to 7.5cm (3in) has been reported in at least one instance for this species. However, a maximum size of around 4cm (1.6in) is generally regarded as being more accurate.

Food: Although this is a predominantly carnivorous species that prefers small livefoods, some commercial preparations will also be accepted, particularly by aquarium-bred specimens.

Tank Conditions: The aquarium should be heavily planted and contain several caves for this retiring species. It is peaceful towards other fish and can, therefore, be kept in a community consisting of small, non-boisterous species, but it will tend to suffer in the company of active tankmates. The water should be soft and acid, although some deviation will be tolerated, and the illumination should be subdued.

Temperature: 24–28°C (75–82°F).

Breeding: Eggs are laid inside a cave and attached to the roof by the parents. Bubbles are usually produced subsequent to spawning, thus supporting the eggs. Hatching can take up to 3 days, and the fry are guarded by the male.

Parosphromenus deissneri (Liguorice Gourami) is a beautiful little fish with a shy retiring nature.

Pseudosphromenus cupanus
(Spike-tailed Paradise Fish)

THE SPIKE-TAILED Paradise Fish (*Pseudosphromenus cupanus*) was formerly known as *Macropodus cupanus*, an indication of its presumed relatedness to the Paradise Fish (*Macropodus opercularis* – see page 168). However, once it was shown that the relationship was rather distant, the original name was re-instated.

For a time, both *P. cupanus* and its closest relative *P. dayi* (see next entry) were also regarded as subspecies of *cupanus*, but they are now considered separate, full species.

P. cupanus is a very adaptable species that occurs in a range of habitats and water chemistry conditions in the wild, including brackish water.

Outside the breeding season, the sexes can be a little difficult to tell apart. However, males have reddish eyes (the colour of which intensifies during courtship and spawning) and the females have a fuller belly.

Natural Range: Probably originated in the areas around the southern coast of India. It is also found in Sri Lanka, and possibly (though there is considerable doubt about this), in Bengal, Burma (Myanmar), Sumatra and Tonkin (North Vietnam).

Size: Around 6cm (2.4in).

Food: Most commercial preparations and livefoods are accepted.

Tank Conditions: *P. cupanus* is a peaceful fish which can be kept in community aquaria, even with members of its own species. However, they should not be kept in the company of boisterous tankmates. The aquarium should be heavily planted, with caves and other shelters provided. A dark substratum helps show off the colours of this species best. Water chemistry is not critical, but relatively soft conditions with pH around neutral suit it well, although some deviation will be comfortably tolerated.

Temperature: From as low as around 20°C (68°F) to 28°C (82°F), or higher for breeding.

Breeding: Bubblenests are usually built in a cave or under a broad leaf. Spawning embraces occur below the nest and the sinking eggs are generally collected by both fish. Females are known to participate in brood care, but these duties are usually carried out by the male. Hatching takes about 2 days.

Pseudosphromenus cupanus (Spike-tailed Paradise Fish).

Pseudosphromenus dayi
(Day's/Brown Spike-tailed Paradise Fish)

The beautiful colours of Pseudosphromenus dayi (Day's Paradise Fish) are best appreciated under subdued lighting.

DAY'S PARADISE FISH (*Pseudosphromenus dayi*) is a slender-looking species in which the males possess delicate extended central rays in their caudal (tail) fin and brilliant greenish-blue edges on the dorsal (back) and anal (belly) fins and on both the top and bottom edges of the caudal.

This is a peaceful fish that can be kept in a community aquarium, as long as the chosen tankmates are neither large nor over-active.

Day's Paradise Fish will hybridize quite easily with its closest relative, *P. cupanus*, to produce fertile hybrids, whose offspring themselves are reported to be fertile. While this clearly indicates a close relationship, other factors (such as distinct differences between the sexes in *P. dayi* – but not in *P. cupanus*) suggest that they are not quite as close to one another as their previous classification, in which they were regarded as subspecies of *P. cupanus*, implied.

Natural Range: The exact distribution of this species outside Sri Lanka and South Vietnam is not known with absolute certainty. There are reports about its occurrence in southern India, Sumatra and Burma (Myanmar).

Size: Up to 7.5cm (3in).

Food: Wide range of commercial and livefoods accepted.

Tank Conditions: A heavily planted aquarium providing additional cover in the form of caves, bogwood, etc., suits this species well. The colours are best appreciated under subdued lighting and against a dark substratum. Water chemistry is not critical, but tannin-stained, soft, slightly acid to neutral water is generally advised.

Temperature: Wide range tolerated, from 16°C (61°F), to 34°C (93°F) – both reported from one locality in the wild. In aquaria, a range of 24–28°C (75–82°F) will be perfectly satisfactory.

Breeding: Bubblenests are built by males, either at the surface, or below a leaf or shelter. In a cold highland habitat in the wild, this species has been reported as spawning on the bottom 'like cichlids'. Both parents are involved in egg/brood care. Hatching takes just over 1 day.

Sphaerichthys osphromenoides
(Chocolate Gourami)

IF APPROPRIATE conditions can be provided (and once some experience has been gained in the finer points of aquarium husbandry), every aquarist should attempt to keep and breed the Chocolate Gourami (*Sphaerichthys osphromenoides*).

It is a truly magnificent little jewel of a fish. . . if, that is, it is in peak condition. At other times, it is usually a pale shadow of what it can be, keeping its fins folded, refusing to eat and slowly fading away.

Without doubt, it is one of the more challenging of the relatively widely available tropical aquarium fish species. It is also one of the more satisfying and rewarding when conditions are to its liking, and one of the most frustrating when they are not.

Natural Range: Peninsular Malaysia, Sumatra and Borneo.

Size: Up to 5cm (2in).

Food: *Sphaerichthys osphromenoides* requires a diet consisting predominantly of small livefoods or their freeze-dried, deep-frozen equivalents. Dry foods are mostly accepted with reluctance.

Tank Conditions: Chocolate Gouramis are timid, retiring fish which should be kept either on their own, or in the company of other gentle species, as long as these can tolerate the water conditions required. These include very soft, acid water (pH values as low as 5 have been recorded in the wild). Tannin-stained water – produced via a peat 'sandwich' (i.e., a layer of peat between layers of other material inside a canister filter), a centrepiece of natural bogwood, or one of the excellent commercial 'blackwater' preparations available – should also be provided, along with heavy plant cover and subdued illumination. Filtration should be efficient, but non-turbulent. Chocolates are sensitive to high nitrate levels in the water. Therefore, frequent partial changes should be carried out using water of equivalent composition to that in the aquarium.

Temperature: 25–30°C (77–86°F).

Breeding: This is a difficult species to breed. It is a mouthbrooder in which the female incubates the eggs and fry for up to two weeks before releasing them.

Sphaerichthys osphromenoides (Chocolate Gourami) is a beautiful, challenging species.

Trichogaster leeri
(Pearl/Lace/Mosaic/Leeri Gourami)

Trichogaster leeri (Pearl Gourami) is among the most beautiful tropical species.

THE PEARL GOURAMI (*Trichogaster leeri*) is a graceful fish and males are among the most beautiful of all tropical aquarium species when in full breeding colours.

Despite the relatively large size that they can attain, Pearl Gouramis are generally good community fish, because of their hardy constitution and peaceful nature. Occasionally males may fight if kept together in a small aquarium, while males which are in the process of nest building will become territorial for a time.

An interesting situation arose in Florida in the early 1990s in which some specimens being grown in outdoor ponds developed golden coloration that intensified as the fish matured. Mysteriously, though, the gold very quickly became patchy once the specimens were transferred to indoor aquaria, eventually reverting to the normal wild-type coloration in the space of a few weeks. At the time of writing, this exciting, but difficult challenge has not been successfully resolved. If it ever is, the resulting fish are certain to enjoy tremendous success the world over.

Natural Range: Peninsular Malaysia, Borneo and Sumatra. It is also reported from Java and Bangkok (Thailand), but there are doubts about the validity of these claims.

Size: Reported up to 15cm (6in), but usually around 12cm (4.7in).

Food: All commercial and livefoods accepted.

Tank Conditions: The tank should be well planted, leaving a central area open for swimming. Cover should also be provided by means of floating vegetation or by submerged plants whose leaves extend along the surface of the water. An aquarium cover/hood should be installed to maintain moist air above the water. Water chemistry is not critical and can range from pH 6.5 to 8.5 and soft to moderately hard.

Temperature: 23–28°C (73–82°F).

Breeding: Males, which colour up spectacularly at breeding time, build surface bubblenests under which spawning occurs. The eggs are guarded by the male who also cares for the fry for a few days. Hatching takes about 1 day.

Trichogaster microlepis
(Moonlight/Moonbeam/Thin-lipped Gourami)

Appropriate tank conditions will encourage Trichogaster microlepis (Moonlight Gourami) to thrive and breed.

DESPITE THE fact that the species name for *Trichogaster microlepis* translates as 'thin-lipped', the first two common names, Moonlight and Moonbeam Gourami are far more descriptive of this silvery, shiny, elegant fish.

While not being as colourful overall as some of its closest relatives, the Moonlight Gourami is a classy-looking fish, whose only 'disadvantage' – in community aquarium terms – is its relatively large size. Its gentle temperament, outside the period of courtship and breeding, allows it to be kept with many other species, but not with fin-nipping types, like some of the barbs, which will find the Moonlight's extremely long and delicate pelvic fins almost irresistible.

In its native waters, this species is so abundant, that it is harvested as a food fish. I have even seen it being used as livefood for large predatory species in the Far East.

Natural Range: Cambodia, Malaysia, Singapore and Thailand.

Size: Up to 20cm (8in) reported, but usually a maximum of 15cm (6in) or less.

Food: All commercial and livefoods accepted.

Tank Conditions: Although it is a relatively large fish, the Moonlight Gourami can be quite timid if kept in conditions that are not to its liking. To get the best results from this species, the aquarium should be deep, i.e., around a minumum of 38–40cm (15–16in) and heavily planted along the sides and back, with a central open swimming area at the front. Surface vegetation and an aquarium cover should also be provided. Some delicate plants will almost certainly be torn during nest building and incorporated among the bubbles. Water chemistry is not critical, but should not be too alkaline or hard.

Temperature: 25–30°C (77–86°F), the top end being best for breeding.

Breeding: Males can build large nests of bubbles interwoven with surface vegetation and (often) bits of submerged vegetation pulled off parent plants. Spawning occurs under the nest. Eggs and fry care (for a few days) are carried out by the male.

Trichogaster pectoralis
(Snakeskin Gourami)

THE SNAKESKIN GOURAMI (*Trichogaster pectoralis*) is the largest species in its genus. It was first imported into Europe in 1896 (at the same time as its relative, *Trichogaster trichopterus* – see page 178), but has never attained the great popularity of either the Pearl Gourami (*T. leeri*) or *T. trichopterus*, itself. No doubt, the large size to which Snakeskins grow has been a major factor. This is a great shame, though, because those aquarists who are able to provide adequate accommodation for this species invariably become enthusiastic fans.

The Snakeskin Gourami is, despite its overall brownish coloration, a very attractive fish indeed when in good condition. It is also graceful and non-aggressive.

In the wild, *T. pectoralis* is found in a wide range of habitats, both within its natural range, as well as the numerous regions into which it has been intentionally or unintentionally introduced, primarily as a food fish. It has even been reported from brackish areas of the Mekong Delta.

Trichogaster pectoralis (Snakeskin Gourami).

Natural Range: Originally from Cambodia, South Vietnam and Thailand, but now widespread in southeast Asia and elsewhere (including Haiti and Sri Lanka).

Size: Up to 20cm (8in).

Food: All commercial and livefoods accepted.

Tank Conditions: Although juvenile specimens may be kept in average-sized aquaria, e.g., around 60cm (24in), sub-adult and mature specimens can only be housed in large tanks. Yet, despite being substantial fish, Snakeskins are gentle and tolerant and can be kept with species considerably smaller than themselves. The tank should be heavily planted around the sides and back and provided with a spacious open swimming area. An aquarium cover and surface vegetation are also recommended. Water chemistry is not critical, as long as the overall quality is good.

Temperature: 23–28°C (73–82°F).

Breeding: Males build relatively small bubblenests, under which spawning takes place. The eggs are guarded by the male who also cares for the fry for several days. Hatching takes about 1 day.

Trichogaster trichopterus
(Two-spot/Three-spot/Blue/Opaline (Cosby)/Amethyst/Lavender/Brown/Gold/Opal (Platinum) Gourami, Hairfin

ALONG WITH the Dwarf Gourami (*Colisa lalia* – see page 164), the Two-spot Gourami (*Trichogaster trichopterus*) dominates the 'Gourami scene'.

This is a tough, versatile, colourful fish which, in addition, is usually tolerant of other species (except at breeding time). It is, therefore, a popular community aquarium choice, especially since it is widely available and reasonably priced.

Males are usually quite aggressive towards one another, so, unless the aquarium provided is large and well designed, only a single male should be kept, along with a number of females.

T. trichopterus is available in a number of colour forms, all of which interbreed easily, giving rise to very interesting 'hybrids' that lend themselves well to studies of the genetics of colour inheritance.

The blue form of the species which occurs naturally in Sumatra, is often regarded as a subspecies: *Trichogaster trichopterus sumatranus*.

Natural Range: Widely distributed in Indochina and the Malaysia, Indonesia and Thailand regions. A blue form occurs in Sumatra (see text above).
Size: Up to 15cm (6in), but usually smaller than this.

Trichogaster trichopterus (Gold Gourami).

Food: All commercial and livefoods accepted.
Tank Conditions: This is the hardiest member of the genus and also (usually) the least timid. Nevertheless, it benefits from a heavily planted, covered aquarium that also provides an open swimming area. Surface vegetation is also appreciated. Water chemistry is not critical, with a pH range as wide as 6.0 to 8.8 being tolerated. However, changes within this range must be made gradually. Water hardness can also be wide-ranging, from soft to hard, but, again, adjustments must not be abrupt.
Temperature: 22–28°C (72–82°F).
Breeding: This is an energetic bubblenest builder, although I have known many males to make little more than a token gesture at constructing a nest prior to spawning. The eggs are guarded by the male who also cares for the fry for a few days after spawning. Hatching takes about 1 day.

Trichogaster trichopterus (Three-spot Gourami).

Trichopsis vittatus
(Croaking Gourami)

THE CROAKING GOURAMI (*Trichopsis vittatus*) was first imported into Europe in 1899. It has always been available, but never in huge quantities, probably because of its rather retiring nature and the existence of other, more active, and perhaps more colourful, labyrinthfishes.

So-called because of the croaking sounds that both males and females can produce, *T. vittatus* is a widespread species whose precise identity is still, after all these years, not fully determined. Contributing factors to the ongoing debate are the numerous colour morphs found in the wild, plus the ease with which it interbreeds with its close relative, the Pygmy or Sparkling Gourami (*T. schalleri*) to produce fertile hybrids.

The matter is further complicated by at least one report that *T. schalleri* itself also produces fertile hybrids when crossed with the Dwarf Croaking Gourami (*T. pumilus*). See also entries for *Colisa fasciata* and *C. labiosa* (pages 162-163), *Macropodus opercularis* and *M. concolor* (page 168) and *Pseudosphromenus cupanus* and *P. dayi* (pages 172-173) for discussion of similar situations.

Natural Range: Widely distributed in southeast Asia, from Vietnam southwards to Java. It is also reported from the island of Borneo. If it occurs in eastern India (as reported in some publicatons), these populations may be introduced, rather than natural.

Size: Up to 7cm (2.8in).

Food: Most commercial and livefoods accepted.

Tank Conditions: The aquarium should be heavily planted, and although some open swimming space is recommended, this need not be over-large, because of the relatively small size of the species and its gentle, slow-moving nature. Croaking Gouramis can be kept in a community aquarium, as long as their tankmates are also peaceful species. Although water chemistry is not too critical, it should avoid extremes of pH and hardness.

Temperature: 22–28°C (72–82°F).

Breeding: A bubblenest is built among vegetation or under an overhang. Eggs are often produced in small clusters and are guarded by the male who also cares for the fry for a few days after hatching (which takes about 1 day).

Trichopsis vittatus (Croaking Gourami) is gentle and slow-moving and will live happily with other peaceful tankmates.

LOACHES

THE SUCKING LOACH (*Gyrinocheilus aymonieri*) and the Clown Loach (*Botia macracantha*) look quite different from one another. The former can be easily distinguished from the latter by its possession of a sucker-like mouth, while, like all the other *Botia* species, the Clown Loach has an almost tube-like mouth adorned with barbels. Yet, despite these and other differences, these loaches possess a number of shared skeletal characteristics which place them both within the superfamily Cobitoidea.

According to most classifications, the superfamily is divided into four families: the Gyrinocheilidae – known as Algae Eaters, the Catostomidae – known as the Suckers, the Cobitidae – known simply as the Loaches, and the Balitoridae or Homalopteridae – known as the River Loaches.

In the pages that follow, I will focus on selected members of two of these families: the Cobitidae and the Gyrinocheilidae.

There are about 100 cobitid loaches, only a few of which have found their way into the hobby in any significant numbers. These fall within three main groups:

the Kuhli-type loaches, which have worm-like bodies, the Botia-type loaches, which are stockier, and the Weather Loach-type species which are superficially similar to the first group, but are somewhat larger.

The shared characteristics of all three types include an elongated body, three to six pairs of barbels (whiskers) around the mouth, an erectile spine either behind or in front of the eye, and one row of pharyngeal (throat) teeth.

When examined in greater detail, the three types actually fall within two groups, each of which is recognised as a subfamily. The Cobitinae possess a single pair of rostral barbels (i.e., at the tip of the snout) and a generally rounded tail, while the Botiinae possess two pairs of rostral barbels and a forked tail. Of the cobitid loaches featured here, the *Botia* species fall within the Botiinae, while all the others belong to the Cobitinae.

The Sucking Loach with its characteristic mouth and feeding/respiratory adaptations, belongs within the family Gyrinocheilidae.

Botia modesta (Orange-finned Loach).

Acanthophthalmus (Pangio) myersi
(Kuhli/Myers'/Slimy Loach)

THE CLASSIFICATION of Kuhli Loaches is in a somewhat 'fluid' state. Debate is focussed on whether certain types constitute valid species, or subspecies, or merely colour morphs.

For example, fish assigned to the species *Acanthopthalmus (Pangio) myersi* – the Slimy, Kuhli or Myers' Loach – can have broad, dark, vertical bands which reach almost to the belly region in the anterior part of the body, while in the posterior half they can encircle the body. Alternatively, specimens can be uniformly dark (except, again, for the belly) with no light bands at all. In yet other specimens, the dark bands can be shallower and the brown pigmentation lighter, and so on.

Generally speaking, though, *A. (P.) myersi* is deeper-bodied than other types of Kuhli Loach, the most popular of which are the Half-banded Kuhli Loach – *A. (P.) semicinctus*, and the Kuhli or Coolie Loach – *A. (P.) kuhlii*.

Note that I have inserted the generic name *Pangio* in brackets to indicate that *Acanthophthalmus* is occasionally referred to as *Pangio* in aquarium literature.

Acanthophthalmus (Pangio) myersi (Kuhli Loach).

Natural Range: Thailand.

Size: Up to 8cm (3.2in).

Food: Most foods accepted, particularly sinking formulations and bottom-living livefoods.

Tank Conditions: On account of the burrowing habits and distinct preference for crawling/burrowing livefoods exhibited by all Kuhli-type loaches, the substratum must be fine-grained and round- or smooth-edged. Kuhlis will also fit through the tiniest of openings, so the aquarium must have a tight-fitting cover. Thick vegetation, rocks, caves, stones and other decor that will provide shelter should also be provided, along with subdued lighting and a thick layer of floating plants. Although often active during the day, this, and related, species are crepuscular (twilight) or nocturnal in their habits, during which time they exhibit tremendous energy. A 'moonlight' fluorescent tube that will allow nighttime observation is therefore recommended. Water chemistry is not critical, but soft, slightly acid conditions seem best.

Temperature: 24–30°C (75–86°F).

Breeding: This is rare in aquaria. The green eggs may be scattered among the roots or stems of floating vegetation.

Acanthopsis choirorhynchus
(Horse-faced/Long-nosed Loach)

THE HORSE-FACED Loach (*Acanthopsis choirorhynchus*) is a delicately marked species whose beauty is sometimes overlooked among the more colourful freshwater tropical fish on offer. In addition, it has the habit of disappearing almost completely from view for long periods, often remaining buried for hours with just its eyes protruding above the substratum.

Provided plants can be protected in some way (see below), the Horse-faced Loach – because of its peaceful nature – can be kept with other similarly sized fish in a community aquarium.

Being a strict bottom-dweller, this species is a poor swimmer. However, it is capable of short, lightning-fast bursts of speed when it feels threatened and can prove a bit of a challenge to net when this becomes necessary. At such times, care must also be taken to prevent specimens from injuring themselves by getting their eye spines entangled in the net.

Natural Range: Southeast Asia.

Size: Up to 22.5cm (8.9in) reported, but usually remains considerably smaller: around 10cm (4in).

Food: All foods accepted, particularly sinking formulations and bottom-dwelling livefoods.

Tank Conditions: Since this species is an active burrower – both when at rest, and when escaping from predators – and since it also likes to search for buried livefoods, the aquarium substratum must be fine-grained and smooth-round-edged. It should also be deep enough to allow large specimens sufficient space to bury themselves completely, with a little room to spare. Plants can be uprooted as a result of the species' burrowing activities and should, therefore, be protected in pots with the surface of the planting medium covered with pebbles. Alternatively, plants rooted in the aquarium substratum should have their bases protected with pebbles. A 'moonlight' fluorescent tube will allow the nighttime activities of this crespuscular/nocturnal species to be fully appreciated. Water chemistry is not critical, but softish, slightly acid water is recommended.

Temperature: 25–28°C (77–82°F).

Breeding: This species has not been bred in aquaria.

Acanthopsis choirorhynchus (Horse-faced Loach).

Botia macracantha
(Clown Loach)

Botia macracantha (Clown Loach) may occasionally lie on its side to rest or to sleep in an unfishlike manner.

IN DAYS gone by, the Clown Loach (*Botia macracantha*) was generally regarded as a small to medium-sized aquarium fish, despite reports of large specimens existing in the wild. Today, improved aquarium technology, foods and husbandry techniques mean that specimens in excess of 20cm (8in) are no longer the rarities they used to be.

In addition to its great beauty, the Clown Loach has at least two other characteristics that make it a little 'different' from most other fish. For instance, it is capable of making quite audible clicking sounds, particularly at feeding time. More unusually, specimens will occasionally lie on their side, apparently half-dead. Disconcerting though this behaviour may appear, such specimens are perfectly healthy and are acting quite normally; they are merely resting or asleep, but doing so in a most unfish-like manner!

In its native lands, this species is regarded both as an aquarium and a food fish.

Natural Range: In flowing waters on the islands of Borneo (Kalimantan) and Sumatra in Indonesia.

Size: Up to 30cm (12in) reported, but usually smaller.

Food: Wide range of foods accepted, particularly sinking commercial preparations and bottom-dwelling livefoods.

Tank Conditions: Clown Loaches can be timid, particularly when kept singly. A small shoal gives them a feeling of greater security and generally makes them bolder. Numerous shelters should be provided and plants should be protected against the burrowing activities of large specimens (see entry for *Acanthopsis choirorhynchus* on the previous page). The substratum should consist of a fine-grained smooth- or round-edged medium and the lighting should be subdued. Like other *Botia* species, *B. macracantha* becomes more active at dusk and during the night (although it is also active during the day). The use of a 'moonlight' fluorescent tube is therefore advisable. Soft, acid water is preferred and raw tapwater must be avoided.

Temperature: 23–30°C (73–86°F).

Breeding: Aquarium spawnings – about which no detailed reports are available – occur from time to time, usually by accident.

Botia sidthimunki
(Chain/Dwarf Loach)

T HE CHAIN or Dwarf Loach (*Botia sidthimunki*) appears to be making something of a comeback after being quite scarce within the hobby during the late 1980s and early 1990s.

This is a delightful fish which looks absolutely captivating when kept in a sizeable shoal in the company of other small species. One

Botia sidthimunki (Chain/Dwarf Loach) is at its best when kept in a small shoal.

great advantage that Chain Loaches have over other Botia species is that they do not appear to mind being kept in a well-lit aquarium. They are also easy to keep, as long as the overall quality of the soft, acid water that they like is good.

Despite their ease of maintenance, these tiny loaches still continue to present an – as yet – unconquered challenge with regard to aquarium breeding.

Natural Range: Reported from northern India and northern Thailand.
Size: Up to 5.5cm (2.2in).
Food: Will accept most small commercial foods, particularly sinking types, but is especially fond of bottom-dwelling livefoods.

Tank Conditions: This is a peaceful fish which does best when kept in shoals in a well planted tank with numerous shelters. The substratum should be fine-grained and free of sharp edges which could injure the species' delicate mouth barbels. Unlike other *Botia* species, *B. sidthimunki* frequently swims in midwater, scuttling around the aquarium at great speed and resting on broad-leaved plants like Amazon Swords (*Echinodorus spp.*). Despite its small size, this species appears to be less timid than some of its closest relatives and is very active both during the day and night. The water should be soft and slightly acid.
Temperature: 25–30°C (77–86°F).
Breeding: This has not been reported in aquaria.

OTHER BOTIA SPECIES

Other *Botia* species currently available and having similar requirements to *B. macracantha* (see previous page) include: *B. beauforti* (Beaufort's Loach), *B. morleti* – formerly *B. horae* (Hora's Loach), *B. lohachata* (Pakistani Loach), *B. modesta* (Orange-finned Loach or Blue Loach) and *B. striata* (Zebra Loach).

Botia lohachata (Pakistani Loach) needs a tank with numerous shelters.

Gyrinocheilus aymonieri
(Sucking Loach, Chinese Algae Eater)

IN THE United States, *Gyrinocheilus aymonieri* is known as the Chinese Algae Eater, a name that appears to be spreading into Europe, where it is beginning to displace the more traditional Sucking Loach name tag. Unfortunately, this is a case where a somewhat inaccurate common name is being pushed out by an equally inaccurate one, since the species is not found in China at all, but in Thailand.

Gyrinocheilus aymonieri, despite its generally unassuming looks, is a remarkable fish that can cling on to rocks and feed and breathe simultaneously without having to release its hold. It is able to do this because, instead of having to take in water for respiratory purposes through its mouth (as other fish do), it does so through a specialized aperture that is located on the top edge of the gill covers.

While encrusting algae undoubtedly form a major part of this species' diet in the wild, its reputation for being able singlehandedly (or 'singlemouthedly'!) to clear an aquarium of these plants is somewhat exaggerated.

In addition to the wild type, there is also a golden form which is gaining popularity.

Natural Range: Thailand.

Size: Up to 27cm (10.6in).

Food: Despite its name and herbivorous habits, most aquarium foods are accepted.

Tank Conditions: The layout should provide numerous resting places, although, even in their presence, these fish will often cling to the aquarium sides. Plants are generally safe, despite the herbivorous tendencies of the species whose mouthparts are more suited for grazing algae than biting vegetation. Juvenile specimens will generally live quite happily together, but adults tend to become territorial and scrappy and should be kept singly. Water chemistry is not critical, as long as the overall quality is good and the oxygen supply is adequate.

Temperature: 21–28°C (70–82°F), but slightly higher temperatures are also tolerated, though not on a longterm basis.

Breeding: No detailed reports of aquarium spawnings are available, although the species has been spawned by commercial breeders.

Gyrinocheilus aymonieri (Sucking Loach) is able to cling on to rocks to feed and breathe at the same time.

Misgurnus anguillicaudatus
(Japanese/Chinese Weather Loach, Dojo)

Misgurnus anguillicaudatus (Weather Loach) is so named because of the change in its behaviour before a storm.

WEATHER LOACHES (both *Misgurnus anguillicaudatus* and its European relative, *M. fossilis*) have been well known in the aquarium hobby for many years. In terms of body shape and coloration (with the exception of the spectacular golden morph), they do not stand out from other fish. In fact, they are generally dull-coloured fish which are often overlooked in shops, particularly since they have the habit of burying themselves in the substratum with only their eyes protruding above the surface.

What has made Weather Loaches strong favourites among aquarists who like something a little out of the ordinary is their 'ability' to forecast stormy weather conditions, hence their common name. I have written 'ability' in quotation marks, because the fact that a drop in barometric pressure (as often experienced prior to storms) causes a corresponding drop in gas pressure inside the swimbladder, which, in turn, makes the fish hyperactive, has nothing to do with genuine ability, but is, rather, the unavoidable end result of a series of interlinked natural events. If the change in pressure is

sufficiently large, Weather Loaches will 'burp', or even break wind!

Natural Range: Widely distributed in northeast Asia.

Size: Around 20cm (8in) reported, but generally smaller than this.

Food: All commercial diets and livefoods accepted.

Tank Conditions: This is an active burrower requiring a fine-grained substratum free of sharp edges. A muddy or silty bottom is sometimes recommended, but, while this poses no problems in the wild, it can create a major water clarity headache in aquaria. Plants need to be protected against being uprooted (see entry for *Acanthopsis choirorhynchus* on page 182). Water chemistry is not critical, with a wide range of pH and hardness being accepted without difficulty.

Temperature: From around 10°C (50°F) to around 18–20°C (64–68°F).

Breeding: Aquarium spawnings have been reported on rare occasions, during which the pair wrap their bodies around each other and scatter eggs among vegetation.

RAINBOWFISHES

RAINBOWFISHES HAVE been deservedly popular among aquarists for over 70 years. Originally, this interest was predominantly concentrated in Australia, the home of many of the rainbows. Today, these active, colourful fish are kept throughout the world and are bred commercially in all ornamental fish-producing regions.

Rainbowfish classification is, like that of many other large groups of fishes, in a somewhat confused state. Some authorities lump most species and genera (but with notable exceptions) within a single family, the Melanotaeniidae, while others split them up into four or more families, with some genera, e.g., *Telmatherina* and *Bedotia* being assigned to one family by some authors, and to another by others.

In the pages that follow, I have adopted the classification published by Nelson, Joseph S. *Fishes of the World**. According to this classification, the genera featured in this book belong to the families in the table above.

Family	Genera
Bedotiidae	*Bedotia*
Melanotaeniidae	*Glossolepis,*
	Iriatherina,
	Melanotaenia
Pseudomugilidae	*Pseudomugil*
Telmatherinidae	*Telmatherina*

Despite skeletal differences which allow us to assign individual genera of rainbows to the various families listed above, they all share a number of features which, taken together, group all these families (and several others) within the order Atheriniformes.

Among these shared characteristics is the possession of two 'genuine' dorsal (back) fins. In contrast, the second small dorsal which characins possess is quite different in composition and is referred to as the adipose fin (see page 69). Indeed, in rainbows, the second, posterior, dorsal fin is usually larger than the anterior one.

In addition, the anal (belly) fin is usually preceded by a single spine, and the lateral line – which is prominent in many other types of fish, particularly the cichlids (see page 121), is either absent or very weak in atherinids.

*(3rd edition), 1994, John Wiley & Sons, Inc., ISBN: 0-471-54713-1.

Telematherina ladigesi (Celebes Rainbowfish)

Bedotia geayi
(Madagascan Rainbowfish)

THE MADAGASCAN Rainbow (*Bedotia geayi*) is the only aquarium rainbowfish to originate from the African region. It is a slender, active, peaceful, shoaling species that does well in community aquaria.

When kept under appropriate conditions (see below), the colours, particularly in males, are resplendent, especially when a sizeable group of adults is housed in a well-planted, long aquarium where they can show off their almost-synchronized swimming behaviour. If a current of water can be created from the outflow of a power filter, the shoaling tendencies of the species will be even better demonstrated.

Although *B. geayi* possesses the two dorsal (back) fins which are characteristic of all rainbowfishes (see previous page), the first of these – which is much smaller than the second – is usually held close to the body, with only occasional flicks revealing its presence. By contrast, the second dorsal fin, as well as the equally brilliantly coloured anal (belly) fin, are frequently extended, both during normal swimming and while displaying between members of the shoal.

Natural Range: Island of Madagascar.

Size: Up to 15cm (6in), but usually around 10cm (4in).

Food: All commercial and livefoods accepted, but only from the surface or midwater; food lying on the bottom of the aquarium will be ignored.

Tank Conditions: This is an active shoaling species which should never be kept as single specimens or pairs. It requires a roomy aquarium with an ample central swimming area. The sides and back should be heavily planted, both to show off the colours of the fish to best effect and to make them feel secure. Although the actual chemical composition of the water is not too critical, the quality must be good, with a composition on the neutral-to-alkaline, medium-hard-to-hard side preferred. Good filtration and regular partial water changes are advisable.

Temperature: 20–25°C (68–77°F).

Breeding: Eggs are scattered among fine-leaved vegetation and take about 7 days to hatch (slightly longer at lower temperatures).

Bedotia geayi (Madagascan Rainbowfish).

Glossolepis incisus
(Red Rainbowfish)

Despite its large size, Glossolepis incisus (Red Rainbowfish) is quite timid and should always be kept in a shoal.

ADULT MALE Red Rainbowfish (*Glossolepis incisus*) are truly impressive, particularly when several are kept as part of a shoal. When in peak condition, these males exhibit intense red coloration (hence the common name for the species) the exact tone and intensity of which – that vary even in individual fish – are difficult to categorize. In some specimens there is an underlying orange tinge, while in others the effect is more wine red; the overall colour has even been described – imaginatively, though perhaps somewhat fancifully – as 'luminous pink'.

At first sight, *Glossolepis* species are similar to their close Australian relatives belonging to the genus *Melanotaenia*. However, *Glossolepis* can be easily distinguished by the pronounced high back profile which fully mature males possess and which makes the head look a little too small for the body.

Despite the large size attained by this species, it is a peaceful – even timid – fish which must always be kept as a shoal.

Three other *Glossolepis* species which have similar requirements are also occasionally available: *G. maculosus*

(Spotted Rainbowfish), *G. multisquamatus* (Sepik Rainbowfish) and *G. wanamensis* (Lake Wanam Rainbowfish or Green Rainbowfish).

Natural Range: Lake Sentani and surrounding areas in Irian Jaya.
Size: Up to 15cm (6in), but often smaller: around 10cm (4in).
Food: While this species will accept commercial dry foods, it has a distinct preference for livefoods.
Tank Conditions: On account of its relatively large size and shoaling habits, *G. incisus* requires a roomy aquarium with ample swimming space. The sides and back can be heavily planted and a shortish fine-leaved or clump-forming plant, e.g., Java Moss (*Vesicularia dubyana*) can be used along the bottom of the swimming area. The water should be either neutral or slightly alkaline and moderately hard.
Temperature: 22–26°C (72–79°F), with the higher end of the range being suitable for breeding.
Breeding: Eggs are scattered among the clumps of Java Moss, or equivalent, e.g., a specially constructed 'spawning mop'. Hatching takes about 7 days.

Iriatherina werneri
(Threadfin Rainbowfish)

Above and left: The fragile-looking Iriantherina werneri (Threadfin Rainbowfish).

DESPITE ITS fragile appearance, the Threadfin Rainbowfish (*Iriatherina werneri*) is quite hardy. Up to the late 1970s, this species was believed to be endemic to Irian Java. Then, in 1978, it was found in the north of Australia (Northern Queensland) around the Jardine River. Two years later, Australian ichthyologist Ray Leggett collected it in the same area in 'quiet backwaters and swamps with dense plant growth and soft, acid water'. Then, in 1985, it was found in similar habitats in another northern river, the Edward.

Although not a particularly rare sight in aquarium shops, *I. werneri* is not generally available as widely as it should be, especially bearing in mind that it is not unduly delicate and travels well. This, sadly, is a fate that is shared by several other small species, as a result of which they are not enjoyed as widely as they deserve. It is a real shame, because Threadfin males in full display mode are astoundingly beautiful.

Natural Range: Irian Java and northern Australia, in the areas around the Jardine and Edward Rivers.

Size: Up to 4cm (1.6in) for males; females usually a little smaller.

Food: Dry foods will be accepted, but livefoods are preferred.

Tank Conditions: This delicate-looking rainbow should be kept in shoals in a well-planted tank where it will tend to occupy the middle and upper sections. It is peaceful and can be kept in a community aquarium, as long as its tankmates are equally peaceful and do not include fin-nippers, such as some of the popular barbs. The water should be slightly acid and relatively soft.

Temperature: 22–29°C (72–84°F).

Breeding: Eggs are scattered among clumps of fine-leaved or fine-stemmed vegetation like Java Moss (*Vesicularia dubyana*); alternatively, spawning mops which consist of strands of non-toxic wool or other fibre attached to a piece of cork floating in the water, may be used. Females will lay eggs over a period of several days. Hatching can take as long as 10–12 days, depending on temperature.

Melanotaenia boesemani
(Boeseman's Rainbowfish)

The strikingly coloured Melanotaenia boesemani (Boeseman's Rainbowfish) breeds very successfully in captivity.

BOESEMAN'S Rainbowfish (*Melanotaenia boesemani*) is a relative newcomer to the hobby, being officially described as recently as 1980. Yet, despite its somewhat brief history when compared to other, longer-established species, this strikingly marked fish has become one of the most popular of all rainbowfishes the world over.

Wild-caught specimens are particularly beautiful, but these are only rarely, if ever, seen these days, such has been the success of captive breeding programmes in all the major fish-producing countries.

Some reports suggest that the brilliant contrasting coloration of wild-caught males is lost after a few generations in captivity. While this may well be true of certain captive-bred populations, I have seen others in countries as widely separated as the USA (Florida) and Sri Lanka, which, to my eyes, are every bit as colourful as the first wild-caught specimens I ever saw during the early 1980s.

Natural Range: Ajamaru Lakes region of Irian Jaya.
Size: Usually reported as attaining 9cm (3.5in) for males and a little smaller for females. However, fully mature males can exceed this size in adequately maintained aquaria.

Food: Most commercial and livefoods accepted.
Tank Conditions: *M. boesemani* is an active, shoaling species which is generally peaceful, even towards smaller fish. On account of its eventual body size, this species should only be kept in large aquaria. This is advisable even when specimens are only half grown, since cramped conditions will inhibit the growth rate. Open swimming areas, bordered by thick vegetation should be provided, along with clumps of Java Moss (*Vesicularia dubyana*) or equivalent along the bottom of the open sections. The water should be soft and neutral or slightly acid. Good filtration is recommended, but this should not create turbulent conditions.
Temperature: 25–30°C (77–88°F), the top end of this range being appropriate for breeding.
Breeding: Eggs are scattered among the Java Moss – or spawning mops – over a period of several days. Hatching takes about 7 days.

Melanotaenia maccullochi
(McCulloch's/Australian/Black-Lined/Dwarf Rainbowfish)

Melanotaenia maccullochi (McCulloch's/Dwarf Rainbowfish) may jump out of the tank unless a cover is used.

McCULLOCH'S RAINBOWFISH (*Melanotaenia maccullochi*) is one of the smaller species of rainbow. It is also possibly the first species of Australian freshwater fish that was ever bred specifically for the aquarium hobby.

For a long time, it was the most popular Australian rainbow kept by aquarists outside its native land. More recently, it has been overtaken in terms of popularity by some of the more colourful, newer species, but is, nevertheless, still a strong favourite.

There are two distinct colour forms of *M. maccullochi*, one with reddish/brownish fins from around the Cairns area, and another, with less colourful finnage, from the Jardine River and southern Papua New Guinea.

Natural Range: Northern Queensland, Australia – around Cairns and the Jardine River; also found in southern parts of Papua New Guinea.

Size: Up to 7cm (2.8in).

Food: Will accept a wide range of commercial formulations and livefoods.

Tank Conditions: This is a peaceful, but active, shoaling species which should be provided with open swimming areas. The sides and back of the aquarium should be heavily planted and a tight-fitting cover must be used to prevent this agile fish from jumping out. Fine-leaved vegetation should also be provided for spawning. The water should be slightly acid or neutral, and soft to moderately hard.

Temperature: 20–26°C (68–79°F).

Breeding: Eggs are scattered among fine-leaved vegetation over a period of several days. Hatching takes 6–10 days, depending on temperature.

OTHER SPECIES

In addition to the above two species, there are quite a few other *Melanotaenia* rainbows available on a more or less regular basis. Sizes vary from around 7cm (2.8in) to 11cm (4.3in), but all are peaceful shoalers with similar requirements. The following are among the best known species: *M. affinis* (North New Guinea Rainbowfish), *M. gracilis* (Slender Rainbowfish), *M. herbertaxelrodi* (Lake Tebera Rainbowfish), *M. lacustris* (Lake Kutubu Rainbowfish), *M. nigrans* (Red-tailed, Black-banded or Dark Rainbowfish), *M. parkinsoni* (Parkinson's Rainbowfish), *M. splendida* (Splendid Rainbowfish) and *M. trifasciata* (Banded Rainbowfish).

Pseudomugil signifer
(Australian/Pacific Blue-Eye)

THE AUSTRALIAN Blue-eye (*Pseudomugil signifer*) is one of several *Pseudomugil* species which are fairly regularly available, the two other most popular species being *P. furcatus*, the Fork-tailed Rainbowfish or Blue-eye, from Papua New Guinea, and *P. gertrudae*, the Spotted Blue-eye, from northern areas of Australia.

As is common among small fish that are found along extensive, but narrow, ranges, *P. signifer* exhibits considerable variation in colour, size and habits in the wild. For instance, fish from the populations found around Townsville in Queensland are quite large, while those from the northernmost areas of the range are said to be more aggressive than those from other regions.

The Australian Blue-eye is a small fish which, despite its diminutive size, can make a brilliant display when kept as a mixed-sex shoal in a well-planted aquarium. A further attraction is that parents are non-cannibalistic and can, therefore, be left with their spawn.

Natural Range: Northern and eastern Queensland, Australia.

Size: Up to 4.5cm (1.8in).

Food: Although some flaked foods will be accepted, freeze-dried, deep-frozen foods, plus livefoods are preferred.

Tank Conditions: This is another shoaling rainbow which is suitable for community aquaria consisting of small, placid tankmates, although some males can become somewhat aggressive (see above text). Open swimming space, bordered on the sides and back by vegetation, is recommended. If possible, position the aquarium so that it can receive some sun during the morning (especially recommended for breeding purposes). The pH of the water should be around neutral and medium hard, with a small amount of salt added (0.5g/litre – 0.1oz/Imperial gallon). This salt is not essential, but may be found beneficial.

Temperature: 20–28°C (68–82°F), with the top end of the range being more suitable for breeding.

Breeding: A few eggs are scattered each day (for up to one week) either among the roots of floating plants or clumps of fine-leaved vegetation. Hatching takes as long as 14–21 days, depending on temperature.

Pseudomugli signifer (Australian Blue Eye) likes a little sunshine on the tank in the morning.

Telmatherina ladigesi
(Celebes Rainbowfish/Sailfish)

Telematherina ladigesi (Celebes Rainbowfish) will remain brilliantly colourful if the water chemistry is correct.

THE CELEBES Rainbowfish (*Telmatherina ladigesi*) is a peaceful shoaling fish which can be kept as a member of a community, as long as its tankmates are comfortable under the water chemistry conditions outlined below. Alternatively, the amount of salt may be gradually reduced to zero over a period of time to make a wider choice of tankmates possible.

T. ladigesi can adapt to a range of pH conditions, but it handles higher values (increased alkalinity) considerably more easily than lower ones (increased acidity). The key factor to bear in mind is to carry out any adjustments in a series of small steps, rather than in one or two major ones.

Under appropriate conditions, this is a beautiful fish with glistening colours and graceful finnage. Kept in poor-quality water, though, or in the company of larger, boisterous species, it will lose much of its brilliance and will tend to hold its fins close to the body.

Natural Range: Island of Sulawesi (formerly Celebes) in Indonesia.

Size: Up to 7.5cm (3in).

Food: Wide range of commercial preparations and livefoods accepted.

Tank Conditions: The Celebes Rainbow is a shoaling fish which should be provided with open swimming space bordered along the sides and back by thick vegetation. It is usually recommended that the tank be placed where it can catch the rays of the morning sun, but this is not essential for everyday maintenance (though advantageous for breeding purposes). Water chemistry is not too critical (but see main text), although neutral to slightly alkaline medium-hard water with about one teaspoonful of salt per 4.5-5 litres (1 Imperial gallon) of water is best.

Temperature: 20–28°C (68–82°F), with the top end of this range being suitable for spawning.

Breeding: Spawning usually takes place during the morning, with eggs being scattered among fine-leaved vegetation over a period of several days. The spawning season can last for several months. Hatching takes 8–12 days, depending on temperature.

GOBIES AND SLEEPERS

DESPITE THEIR overall similarities, gobies and sleepers (often also referred to as sleeper gobies) belong to two distinct families, the Gobiidae and Eleotridae respectively.

Together with a number of other families, gobies and sleepers form part of the suborder Gobioidei, which is characterized, among other shared features, by the lack of a swimbladder, the frequent occurrence of pelvic (hip) fins which are to a greater or lesser extent united and are located under the pectoral (chest) fins, and the possession of a unique sperm gland.

In terms of the aquarium hobby, gobies and sleepers can be told apart by the possession of united pelvic fins, which form a sucker, in gobies, but are separate (although their bases may be united) in sleepers. Although, as a result, sleepers do not possess a sucker, they do, nevertheless, exhibit considerable variation in the degree of union of the pelvic fin bases.

There are still many unanswered questions regarding the taxonomy of the Gobiidae, but – if and when these are eventually resolved – this family could contain even more than the 212 genera and around 1,900 species currently recognized, thus making it the largest family of vertebrates known (see also the entry entitled CYPRINIDS on page 48).

In marked contrast, the family Eleotridae contains only some 35 genera, with about 150 species – still a respectable number by most standards, but small when compared to the more wide-ranging true gobies.

Despite the undoubted species richness of the Gobiidae, very few of these are kept with any regularity within the freshwater aquarium hobby. Indeed, almost as many sleepers are kept in aquaria as true gobies.

In the pages that follow, the Gobiidae is represented by just two species: the Bumblebee Goby (*Brachygobius xanthozona* and close relatives) and the Knight Goby (*Stigmatogobius sadanundio*), while the Eleotridae is represented by three: the Striped/Fat Sleeper, Spotted Goby (*Dormitator maculatus*), the Emperor Goby/Gudgeon (*Hypseleotris compressa*) and the Peacock Goby (*Tateurndina ocellicauda*), with passing reference to other species.

Bumblebee Goby showing sucker fins. See page 196.

Brachygobius xanthozona
(Bumblebee Goby)

Brachygobius xanthozona (Bumblebee Goby) is a shy species which spends much of its time hiding in caves.

*B*RACHYGOBIUS XANTHOZONA is one of several species of small black and yellow/golden gobies collectively known as Bumblebee Gobies. Pigmentation varies considerably, even within a single species, making naming of species uncertain.

In addition to *B. xanthozona* (a name which is disputed by some authors), other 'species' which appear in aquarium literature are *B. nunus* (believed by some to be a synonym of *B. doriae*) and *B. aggregatus*. All require the same basic conditions.

Unlike many other fish from brackish environments, Bumblebees do not take kindly to water that lacks a certain amount of salt, and, although the exact quantity can vary, its presence appears to be essential for the long-term well-being of these strikingly marked little gobies.

Natural Range: Southeast Asia.

Size: Around 4.5cm (1.8in).

Food: This is a predominantly carnivorous species which will accept a wide range of deep-frozen and livefoods. Freeze-dried foods are also accepted, usually once they become waterlogged, but dry foods will only rarely be accepted.

Tank Conditions: Bumblebees are shy, retiring creatures which spend much of their time hiding in caves, often with just their heads projecting from the entrance. Although larger caves will be occupied when no other options are available, some smaller shelters should also be provided. Owing to their diminutive size and their unsuitability as community aquarium fish (because of their requirements, rather than behaviour), this, and allied, species should be kept in a small planted aquarium set aside specifically for them. Other small, peaceful salt-tolerant species, such as Glassfish (*Chanda spp.*) can, however, be housed with Bumblebees, but as males become territorial, only one should be kept per tank, unless adequate provision for separate territories can be provided. The water should be hard and alkaline, with as much as one tablespoon of salt added to each 4.5-5 litres (1 Imperial gallon) of water.

Temperature: 24–30°C (75–86°F).

Breeding: Eggs are laid in caves (often, a large snail shell will suffice) and are guarded by the male. Hatching takes about 4 days.

Dormitator maculatus
(Striped/Fat Sleeper Goby, Spotted Goby)

THE STRIPED Sleeper Goby (*Dormitator maculatus*) is a sturdy-looking fish which is attractively marked and is usually offered at a relatively small size as a suitable choice for a brackish set-up.

Unlike many other brackish water species, Striped Sleepers do not adapt to total freshwater conditions. Therefore (and bearing in mind their predatory instincts), these sleepers should either be housed on their own, i.e., in a species tank, or with other brackish species of a sufficiently large size to be disregarded as food items.

Without a doubt, the Striped Sleeper presents a bit of a challenge, but once this is successfuly negotiated, its longevity and the ease with which it becomes tame, will pay rich dividends.

Natural Range: Atlantic coast of tropical regions of South America.

Size: Up to 25cm (10in), but usually smaller. Sexual maturity is attained at less than half the full reported adult size.

Food: This is a carnivorous/piscivorous species which will only accept livefood or deep-frozen/freeze-dried formulae, the last of which is (mostly) accepted with reluctance.

Tank Conditions: Being a predator that is not built for chasing its prey, but rather lies in wait for it, *D. maculatus* should be provided with numerous caves in a large aquarium. These caves should be sufficiently spaced out to allow individual fish to establish their own territories. The substratum should be relatively fine-grained to cater for the species' burying tendencies. Plants – which should be salt-tolerant, e.g., Java Fern (*Microsorum pteropus*) or artificial – must be protected against the digging activities of these robust fish, either by being potted up with pebbles covering the planting medium, or by having pebbles placed around the stems (if planted in the aquarium substratum). The water should be well filtered, alkaline and hardish, with one to two teaspoonfuls of salt added to each 4.5–5 litres (1 Imperial gallon).

Temperature: 22–25°C (72–77°F).

Breeding: Eggs are laid on a pre-cleaned stone and hatch in 1 day. Aquarium spawnings are rare.

Dormitator maculatus (Striped Sleeper Goby) is a tough-looking species.

Hypseleotris compressa
(Empire Goby/Gudgeon, Carp Gudgeon)

Hypseleotris compressa (Empire Goby) is a strikingly marked fish.

WITH THE exception of *Tateurndina ocellicauda* (see page 200), *Hypseleotris compressa*, the Empire Goby or Gudgeon is the most colourful of a number of *Hypseleotris* species currently available.

It is also, because of its ability to tolerate both freshwater and brackish conditions, considerably more adaptable than some other sleepers. Its temperament, too, is much more suitable for mixed collections. All in all, if you would like to take up keeping sleeper gobies, this species should be your first choice, since it is the perfect introduction to this interesting and often challenging family,

Other *Hypseleotris* species which are also available from time to time include *H. aureus* (Golden Goby or Gudgeon), *H. cyprinoides* (Minnow Goby or Gudgeon) and *H. galii* (Firetail Goby or Gudgeon).

Natural Range: Australia and Papua New Guinea.

Size: Up to around 11cm (4.3in), but often smaller.

Food: This is a predominantly carnivorous species which prefers livefoods above all other types. However, deep-frozen and freeze-dried foods are also accepted, along with dry foods, such as flakes and meat-based pellets.

Tank Conditions: Because of its relatively large size, this species should only be housed in a roomy aquarium. It is considerably less aggressive and territorial than *Dormitator* and is, therefore, easier to keep with other species. In addition, *H. compressa* can tolerate a gradual transition from brackish to freshwater conditions, thus offering considerably more possibilities with regard to tankmates. The aquarium decor should include planted and sheltered areas, as well as open ones containing one or more large flat or rounded stones. The pH of the water should be neutral or slightly alkaline and moderately hard, with (ideally) some salt – about one teaspoonful per 4.5-5 litres (1 Imperial gallon) – added.

Temperature: This species can tolerate a very wide range, which, reportedly, extends from as low as 12°C (54°F) to around 28°C (82°F).

Breeding: Eggs are laid on a pre-cleaned site and are guarded by the male. Hatching takes less than 1 day. Fry should be fed on the smallest foods, e.g., rotifers.

Stigmatogobius sadanundio
(Knight Goby)

THE KNIGHT GOBY (*Stigmatogobius sadanundio*) is probably the most frequently imported member of the Gobiidae. Mature males, with their attractive black spots, are particularly impressive. Females are generally smaller and have a yellowish tinge on their bodies.

Knight Goby males are territorial, even outside the breeding season. However, if the accommodation provided is roomy enough and the caves or other forms of shelter are well spaced out, more than one specimen can be kept in the same aquarium.

Knight Gobies are bottom-dwellers which are relatively peaceful towards other similarly sized species and can, therefore, be kept in a community aquarium. It would be sensible, though, to avoid choosing too many other bottom-dwelling species for a community containing more than one *S. sadanundio*.

Although this species is often found in freshwater habitats in the wild and so can adapt to such conditions in aquaria, it is advisable to provide hardish conditions, rather than soft, for their long-term health. Indeed, some authorities advise very vigorously against even attempting to keep Knight Gobies in soft water.

Personally, I have always maintained hard, alkaline water with some salt whenever I have kept this interesting fish.

Natural Range: Indonesia and the Philippines.
Size: Up to 8.5cm (3.4in).
Food: Will eat a wide range of livefoods, freeze-dried and deep-frozen diets, as well as algae.
Tank Conditions: The tank should contain a sandy or other fine-grained substratum and be liberally supplied with rock shelters. Plants should be salt-tolerant, e.g., Java Fern (*Microsorum pteropus*), Water Star (*Hygrophila polysperma*), Tape Grass or Vallis (*Vallisneria spp.*) or one or other of the Sagittarias (*Sagittaria spp.*). The water should be well-filtered and hard and alkaline, with some added salt (one teaspoonful per 4.5–5 litres/1 Imperial gallon), although freshwater will also be tolerated.
Temperature: 20–26°C (68–79°F), slightly higher for breeding.
Breeding: Eggs are laid on the roof of a cave and guarded by both parents.

Stigmatogobius sadanundio (Knight Goby) showing the attractive black spots characteristic of this popular species.

Tateurndina ocellicauda
(Peacock Goby / Gudgeon)

UNTIL THE 1980s, the Peacock Goby (*Tateurndina ocellicauda*) was only occasionally seen in shops. Gradually, though, it has become more popular, but is still never available in large numbers.

Although the sexes can be easily told apart (males are slimmer than females, which seem to be permanently full of eggs; they also possess a thicker and larger head than females), both are almost equally colourful and fully live up to their name. The Peacock Goby is a delight to keep and breed, as long as one caters adequately for its needs.

Natural Range: Papua New Guinea.

Size: Up to 7.5cm (3in) reported, but is mature at around 5–5.5cm (2–2.2in).

Food: Will accept a wider range of foods than other sleepers and gobies and, although livefoods are preferred, even flaked foods will be taken by most specimens. Some, though, refuse all dry foods.

Tank Conditions: Unusually for a sleeper, *T. ocellicauda* is found in soft water in the wild. These conditions should, of course, be replicated in aquaria, but some deviation will be tolerated, as long as it is not extreme and any changes are carried out gradually. The pH should be around neutral, i.e., approximately 7. This is a peaceful species which will tolerate the presence of other fish. However, tankmates should be chosen to fit in bearing in mind the rather slow, sedentary nature of the Peacock Goby. If this is not possible, a special aquarium should be set up. Either way, there should be plenty of vegetation and numerous hiding places.

Temperature: 22–27°C (72–81°F), the top end of the range being suitable for spawning.

Breeding: Eggs are attached by 'threads' to the roof of a cave or other shelter. There are also reports of this species spawning in the open, but, given the choice, they usually opt to spawn under cover. The eggs are guarded by the male. Hatching takes about 7 days and the fry accept brine shrimp (*Artemia*) from the outset.

Tateurndina ocellicauda (Peacock Goby).

KILLIFISH

KILLIFISH HAVE been referred to as 'the jewels of freshwaters', such is the brilliance of their coloration. Traditionally, killifish have been termed egg-laying toothcarps, while livebearers (see pages 230 and following) have been referred to as livebearing toothcarps. This holds true for most species of killifish, but there are a few – most notably, *Cynolebias melanotaenia* and *C. brucei* – which, while laying eggs, employ internal fertilization, a characteristic of the livebearers, among which we also find a few species that exhibit these same characteristics. Clearly, therefore, there is no sharp distinction between these two groups.

Old classifications placed all the killifish species within a single family, the Cyprinodontidae. However, as new discoveries have been made, a number of revisions have taken place. No doubt, further ones will follow, since universal agreement on how to classify these fish has not been reached.

One of the more recent (and more widely, but not universally, accepted) classifications is that of Lynne Parenti (1981), which is the one I adopt here. According to this classification, the species featured in the next few pages, belong to the families listed in the table below.

Killifish spawn either by burying their eggs in the substratum, or by scattering them among plants. In some species, these eggs will hatch out within a short time, but in many others (especially the so-called 'annual species'), the eggs spend a period of time buried in the mud at the bottom of dried-up ponds until the next rains arrive. Once this happens, these eggs will hatch in a matter of hours. It is this fascinating method of reproduction that, from the aquarium hobby point of view, is the most characteristic feature of killifish.

Pachypanchax playfairi (Playfair's Panchax). See page 111.

Family	Genera
Aplocheilichthyidae	*Aplocheilichthys macrophthalmus*
Cyprinodontidae	*Jordanella floridae*
Aplocheilidae	*Aphysemion australe, A. gardneri,*
	Epiplatys (Aplocheilus) annutalus,
	Nothobranchius guentheri, N. rachovii,
	Pachypanchax playfairi
Rivulidae	*Cynolebias bellotti, C. nigripinnis,C. whitei*

Nothobranchius guentheri (Günther's Nothobranch). See page 209.

Aphyosemion australe
(Cape Lopez Lyretail, Lyretailed Panchax, Lyretail)

THE CAPE Lopez Lyretail (*Aphyosemion australe*) is a splendid, small peaceful fish which does well in aquaria set up to meet its needs. It is also a relatively long-lived species (for a killifish) with a lifespan of around three years, indicating that its native waters do not dry up seasonally, as they do in many of the habitats occupied by annual killifish (see, for example, *Cynolebias bellotti* – page 206).

In Lyretails, the characteristic caudal (tail) fin extensions, which are responsible for the common names given to the species, are exhibited only by the males. Females lack these and are generally less colourful overall.

Several naturally-occurring geographical colour morphs of *A. australe* are available, as well as a number of aquarium-created varieties.

Natural Range: Western Africa: Gabon, Cameroon, southern Congo.

Size: Around 6cm (2.4in) for males; females are smaller.

Food: Although this is predominantly a livefood feeder, it will also accept deep-frozen and freeze-dried diets, as well as flakes.

Tank Conditions: Ideally, the aquarium should have a dark substratum incorporating some peat. Alternatively, tannin-stained water may be produced using a peat 'sandwich' in a canister-type filter, i.e., a layer of aquarium peat sandwiched between two layers of another type of medium, or by means of one of the widely available commercial 'blackwater' preparations. Using a piece of natural bogwood as part of the aquarium decor will also help. Chemically, the water should be non-turbulent, soft and acid, and the aquarium should be heavily planted and the lighting relatively subdued. This is a peaceful fish which can be kept with other small, equally peaceful species.

Temperature: From around 18°C (64°F) to 24°C (75°F), but the lower temperatures should not be maintained for long periods.

Breeding: Eggs are scattered among clumps of fine-leaved vegetation or a special spawning mop (consisting of strands of non-toxic wool or other fibre attached to a piece of cork and allowed to float in the water). Hatching takes about two weeks.

Aphyosemion australe (Cape Lopez Lyretail) male exhibiting tail fin extensions responsible for its common name.

Aphyosemion gardneri
(Steel-Blue/Gardner's Aphyosemion)

THE STEEL-BLUE Aphyosemion (*Aphyosemion gardneri*) is one of the most variable and confusing of the killifish. There are so many different fish found in isolated localities in Nigeria and Cameroon which fit the overall morphological description for the species, that, inevitably, a profusion of names has evolved over the years.

The result is that some of these morphs or types are regarded as subspecies by some authorities, while others even place them in another genus altogether *(Fundulopanchax)*. Four such 'gardneris' which have, basically, similar requirements and are variously available are: *Aphyosemion (Fundulopanchax) gardneri gardneri* (the Steel-Blue or Gardner's Aphyosemion), *A. (F.) gardneri lacustre* (Ejagham Aphyosemion), *A. (F.) gardneri mamfense* (Mamfe Aphyosemion) and *A. (F.) gardneri nigerianum* (Nigerian Aphyosemion).

Natural Range: Nigeria and western Cameroon (but see above text).

Size: Around 6cm (2.4in).

Food: Predominantly livefoods, but some dry foods will also be accepted.

Tank Conditions: In general, conditions should be similar to those provided for *Aphyosemion australe* (see previous entry). However, *A. gardneri* is a generally intolerant species; in particular, males will often fight among themselves. A species tank is therefore recommended for this annual species, with numerous hiding places and thick vegetation provided.

Temperature: 22–25°C (72–77°F), slightly higher for breeding.

Breeding: Eggs are scattered among clumps of fine-

There are many beautiful Aphyosemion gardneri (Steel Blue Aphyosemion) species.

leaved vegetation or spawning mops and hatch after 14–21 days. Alternatively, eggs may be kept in moist peat for 28–30 days and then re-soaked, after which they will hatch within a few hours.

SOME OTHER APHYOSEMION SPECIES

Among the many beautiful species of *Aphyosemion* which are available – especially through specialist outlets or from members of a killifish society – the following are (perhaps) the best known.

A. bitaeniatum (Two-striped Aphyosemion), *A. bivittatum* (Red or Two-banded Aphyosemion), *A. calliurum* (Banded Lyretail or Aphyosemion), *A. cameronense* (Cameroon Aphyosemion – several subspecies/morphs), *A coeleste* (Sky-Blue Aphyosemion), *A. congicum* (Congo or Goldstein's Aphyosemion), *A. fallax* (Kribi Aphyosemion), *A. filamentosum* (Blue Aphyosemion), *A. gulare* (Gulare), *A. liberiense* (Liberian Aphyosemion), *A. mirabile* (Miracle Aphyosemion), *A. ogoense* (Ogowe Aphyosemion) and *A. sjoestedti* (Blue Gularis).

Aplocheilichthys macrophthalmus
(Lamp-Eye Panchax, Big-Eye/Iridiscent Lampeye)

THE LAMP-EYE Panchax (*Aplocheilichthys macrophthalmus*) is a delicately coloured killifish which is not seen too regularly in shops. When it does appear, it is often kept in brightly lit aquaria which do no justice to the iridescent blue coloration which males possess. Perhaps this is the main reason why this species is not as popular as it deserves to be. Maintained in a shoal under the conditions outlined below, it makes a most impressive display, especially when kept with other peaceful shoaling fish.

Most books refer to the Lamp-eye Panchax by its long-established name of *Aplocheilichthys macrophthalmus*, but some of the more recent publications (but by no means all) are reverting to the older specific name of *luxophthalmus*, which was used when the species was regarded as belonging to the genus *Fundulopanchax*.

The newer nomenclature recognizes two subspecies: *A. luxophthalmus luxophthalmus* and *A. luxophthalmus hannerzi* which carries the common name of Hannerz's Lampeye and is the type found in the Lower Cross River drainage (see below). These are the same fish which appear as *A. macrophthalmus macrophthalmus* and *A. macrophthalmus hannerzi* in the majority of aquarium books.

Natural Range: West Africa, including Cameroon, Togo and the Lower Cross River drainage and Niger delta in Nigeria.

Size: Up to 4cm (1.6in).

Food: While livefoods are preferred, deep-frozen, freeze-dried and dry formulations are also accepted.

Tank Conditions: This is an active, shoaling species which should be provided with ample open swimming space, bordered on the sides and back, by heavily planted areas. Ideally, the substratum should be dark and the lighting subdued, either by using low-voltage lamps or, preferably, by covering the water surface with floating plants. The water should be neutral or slightly alkaline and medium-hard.

Temperature: 22–26°C (72–79°F).

Breeding: Eggs are scattered among fine-leaved vegetation or the feathery roots of floating plants and take 10-14 days to hatch.

Aplocheilichthys macrophthalmus (Lamp-Eye Panchax) showing its characteristic iridescent blue coloration.

Aplocheilus annulatus
(Clown Killifish, Comet/Rocket Panchax)

Subdued lighting is recommended for the attractive Aplocheilus annulatus (Clown Killifish).

THE CLOWN KILLIFISH (*Aplocheilus annulatus*) is still referred to in many books by one or other of its two older, more traditional, names: *Epiplatys annulatus* or *Pseudepiplatys annulatus*. In more recent years, the affinities between this species (and its small group of close relatives) and those of the genus *Aplocheilus* have been recognized with the adoption of this generic name.

There are also a number of skeletal differences which the Clown Killifish shares with members of the *Nothobranchius* genus, while haemoglobin studies indicate similarities with *Aphyosemion* and *Rivulus*. These distinctive features have resulted in some authorities regarding the species as belonging to the subgenus *Pseudepiplatys* of the genus *Aplocheilus*.

Other relatives of the Clown Killifish which are occasionally available (and which have the same basic requirements) include: *A. chevalieri* (Chevalier's Panchax), *A. dageti* (Black-lipped Panchax), *A. fasciolatus* (Orange Panchax) and *A. sexfasciatus* (Six-barred Panchax). *Pachypanchax playfairii* (see page 211) is also believed to be an *Aplocheilus* by some authors.

Natural Range: West Africa: Guinea, Sierra Leone, Liberia.

Size: Up to 4cm (1.6in) reported, but usually a little smaller.

Food: Although some dry formulations will be accepted, the diet should consist primarily of livefoods.

Tank Conditions: On account of its small size and peaceful nature, the Clown Killifish should be kept either exclusively with members of its own species, i.e., in a species tank, or only with other small, peaceful fish which like soft, slightly acid water (a little more so for breeding). The use of a peat substratum is often recommended, but this is not essential if appropriate water chemistry conditions can be otherwise provided. Subdued lighting is also recommended – a thick surface layer of floating plants will help provide this.

Temperature: 23–26°C (73–79°F).

Breeding: Eggs are deposited among fine-leaved plants or spawning mops and are ignored by the parents. Hatching takes 8–10 days. Alternatively, eggs may be stored in moist peat for two weeks (see *Cynolebias* – next two pages – for further details of this method).

Cynolebias bellotti
(Argentine Pearl)

THE ARGENTINE PEARL (*Cynolebias bellotti*) is an annual fish which hatches, grows, reproduces and dies in a single season. In its native habitat, the bodies of water in which this species is found tend to dry up during the hot season, wiping out all the adults in the process. However, by then, the fish will have spawned and their eggs will remain buried in the substratum and will hatch when the rains return several months later. This single-season lifespan is maintained even in aquaria.

Natural Range: Rio de la Plata Basin in Argentina.
Size: Up to 7cm (2.8in); females slightly smaller.
Food: Will accept flaked foods and other dry formulations, but prefers live, deep-frozen and freeze-dried foods.
Tank Conditions: The Argentine Pearl is better suited to species, rather than community, aquaria. The substratum should consist of aquarium peat which should be rinsed thoroughly to eliminate the finest particles and then soaked to waterlog it and allow it to sink to the bottom of the tank. Some fine-leaved plants like *Cabomba spp.* or

Myriophyllum spp. can be added as decor and to provide females with some degree of shelter. The water should be soft and slightly acid (the peat will help to establish these conditions).

Temperature: This species has been known to survive temperatures as low as 4°C (39°F) and as high as 30°C (86°F). However, a more tolerable range is anything between 15–22°C (59–72°F) for general maintenance and slightly higher for breeding purposes.

Breeding: A trio consisting of one male and two females should be used. Eggs are laid within the bottom layer of peat. After spawning, the breeders should be separated, since the male will be ready to spawn again straightaway. The peat containing the eggs should be squeezed to remove excess water (the eggs are very resistant) and stored in a moist condition in the dark in a suitable receptacle (a small plastic tub with lid, or even, a polythene bag will do) for 3–4 months. On re-soaking after this period, the eggs will begin hatching almost straightaway.

Cynolebias bellotti (Argentine Pearl): one of the so-called 'annual' species.

Cynolebias nigripinnis
(Black-Finned/Dwarf Argentine Pearl)

Cynolebias nigripinnis (Black-finned Argentine Pearl) is a beautiful single-season fish.

THE BLACK-FINNED Argentine Pearl (*Cynolebias nigripinnis*) is, like its larger relative, *C. bellotti*, a single-season fish which hatches, grows to maturity, breeds and dies in less than one year.

A further similarity between the two species is that a pair or trio will spawn over an extended period of time: about eight to ten days in *C. nigripinnis* and up to three weeks in *C. bellotti*.

Best breeding results are obtained with all *Cynolebias* species if the sexes are kept separated and conditioned on a nutritious diet for several weeks. Once spawning has been completed, the females should be removed, otherwise they will be harrassed by the males which, because of their short lifespan, are capable of breeding virtually on a continuous basis.

Natural Range: Rio de la Plata and Rio Panama regions of Argentina.

Size: Up to 5cm (2in) for males; females are smaller.

Food: Will accept dry formulations, but prefers deep-frozen, freeze-dried and livefood diets.

Tank Conditions: The tank should be prepared along similar lines as those recommended for *C. bellotti* (see previous entry). Like *C. bellotti*, Dwarf Argentine Pearl males are aggressive, not only towards males of their own species, but also towards females, though to a lesser degree.

Temperature: Between 18–25°C (64–77°F), but slightly higher and lower temperatures will be tolerated.

Breeding: Follow the guidelines given for *C. bellotti*, keeping the eggs in moist peat for a minimum of three months.

SOME OTHER CYNOLEBIAS SPECIES

Although *Cynolebias* killifish are not always easily available in general aquatic shops, stocks may be obtained either via specialist outlets or members of killifish societies. Here are some species worth looking out for:

C. adloffi (Banded Pearl), *C. boitonei* (Brazilian Lyretail), *C. brucei* (Turner's Gaucho – the eggs of this species are fertilized internally, although it is an egglayer), *C. constanciae* (Featherfin Pearl), *C. elongatus* (Blue Pearl), *C. melanotaenia* (Fighting Gaucho – also uses internal fertilization), *C. opalescens* – also known as *C. minutus* (Myer's Gaucho) and *C. whitei* (White's Pearl).

Jordanella floridae
(American Flagfish)

Jordanella floridae (American Flagfish) is a tough, active fish with an appetite for decorative plants.

THE AMERICAN Flagfish (*Jordanella floridae*) has been known in the European hobby for over 80 years, following its introduction as a colourful American species that could be kept in coldwater aquaria.

Over the years, it has been 'adopted' by the tropical side of the hobby, so much so that it often comes as a surprise to new aquarists when they learn that this species can be kept in unheated aquaria.

This is a tough, active fish which should, therefore, be kept in a community of other robust species, rather than delicate or timid tankmates. To counter its partially herbivorous habits, the plants provided for decor should also be tough...or unpalatable.

Natural Range: From Florida southwards to Yucatán in Mexico.

Size: Up to 6.5cm (2.6in) for males; females are smaller.

Food: All types of food accepted, but should include a vegetable component.

Tank Conditions: Although males are often aggressive towards other males of their own species, they are generally tolerant of other species and can therefore be kept in community aquaria. The main limiting factor in this respect is temperature (see below). Open swimming space should be provided along the front of the aquarium, with thick, tough vegetation along the sides and back. The substratum should be fine-grained to allow males to dig spawning depressions (see below). It is often recommended that the aquarium be placed in a spot that receives some sunlight, but this can make temperature control quite difficult. Water chemistry is not critical, as long as the overall quality is good.

Temperature: 19–25°C (66–77°F), the lower end being preferred on a long-term basis, the higher being reserved for breeding purposes.

Breeding: Flagfish can use two different methods of spawning: they can either scatter their eggs among fine-leaved vegetation, or lay them in a depression excavated by the male in the substratum. Either way, the male guards the eggs until they hatch 6–9 days later, depending on temperature.

Nothobranchius guentheri
(Günther's Nothobranch)

GÜNTHER'S NOTHOBRANCH (*Nothobranchius guentheri*) is one of the many exuberantly coloured *Nothobranchius* species which are only occasionally available in general aquatic shops, but more often obtainable either in specialized outlets or through members of a killifish society.

The species' natural range appears to be the island of Zanzibar, but is also often quoted as occurring on the Tanzanian mainland. Its size is also variously quoted as around 5cm (2in), or up to 6.5–7cm (2.6–2.8in). Both in the case of the Tanzanian claims and the larger sizes, it now appears as if the species in question could be the similar-looking *N. melanospilus* (the Beira Nothobranch).

Much confusion surrounds the actual classification of the genus *Nothobranchius* and its constituent species, as a result of which conflicting reports can easily arise.

Natural Range: East Africa: island of Zanzibar – see also main text.

Size: Around 5cm (2in) – see also main text.

Food: Although flakes and other dry formulations may be accepted, the diet should be predominantly livefood-based.

Tank Conditions: On account of the aggressive tendencies of *N. guentheri* males towards other males of their own species, they should be kept singly in a species tank in the company of several females. Should the aquarium be sufficiently large and well planted for several males to be able to set up non-overlapping territories and for adequate shelter to be provided, the collection can be expanded and will result in a community of continuously displaying males – a situation not unlike that found in the wild. There should be open swimming areas separated by thickets of vegetation, bogwood, roots or their equivalents. The substratum should be dark and soft, e.g., peat – see entries for *Cynolebias* on pages 206, 207 – and the water should be soft and slightly acid.

Temperature: 22–26°C (72–79°F).

Breeding: This is an annual species which buries its eggs in the substratum (peat). These should be maintained in a moist condition (see *Cynolebias*) for three to four months before being re-soaked.

Nothobranchius guentheri (Günther's Nothobranch).

Nothobranchius rachovi
(Rachow's Nothobranch)

The colourful Nothobranchius rachovi (Rachow's Nothobranch) is one of around 30 species available in the hobby.

RACHOW'S NOTHOBRANCH (*Nothobranchius rachovi* – also spelt *rachovii* in many publications) is a colourful annual species which occurs in numerous colour forms in the wild.

Jorgen Scheel, who during his lifetime carried out one of the most intensive (if not *the* most intensive) genetic studies of African and Asian killifish, states that *N. rachovi* has the most specialized complement of chromosomes in the whole genus. He also comments that the males of this species from the northern part of the range are 'by far the most colourful'.

Two other *Nothobranchius* species are found in the same localities as *N. rachovi*: *N. orthonotus* (the Dusky Nothobranch) and *N. kuhntae* (the Pungue Nothobranch), the former being more frequently seen in the hobby than the latter.

Despite being an annual species, some *N. rachovi* males can take as long as three months to attain full maturity.

Natural Range: Reported from Quelimane in southern Mozambique, southwards to the northern parts of the Kruger Park in South Africa.
Size: Up to 5cm (2in) for males; females are smaller.
Food: Will accept some dry formulations, but the diet should consist primarily of small livefoods.
Tank Conditions: Despite its generally peaceful behaviour towards other species, males can be territorial and very aggressive towards each other. Tank conditions should be similar to those provided for *N. guentheri* (see previous entry).
Temperature: 20–24°C (68–75°F).
Breeding: This will occur even at temperatures below the maximum recommended above, i.e., higher temperatures are not necessary. Eggs are laid in the soft substratum, after which they should be stored in moist peat for about three months before being re-soaked.

SOME OTHER NOTHOBRANCHIUS SPECIES

The genus *Nothobranchius* consists of around 30 species (the exact number is not known with any certainty), many of which can be obtained with varying degrees of difficulty. Among those most frequently encountered are: *N. foerschi* (Foersch's Nothobranch), *N. furzeri* (Furzer's Nothobranch), *N. lourensi* (Green Nothobranch), *N. korthausae* (Korthaus' Nothobranch), *N. palmqvisti* (Palmqvist's Nothobranch), *N. polli* (Poll's Nothobranch) and *N. rubripinnis* (Mbezi Nothobranch).

Pachypanchax playfairi
(Playfair's Panchax)

PLAYFAIR'S PANCHAX has traditionally been referred to as *Pachypanchax playfairi* or *playfairii*. More recently, some authorities have assimilated it within the genus *Aplocheilus*, under which name it has begun appearing in aquarium literature.

Certainly, there are scalation, neuromast (sensory cells), haemoglobin and chromosome characteristics that it shares with several *Aplocheilus* species, but there are also distinct differences in the detailed structures and arrangements within the overall similarities. It is, therefore, possible that, while belonging to *Aplocheilus*, Playfair's Panchax, along with a couple of other species, also constitute a subgenus of their own. If so, the full scientific 'label' should read: *Aplocheilus (Pachypanchax) playfairi*.

Natural Range: Island of Zanzibar, Seychelles and Madagascar.

Size: Up to 10cm (4in) for males; females are smaller.

Food: Will accept dry, deep-frozen and freeze-dried formulations, but prefers livefoods.

Tank Conditions: Because of its relatively large eventual size, it would be natural to assume that this species requires a roomy aquarium. However, since it is aggressive towards its own kind and will prey on smaller fish, it can be housed in a 60cm (24in) aquarium if it is being kept on its own. Kept in a community of fish its own size, though, it will require larger quarters. There should be open swimming spaces bordered, along the sides and back, by thick vegetation. The substratum should, ideally, be fine-grained and the lighting subdued. Hiding places should also be provided, as well as a tight-fitting aquarium cover (this species is an excellent jumper). The water should be slightly acid or neutral and can vary from soft to medium-hard.

Temperature: 22–25°C (72–77°F).

Breeding: Eggs are scattered among fine-leaved vegetation over an extended period of around 7 days. This species has a distinct liking for its own eggs and should, therefore, be separated from its spawn. The easiest way of doing this is by providing separate clumps of, e.g., Java Moss (*Vesicularia dubyana*) which can be removed on a daily basis. Hatching takes 10–12 days.

Pachypanchax playfairi (Playfair's panchax).

EELS AND REEDFISH

Despite their elongated, snake-like shape, spiny eels are not true eels.

THE TERM 'EEL' is used in aquarium literature to refer to a number of fish whose only shared characteristic is an elongated, snake-like body. Other than that, they are often as closely related to one another as a Guppy is to an Angler Fish!

Within both the freshwater and marine hobbies, several types of eels are encountered from time to time, varying from the freshwater Swamp or Marbled Eel (*Synbranchus marmoratus*, family Synbranchidae) and Electric Eel (*Electrophorus electricus*, family Electrophoridae), to the Snowflake Moray (*Echidna nebulosa*, family Muraenidae) and the 'Common' Eel (*Anguilla anguilla*, family Anguillidae).

The species of 'eel' featured in the pages that follow are not true eels in the strict sense of the word; they are only eel-like in overall body form. They belong to the family Mastacembelidae, which are more correctly referred in non-scientific parlance as spiny eels.

These interesting fish are characterized by a row of isolated spines (numbering between nine and 42,

depending on species) that precede the long soft dorsal (back) fin which, itself, possesses between 52 and 131 soft rays (again, depending on species). In addition, all species have a long, downward-pointing snout adorned by fleshy growths known as rostral appendages. Many spiny eels are regarded as food fish in their native lands, but a few of the 67 or so species are also popular as aquarium fish.

The Reedfish, Ropefish or Snakefish (*Erpetoichthys calabaricus*) is not an eel, but has the characteristic elongated body associated with eels and is, as a result, wrongly regarded as such by some aquarists. Biologically, though, it belongs to the family Polypteridae, some species of which – most notably the various bichirs of the genus *Polypterus* – are also occasionally encountered in aquarium shops.

Like its close relatives, the Reedfish carries the most easily distinguishable family characteristics consisting of a dorsal fin made up of a series of finlets, each preceded by a single spine.

Erpetoichthys calabaricus
(Reed / Rope / Snakefish)

THE REEDFISH (*Erpetoichthys calabaricus*) was formerly known as *Calamoichthys calabaricus* and often still appears as such in aquarium literature. Retention of the old name (for the sake of stability) is supported by several leading ichthyologists, some of whom believe that the species should, in fact, be regarded as a *Polypterus*, i.e. a bichir.

While sharing many characteristics with the bichirs – including an ability to use its swimbladder as an auxiliary respiratory organ, and the dorsal (back) fin being divided into finlets (7–13) – the Reedfish differs from its closest relatives in that it does not have any pelvic (hip) fins.

As long as the air is humid, to the extent that their body surface does not dry out completely, Reedfish can survive out of water for several hours.

The easiest way to separate the sexes is by the number of bars on the caudal (tail) fin: in females, there are nine and in males, 12 to 14.

Erpetoichthys calabaricus (Reedfish).

Natural Range: Cameroon and Nigeria, particularly the Niger Delta, West Africa.

Size: Up to 40cm (15.7in), but often smaller.

Food: This is a carnivorous species which takes livefoods and meat-based diets, but not dry formulations.

Tank Conditions: Because its size, the Reedfish must be kept in relatively large aquaria. It is peaceful towards all fish that are too large to be regarded as food and so can be kept as part of a selected community. The substratum should be fine-grained to allow specimens to bury themselves. Plants should be protected against this, either by being potted, with pebbles on the soil/medium surface or – if planted in the substratum – by having pebbles strategically placed around their stems. A tight-fitting aquarium cover is essential to prevent escapes, and hiding places should be provided for this sometimes retiring species. A 'moonlight' fluorescent tube will make noctural activities easy to observe. The water should be slightly acid and medium-hard.

Temperature: 22–28°C (72–82°F).

Breeding: This species has not been bred in aquaria.

Macrognathus aculeatus
(Lesser Spiny Eel)

WHEN KEPT with just one or two other members of its own species, the Lesser Spiny Eel (*Macrognathus aculeatus*) is aggressive. However, when kept in a large group, this aggression generally subsides to the extent that 'bundles' of spiny eels with intertwined bodies can be seen draped over a piece of bogwood or other aquarium decor, or crammed inside a cave.

This behaviour applies more to half-grown individuals than fully grown ones and is most often seen in shops, since home aquaria are not usually large enough to accommodate a collection of ten or more specimens. It is, therefore, safer to keep just single specimens.

Natural Range: Fresh and brackish waters in southeast Asia.
Size: Up to 35cm (13.8in), but usually smaller.
Food: While some commercial dry sinking foods may be accepted, this species should be fed primarily on bottom-dwelling livefoods.
Tank Conditions: Spiny eels (not just this species) spend much of their time completely buried in the substratum with, if anything, just the tip of the snout and eyes showing. The tank should have a fine-grained bottom to allow these eel-like species to follow their instincts. On account of the size attained by these fish, the substratum layer must also be deep enough to accommodate the full body depth of large specimens. Plants must be protected, using the technique outlined on the previous page for Reedfish (*Erpetoichthys calabaricus*). Lighting should be subdued during the day, with a 'moonlight' fluorescent tube allowing the crepuscular (twilight) and nocturnal activities of the species to be observed. Hiding places should also be provided. The water should be around neutral and medium-hard. The addition of a little salt – about one teaspoonful per 9–10 litres (2 Imperial gallons) – is often recommended, but this is not essential.
Temperature: 23–28°C (73–82°F).
Breeding: Only occurs very rarely in aquaria. Vigorous courting is followed by the scattering of up to 1,000 eggs which hatch after about 3 days.

Macrognathus aculeatus (Lesser Spiny Eel).

Mastacembelus erythrotaenia
(Fire/Spotted Fire/Asian Fire Eel)

Mastacembelus erythrotaenia (Fire Eel) is an attractively marked, large species.

T HE FIRE EEL (*Mastacembelus erythrotaenia*) is the most colourful of the spiny eels. It is also the largest of the so-called aquarium species, although most specimens seen in shops, and even in established home aquaria, are nowhere as large as the maximum size reported for the species.

M. erythrotaenia is a nocturnal predator which can only be housed with tankmates that are too large to be regarded as food. It is also intolerant of members of its own species (see entry for *Macrognathus aculeatus* for further discussion of this point).

Despite usually being more widely available than most other spiny eels, the Fire Eel is not the easiest of the group to maintain in a healthy state on a permanent basis, owing to its susceptibility to injuries and parasites. Water quality must, therefore, be good at all times to minimize risks.

Natural Range: Southeast Asia: Borneo, Myanmar (Burma), Sumatra and Thailand.

Size: Up to 1 metre (39in) reported, but even large aquarium specimens are rarely over 35–50cm (13.8–20in) in length.

Food: This is a carnivorous species which only rarely takes dry foods. Deep-frozen and freeze-dried diets will, however, be accepted.

Tank Conditions: In general, aquarium conditions should be as described for *Macrognathus aculeatus* on the previous page. Howevever, as *Mastacembelus erythrotaenia* is even larger, appropriate allowances must be made for this.

Temperature: 22–28°C (72–82°F).

Breeding: This has not been recorded in aquaria.

SOME OTHER SPINY EELS AVAILABLE

The names *Macrognathus* and *Mastacembelus* are often used interchangeably, leading to a certain degree of confusion. The following list uses the nomenclature suggested by Robert Travers in 1984.

Afromastacembelus moorii (Mottled Spiny Eel – 16cm/6.3in), *A. tanganikae* (Tanganyika Spiny Eel – 15cm/6in) *Macrognathus circumcictus* (Banded Spiny Eel – 25cm/10in), *M. maculatus* (Spotted or Black Spotted Spiny Eel – 45cm/17.8in), *M. pancalus* (Common, Deep-bodied or Spotted Spiny Eel – 20cm/8in), *M. siamensis* (Clown or Siamese Spiny Eel – 35cm/13.8in), *M. zebrinus* (Zebra Spiny Eel – 45/17.8in), *Mastacembelus armatus* (Giant, Car-track or Tyre-track Spiny Eel – 75cm/29.5in).

GLASSFISHES,
PUFFERS AND ARCHERS

Puffers, such as this Tetraodon fluviatilis (Green Puffer) are often aggressive to other fish in a communal aquarium.,

IN GLASSFISHES, puffers and archers, we have three families of fish which are generally regarded as occurring predominantly in brackish and marine environments. This is not strictly true (see below), but the occurrence of some of the best-known species in such environments has led to all three types being regarded as more suitable for brackish, rather than freshwater, aquaria.

The Asiatic glassfishes constitute the family Chandidae, which is sometimes referred to by its alternative name, Ambassidae. As their common name implies, glassfishes are characterized by possessing an almost-transparent body. As a result, the skeleton, particularly the vertebral column (backbone), is clearly visible through the unpigmented body musculature.

Other features which separate the Chandidae from their nearest relatives include the possession of 7 or 8 spines and 7 to 11 soft rays in the dorsal (back) fin, with 3 spines and 7 to 11 soft rays in the anal (belly) fin. There

are 8 genera in the family, with around 40 species, about half of which are confined for freshwater habitats.

The puffers we find in freshwater and brackish aquaria belong to the family Tetraodontidae, which is characterized by the possession of four fused teeth and the ability to inflate the body when threatened. Within the Tetraodontidae, the species that are included here belong to the subfamily Tetraodontinae which have a rounded body and one or two conspicuous nostrils on either side of the snout.

The archers constitute the family Toxotidae, which contains just one genus, *Toxotes*, and six species. In archers, the dorsal profile of the part of the body stretching from the tip of the snout to the anterior edge of the dorsal fin is straight, allowing these fish to swim directly below the surface of the water in search of aerial prey. Once they find a suitable victim, archers shoot it down with a jet of water, hence their common name.

Chanda ranga
(Indian Glassfish)

THE INDIAN Glassfish (*Chanda ranga*) – also now referred to as *Parambassis ranga* – used to be the most popular member of its genus. Today, a second, larger species, *C. wolffii*, has made considerable inroads into this popularity.

During the 1980s and earlier part of the 1990s, glassfishes became very widespread in the hobby, following the introduction of gaudily 'painted' (injected) specimens from the Far East. Gradually, though, demand for these artificially coloured fish has declined, as a growing number of both aquarists and dealers have chosen not to buy or stock these varieties.

In addition, dye-injected fish have been shown to be more susceptible to lymphocystis – a virus infection often referred to as 'Cauliflower Disease' – than non-injected ones.

Natural Range: India, Myanmar (Burma) and Thailand.
Size: Up to 8cm (3.2in) reported, but usually around 6cm (2.4in).
Food: Although flaked food and some other dry formulations are accepted, livefoods are preferred, along with deep-frozen and freeze-dried diets.

Tank Conditions: This is a shoaling species which should be kept in groups. It is generally timid, but can be housed with other peaceful, smallish species. The tank should be heavily planted, contain shelters and have a dark substratum. This seems to show off the subtle colours of the species to best effect, but only if the water conditions are suitable, i.e., hard, alkaline water with some salt added (preferably a good-quality marine mix). The actual concentration of salt can vary from around one to three teaspoonsful per 4.5–5 litres (1 Imperial gallon). The water should also be mature, rather than freshly drawn or raw.
Temperature: 18–30°C (64–86°F), with the higher end being more suitable for breeding.
Breeding: Eggs are scattered among vegetation, often after the tank has received some morning sun. Hatching takes about 1 day. Newly hatched glassfish are tiny and should therefore be fed on microscopic food such as rotifers. Owing to their very small size, these fry are difficult to raise.

The beautiful Chanda ranga (Indian Glassfish) is a shoaling species which should therefore be kept in groups.

Tetraodon fluviatilis
(Green Puffer)

THE GREEN PUFFER (*Tetraodon fluviatilis*) can, as indicated by its species name, be found in rivers. However, this must not be taken as meaning that it is ideally suited for freshwater environments, at least not for breeding purposes (see guidelines given below). The only occasional breeding successes that have been reported have all occurred under brackish conditions.

Tetraodon fluviatilis (Green Puffer).

All puffers, not just this species, look placid and appealing, but their slow swimming movements belie an underlying aggression that, allied to the powerful dentition, can result in serious injury to more delicate, smaller tankmates.

In additon to the Green Puffer, four other species are regularly available: *T. biocellatus* (Figure-of-Eight Puffer), *T. mbu* (Giant Puffer), *T. schoutedeni* (Spotted Congo Puffer) and *T. steindachneri* (Steindacher's Puffer).

Natural Range: Widely distributed in freshwater and brackish habitats in southeast Asia.

Size: Up to 17cm (6.7in) reported.

Food: Will eat a wide range of foods, including snails (they are excellent at ridding aquaria of infestations of these molluscs). Plant matter, e.g., lettuce and some aquarium plants, also accepted, as well as some commercial tablet and pellet diets.

Tank Conditions: Juvenile specimens are generally peaceful, but become progressively more aggressive, particularly towards their own kind, as they grow. Adult specimens must, therefore, be kept either on their own, or in a community of similarly-sized, tough tankmates. Despite their affinity for plants, the aquarium should contain thickets of vegetation around the sides and back, with an open swimming space along the front. Use either tough and/or unpalatable types like Anubias, e.g. *Anubias nana*, and some of the ferns, e.g., Java Fern

(*Microsorum pteropus*), or artificial plants. Several shelters should also be provided. The water should be neutral to slightly alkaline and hard, with some salt added (about one teaspoonful per 4.5–5 litres/1 Imperial gallon).

Temperature: 24–28°C (75-82°F).

Breeding: Eggs are laid on a stone and are guarded by the male. Hatching takes 6–7 days.

Toxotes jaculator
(Archer Fish)

THE ARCHER FISH appears under two different names in aquarium literature: *Toxotes jaculator* and *Toxotes jaculatrix*.

This remarkable fish, which can shoot down prey from a distance of up to 1.5m (5ft), also has the ability to make allowances for the refraction ('bending') of light rays that occurs between air and water. If a fish were to shoot at a target as it sees it from under the water, i.e., without making a refractive adjustment, it would invariably miss. The fact that this does not happen too often indicates that Archer Fish are able to angle their shots to take account of this optical phenomenon which makes an object (or prey) appear to be where it is not.

Of the other five species in the genus, one is found in shops considerably more frequently than the rest: *T. chatareus* (Seven-spot Archer Fish).

Natural Range: Widely distributed in estuarine waters from the Gulf of Aden, through India and southeast Asia, to Australia.

Size: Up to 25cm (10in) reported, but usually smaller in aquaria.

Food: This is a carnivorous species which requires either livefoods or freeze-dried preparations that float on the surface of the water. It will also shoot down insects from above the water surface (see below).

Tank Conditions: Ideally, Archer Fish require a deep tank that can be arranged to provide a water depth of around 20cm (8in) or more and an equal space above it, topped by a tight-fitting aquarium cover. Twigs and branches projecting from the water into this space can be used as perches by insects, such as flies, introduced to act as food items. Such an arrangement is, however, difficult to organize and provision of a continuous supply of flying foods can pose a considerable challenge. Fortunately, Archer Fish will happily feed on floating foods instead. Submerged plants should be salt-tolerant or artificial. The water should be neutral to alkaline and medium-hard with some salt added (about one teaspoonful per 4.5–5 litres/1 Imperial gallon).

Temperature: 25–30°C (77–86°F).

Breeding: This has not yet been recorded in aquaria.

The remarkable Toxotes jaculator (Archer Fish).

Monos and Scats

Psettus (Monodactylus) sebae, the deep-bodied Seba Mono.

The Monodactylidae are referred to as monos, moonfishes or fingerfishes. All species possess a strongly compressed, silvery body, which in some species, such as *Psettus (Monodactylus) sebae*, can be deeper than long. As monos grow, a very interesting change occurs in that the fully formed pelvic (hip) fins which are present in juveniles, gradually disappear or shrink to mere vestiges in adults.

The dorsal (back) fin in monos has a long base which is covered in scales and possesses 5 to 8 short spines in front of the softer part of the fin. The anal (belly) fin has only 3 spines. There is no adipose or second dorsal fin, as found in, e.g., characins (page 69) or rainbowfishes (page 187).

The Scatophagidae, so-named because of their reputation as detritus feeders ('scatophagus' means 'foul feeder') are attractive fish which have long been popular with aquarists. As with monos, the body is compressed, but in this case the overall shape is more rounded or squarish. In the Scatophagidae, the pelvic fins are present in both juveniles and adults and the dorsal is deeply notched.

MONOS AND SCATS belong to two distinct families, the Monodactylidae and the Scatophagidae, respectively. Despite their biological differences, they share a common feature in that they spend most of their adult lives in marine environments, where most of them breed, but also spend time in brackish and freshwater environments during their juvenile/sub-adult stages.

There are venomous glands at the base of each fin spine and these can inflict painful wounds, so extreme caution should be exercised when handling these fish.

One of the species in the genus *Scatophagus*, *S. tetracanthus*, differs from the others in that it can not only survive in freshwater, but even breed under such conditions.

Monodactylus argenteus
(Mono, Moon/Finger Fish; in Australia: Silver Batfish, Butter Bream)

THE MONO (*Monodactylus argenteus*) was first imported into the European hobby during the first decade of the twentieth century and, despite its increasingly demanding requirements as it matures, it has always been popular with aquarists.

The large number of common names reflects the wide distribution of the species, but, even so, only represents some of the English-language versions from a long list of local names by which this beautiful shoaling fish is known. One of these names, Finger Fish, is particularly interesting because it refers to the long, almost fingerlike dorsal (back) and anal (belly) fins. The scientific name for the genus, *Monodactylus*, actually means 'one finger'.

A second species, *Psettus (Monodactylus) sebae*, known as the Seba Mono, is also available. Its body is deeper than long, particularly in juvenile specimens. It has the same basic requirements as *M. argenteus*, with a little less tolerance for freshwater.

Monodactylus argenteus (Mono).

Natural Range: Widely distributed in tropical brackish environments (but see below), ranging from Africa to Asia, to Australia.

Size: Up to 25cm (10in), but usually smaller in aquaria.

Food: Virtually all foods accepted, some of which must include a vegetable component.

Tank Conditions: This species requires a progressively higher saline environment as it grows. It is, therefore, the ideal fish for the aquarist who possesses both freshwater and (large!) marine tanks, or can maintain 'salty' brackish conditions. Young specimens do well in freshwater, but still prefer some salt (about one teaspoonful per 4.5–5 litres/1 Imperial gallon) for longterm health. This is a shoaling fish which should be kept in groups in a deep tank. Plants should be matched to the salt content of the water and can even consist of marine or estuarine species in the more saline environment required by sub-adults and adults. For general maintenance of juveniles, the water should be neutral to alkaline and hard.

Temperature: 24–28°C (75–82°F).

Breeding: This species has not been bred in aquaria.

Scatophagus argus
(Scat, Argus Fish)

ALTHOUGH THE Scat (*Scatophagus argus*) is an attractively marked fish when adult, it is even more strikingly patterned when juvenile. However, unless suitable accommodation can be provided on a long-term basis, the temptation to buy more than two or three such specimens should be resisted.

If well looked-after, juveniles will outgrow a modestly sized aquarium in a remarkably short time, thus presenting the unprepared aquarist with a 'sizeable' challenge. Another point worth considering is that Scats will consume large amounts of vegetation, so the plants chosen should be tough, e.g., *Anubias* or the various aquatic ferns (but see below).

A reddish type – often referred to as *Scatophagus 'rubrifrons'* or *Scatophagus argus atromaculatus* – is also available and is generally regarded to be a colour variety of *S. argus*.

Natural Range: Adults are widely distributed in coastal brackish and marine waters in the Indian and Pacific Oceans. Juveniles often enter freshwaters.

Size: Up to 30cm (12in).

Food: All foods accepted, from dry formulations to live diets; a vegetable component must be included.

Tank Conditions: On account of the size attained by this shoaling species, only juveniles may be kept in most home aquaria. Adults require not just a large swimming area, but sufficient water depth as well. In addition, there should be thickets of salt-tolerant or artificial vegetation along the sides and back. It has been reported that one such plant, Java Fern (*Microsorum pteropus*), is believed to be poisonous to Scats when ingested and so is best avoided. Juvenile specimens can be kept in well filtered, alkaline, hard water, but require the addition of salt as they grow, beginning with around one teaspoonful per 4.5–5 litres (1 Imperial gallon) and gradually increasing this to double the amount. Eventually, if adults are to be maintained successfully, they will require even better filtered water, more salt or, preferably, full marine conditions.

Temperature: 20–28°C (68–82°F).

Breeding: This species has not been bred in aquaria.

Scatophagus argus (the Scat) has wide-ranging tastes in food.

Selenotoca multifasciata
(Silver/Striped Scat; in Australia: Striped Butterfish)

THE SILVER Scat (*Selenotoca multifasciata*) is superficially like the Scat or Argus (*Scatophagus argus*) – see previous entry. It is, however, even larger when fully mature. The vertical black stripes that adorn the top half of the body from the snout to the tail, combined with the spots that occur on the lower half – all against a silvery background – make this a very attractive fish.

Adults are known to live in estuaries and the lower reaches of rivers, but the young migrate upstream into freshwater for a time, moving down towards the saltier reaches as they grow.

Natural Range: Indo-Pacific region and coasts of Australia, from the southeast corner, northwards, all along the north coast and about halfway down the west coast.

Size: Up to 41cm (16.1in) reported from the wild.

Food: All commercial and live diets accepted; must include a vegetable component.

Tank Conditions: Owing to the large size attained by this species, only juveniles can be considered suitable for smallish or medium-sized aquaria. Most plants will be eaten, so only particularly tough, unpalatable and salt-tolerant natural plants can be considered suitable. Artificial plants are easier to obtain than the above and may therefore constitute a better all-round choice. Some salt should be added to the water – around one teaspoonful per 4.5-5 litres (1 Imperial gallon), gradually increasing this concentration as the fish grow, as suggested for *Scatophagus argus* (see previous entry).

Temperature: 20-28°C (68-82°F).

Breeding: No information is available about the detailed breeding habits of this species.

Selenotoca multifasciata (Silver or Striped Scat).

MISCELLANEOUS SPECIES

B Y DEFINITION, no selection of egglaying species can be all-embracing or exhaustive. Inevitably, personal preferences – whether adopted consciously or otherwise – influence decisions regarding which species are included and which are omitted. However, despite these, plus additional unavoidable restrictions that space and other factors impose, I hope to have provided a

sufficiently representative selection covering all the families of egglayers that we most commonly encounter in aquarium shops.

In the pages that follow, there is a further limited selection of species which are regularly available, but which do not fall within the families so far described in this book.

Badis badis
(Chameleon Fish, Badis)

D EPENDING ON which classification is adopted, the Chameleon Fish (*Badis badis*) either belongs to the subfamily Badinae of the family Nandidae, which also includes the leaf-fishes, or else constitutes the sole representative of the family Badidae.

The name Chameleon Fish refers to the ability of males to change colour according to mood. It may also be in recognition of the two colour forms which are known from the wild. Indian populations are generally bluish in overall coloration and are sometimes referred to as the subspecies, *Badis badis badis*, while those from Myanmar

are redder and are regarded by some as a separate subspecies, *B.b. burmanicus*.

Natural Range: India and Myanmar (Burma).
Size: Up to 8cm (3.2in) for males; females are a little smaller.
Food: Wide variety of dry formulations and livefoods accepted.
Tank Conditions: This is a generally peaceful community fish (although it can become territorial) which likes heavily planted aquaria provided with numerous shelters. Water chemistry is not critical, as long as the overall quality is good.
Temperature: 23–28°C (73–82°F) with the top end being more suitable for breeding.
Breeding: Eggs are laid under cover and are guarded by the male who also cares for the fry for a few days until their yolk sacs are absorbed. Hatching takes about 3 days.

Badis badis,
(Chameleon Fish).

Gnathonemus petersii
(Elephantnose, Peter's Elephantnose)

I N THE 1950s and 60s, the Elephantnose (*Gnathonemus petersii* – family Mormyridae) was a rarity. It was not until the 1980s that larger numbers begun to appear as demand for African fish, particularly from Nigeria, increased.

Today, this remarkable fish, which uses weak electrical impulses to communicate with other members of its species, as well as to find its way around the sometimes murky waters of its native environment, is no longer rare. We now underestand its requirements more thoroughly and this, allied to the high quality and extensive range of fish foods available these days, means that keeping Elephantnoses successfully is no longer a major challenge.

Nevertheless, they are somewhat more demanding than many other species, since they are susceptible to any deterioration in water quality (fortnightly or monthly partial changes are therefore necessary).

In addition to *G. petersii*, several other species – some without a 'nose' and often referred to as 'whales' – are imported, among them, *G. elephas* (Blunt-nosed or Blunt-jaw Elephantnose), *G. tamandua* (no common name), *Marcusenius angolensis* (Spotted Whale or Elephantnose) and *Brienomyrus* (*Marcusenius*) *brachyistius* (Whale).

Natural Range: Central and West Africa, including Cameroon, Democratic Republic of Congo and Nigeria.

Size: Up to around 23cm (9in) reported.

Food: Will accept flaked and dry foods, but has a distinct preference for livefoods, as well as deep-frozen and freeze-dried formulations.

Tank Conditions: Because of the delicate nature of the lower jaw, which is extended into a fleshy proboscis-like growth that the fish uses to search for bottom-dwelling foods, the substratum must be fine-grained. Caves and hiding places must also be provided, along with thickets of vegetation for this predominantly crepuscular (twilight) and nocturnal species. Night-time foraging activities are best observed using a 'moonlight' fluorescent tube. Although water chemistry is not too critical, good quality, mature, slightly acid to neutral water is recommended.

Temperature: 22–28°C (72–82°F).

Breeding: This species has not been bred in aquaria.

Gnathonemus petersii (Elephantnose).

Notopterus chitala
(Clown Knifefish)

THE CLOWN KNIFEFISH (*Notopterus chitala*) is, perhaps, the most commonly seen knifefish in the aquarium hobby. It is often sold as very attractively marked 10–15cm (4–6in) juveniles backed up by a cautionary note from responsible dealers that they will eventually grow into giants with voracious appetites.

All knifefish are predatory, irrespective of their size, and the various 'aquarium' species belonging to the family Notopteridae all attain lengths of 30cm (12in) or more. Among those species available on a fairly regular basis are *Papyrocranus* (*Notopterus*) *afer* (African Knifefish or Featherfin: 60cm/24in), *Notopterus notopterus* (Asian Knifefish: 35cm/13.8in) and *Xenomystus nigri* (also known as African Knifefish: 30cm/12in).

Natural Range: Southeast Asia, including island of Borneo (incorporating Kalimantan), India, Myanmar (Burma), Malaysia and Sumatra.

Size: Specimens measuring up to 1m (39in) have been recorded in the wild. Large aquarium specimens usually attain 70-80cm (28-32in) under optimal conditions.

Food: This is a carnivorous/piscivorous species which requires a meat- or fish-based diet. Deep-frozen and freeze-dried foods will also be accepted, particularly by juveniles, some of which will accept dry formulations as well.

Tank Conditions: Several juveniles may be kept together in a large aquarium if a hierarchy is allowed to become established and the fish are not overcrowded. Otherwise, specimens must be kept on their own, or with tankmates of other large and robust species. Efficient water filtration is essential and the decor must be uncluttered and free of sharp edges. Large pieces of bogwood (or equivalent) that can provide shelter are recommended, along with subdued lighting. The nighttime activities of this species are best observed using a 'moonlight' fluorescent tube, Water chemistry is not critical, but the quality must be good.

Temperature: 24–30°C (75–86°F).

Breeding: In the wild, eggs are laid on a prepared surface and guarded by the male. Hatching takes about 5–7 days. No documented reports of aquarium spawnings are available.

Notopterus chitala (Clown Knifefish) grows to a large size.

Oryzias latipes
(Japanese Medaka/Ricefish, Golden Medaka, Geisha Girl)

Oryzias latipes (Japanese Medaka) exhibits unusual breeding characteristics.

THE WILD TYPE of the Japanese Medaka (*Oryzias latipes* – family Oryziidae – but also often referred to as Oryziatidae) is only rarely seen in shops these days, its place being taken almost exclusively by the commercially developed golden morph. In fact, the original common name, Japanese Medaka, has now been almost universally replaced by Golden Medaka.

One of the most unusual characteristics of all ricefish species is that females will carry their egg clusters – looking almost like a tiny bunch of grapes – around with them, attached to their anal/genital aperture until they deposit them, usually in clumps, among fine-leaved vegetation. Another unusual feature is that the eggs may be fertilized externally (as in true egglayers) or internally (as in livebearers).

Other species of ricefishes include: *O. celebensis* (Celebes Medaka), *O. javanicus* (Javanese Medaka), *O. melastigma* (Spotted Medaka) and the rarely seen *O. nigrimas* (Black Medaka).

Natural Range: China, Japan and South Korea. Also reported from Java and Malaysia.

Size: Up to 4cm (1.6in).

Food: Most commercial diets and livefoods accepted.

Tank Conditions: This is an active, peaceful shoaling species which prefers the upper reaches of the water column and can be kept in a community aquarium. Although some floating plants can be included in the decor, some clear areas of surface should also be provided. Submerged vegetation should be primarily arranged along the sides and back of the aquarium, with an open swimming space along the front. Good filtration with some water movement is appreciated by Medakas. Water chemistry is not too critical but a pH around neutral and moderately hard water is most suitable.

Temperature: Wide range tolerated, from below 15°C (59°F) to over 28°C (82°F), but neither extreme should be maintained on a permanent basis.

Breeding: The eggs may be fertilized either internally or externally, and are carried for a time by the female attached to her vent, before being deposited among vegetation. Hatching takes about 7–10 days, depending on temperature.

Osteoglossum bicirrhosum
(Silver Arowana)

Osteoglossum bicirrhosum (Silver Arowa) can be an aggressive fish and could grow up to 1m (39in) long.

THE SILVER Arowana (*Osteoglossum bicirrhosum* – family Osteoglossidae) is one of two Amazonian Arowana regularly imported, the other species being the Black Arowana (*O. ferreirai*).

Both are usually offered as juveniles, often with their yolk sacs still present (it takes many weeks for young fish to use up their supply of yolk). These young fish are quite easy to acclimatize successfully and will begin feeding as soon as their in-built food supply is used up.

As they grow, they will become progressively more intolerant of each other and will, eventually, need to be separated (see below).

Captive-bred certificated specimens of the closely related and protected Asian Dragon Fish (*Scleropages formosus*) – also often referred to as the Asian Arowana – are now available from several registered Far East fish farms.

Natural Range: Amazon drainage, western Orinoco, Guyana.

Size: Up to 1m (39in) reported, but most specimens are usually smaller.

Food: 'Substantial' livefoods and meat- or fish-based diets, e.g,. home-made fish paste, fish chunks, etc. Some deep-frozen foods will also be accepted, along with shelled prawns and large insects.

Tank Conditions: Both species of Amazonian Arowana, as well as their *Scleropages* counterparts from the Far East and Australia, are aggressive fish, even when juvenile. It is, nevertheless, possible to keep a group of juveniles together, as long as they are well matched. The tank must be large with plenty of swimming space and few decorations. A gravel bottom can be provided for aquaria housing young fish, but is often omitted from the even larger accommodation required for sub-adults and mature specimens which should be kept singly or with robust, large tankmates. A tight-fitting cover is essential, as is efficient filtration. Soft, slightly or moderately acid water is recommended.

Temperature: 24–30°C (75–86°F).

Breeding: There are only a few reports of aquarium spawnings, but commercial breeding is becoming established. Fertilized eggs and developing young are incubated orally by the male for up to 60 days. Feeding of young must be delayed until the yolk sac has been fully absorbed.

Pantodon buchholzi
(Butterflyfish)

THE BUTTERFLYFISH (*Pantodon buchholzi*) is the only representative in its family, the Pantodontidae. It has been known in the hobby for over 90 years, but has never been available in large numbers, partly because of its requirements (see below), partly because of its distribution – which covers countries from which exports of fish have not been particularly high until relatively recently – and partly owing to the difficulty of breeding the species in commercial quantities.

Despite its placid appearance, the Butterflyfish is a predator with a sizeable mouth. Therefore, caution must be exercised when choosing tankmates to ensure that they are too large to be considered as food items.

There are reports of the species' being able to fly, but they are a little misleading since – when it does happen – no flapping of the pectoral fins occurs, as a result of which the fish glide, rather than fly (see the entry of *Gasteropelecus sternicla* on page 75 for further discussion of 'flying fishes').

Pantodon buchholzi (Butterflyfish).

Natural Range: West Africa, particularly Cameroon, Democratic Republic of Congo and Nigeria.
Size: Up to 10cm (4in).
Food: May accept some pelleted and flaked foods, but is predominantly carnivorous/piscivorous, preferring livefoods and deep-frozen or freeze-dried formulations.
Tank Conditions: Butterflyfish are strict surface dwellers which must be provided with open areas clear of vegetation, although some floating plants can be provided. A tight-fitting aquarium cover is essential to prevent specimens from jumping out. Other surface-living species will generally not be tolerated, but midwater and bottom dwellers are usually ignored. Soft, slightly acid water, preferably tannin-stained, is recommended (use a 'peat sandwich' in a canister filter to achieve this; similar results can be obtained using a commercial 'blackwater' preparation).
Temperature: 23–30°C (73–86°F).
Breeding: Floating transparent eggs are produced over a period of several days. After 8–10 hours, the eggs turn brown or black, and hatch after 36–48 hours.

LIVEBEARERS

ALL THE SPECIES so far dealt with in this book are regarded as egglayers because, as the term implies, they produce eggs. In the vast majority of cases, these eggs are fertilized externally, i.e., both eggs and sperm are ejected into the water where fertilisation occurs. In a few instances, though, fertilization is known to be internal (at least, occasionally), with the fertilized eggs subsequently being released into the water by the females (see page 201 – Killifishes, and page 227 – *Oryzias latipes*).

Where internal fertilization occurs, questions can be raised as to whether such species are true egglayers or not, since internal fertilization is a characteristic of livebearing fishes. Livebearers also differ from egglayers in that instead of producing eggs, females retain these within their bodies until they hatch and the new-born young (fry) can be released.

However, as in egglayers, there are a few exceptions to this generally applicable 'rule'. The most notable of these exceptions is a fish which belongs to the family Poeciliidae (the family to which the most popular aquarium livebearers, such as the Guppy – *Poecilia reticulata* – belong). *Tomeurus gracilis* exhibits internal fertilization, but then releases the eggs into the water, a situation regularly found in so-called egglayers such as the two killifish species *Cynolebias brucei* and *C. melanotaenia*, and occasionally in the Medaka (*Oryzias latipes*).

These, and a few other, exceptions notwithstanding, aquarium livebearers can be split into four main groups:

a) Poeciliids – family Poeciliidae
b) Anablepids – family Anablepidae
c) Goodeids – family Goodeidae
d) Halfbeaks – family Hemirhamphidae

Alfaro cultratus (Knife Livebearer) will do well in a community of non-aggressive species. See page 232.

Poecilia reticulata (Double Sword Guppy). Page 240.

POECILIIDAE

There are several characteristics which distinguish poeciliids from other livebearers. Most easily detectable externally is the modification of the anal (belly) fin in males into a mating organ known as the gonopodium. Some of the anal fin rays are extended and carry specialized structures called hooks, claws and blades, so that when the gonopodium is swung forward during mating, they form a channel along which the packets of sperm (spermatozeugmata) travel and through which they are transferred into the female's body to effect internal fertilization of eggs.

Another distinctive feature of poeciliids is that the females can store these packets of sperm and use them as needed to fertilize a series of egg batches as they ripen. Therefore, following a single mating, poeciliid females can produce a number of broods of fry at regular intervals.

The various genera of poeciliids discussed in the pages that follow all belong to the subfamily Poeciliinae (following Lynne Parenti's 1981 revision): *Alfaro, Gambusia, Limia, Poecilia* and *Xiphophorus*.

ANABLEPIDAE

In the Anablepidae, the fin rays of the gonopodium are twisted around each other to form a tube.

During development, anablepid embryos experience large increases in weight, unlike those of the poeciliids which weigh about the same, or even less, than the eggs from which they develop.

The two genera of anablepids featured here: *Anableps* and *Jenynsia*, belong to the subfamily Anablepinae.

GOODEIDAE

The most easily distinguishable external characteristic of goodeid males is that their anal fin is not modified into a gonopodium, but carries a distinctive notch produced by a bunching together and shortening of the first five to seven rays (the spermatopodium).

Following fertilization of eggs, female goodeids actually ovulate and the embryos complete their development inside the ovarian cavity, which acts as a womb. During development, very large weight increases are experienced by the embryos as a result of deriving nourishment through specialized feeding structures known as trophotaeniae.

Goodeid females cannot store sperm. Therefore, each batch of offspring requires a separate mating.

The genera discussed in this book: *Ameca, Characodon* and *Xenotoca*, all belong to the subfamily Goodeinae.

HEMIRHAMPHIDAE (HALFBEAKS)

In the halfbeaks, the mating organ of males is known as an andropodium. It contains several distinctive features, such as a knee-like structure (the geniculus), two laterally-spread spines (the tridens flexilis), a so-called spiculum (part of the second ray) and a pouch-like skin fold (the physa).

The three genera discussed here: *Dermogenys, Hemirhamphodon* and *Nomorhamphus*, all belong to the subfamily Hemirhamphinae.

Anableps anableps (Four-Eyed Fish) can see above and below the water. See page 246.

POECILIIDS

Alfaro cultratus
(Knife Livebearer)

THE KNIFE Livebearer (*Alfaro cultratus*) is a lively, though often timid, fish, which can do well in a community of non-aggressive species. Alternatively, it can be kept in a shoal, as long as adequate shelter is provided so that non-dominant males can seek refuge if required. Reports of dominant males being excessively aggressive are somewhat exaggerated.

The common name, Knife Livebearer, refers to the keel-like feature created by a series of scales along the lower edge of the body, extending from behind the vent, to the base of the caudal (tail) fin.

Alfaro cultratus and its close relative, *A. huberi* (the Orange Knife Livebearer or Orange Rocket), are the only two members of the genus, which is believed to exhibit a primitive form of gonopodial structure in which the hooks and other adornments (see previous page) are not as intricately developed as in other poeciliids.

Natural Range: Costa Rica, Nicaragua and Panama.
Size: Up to around 9cm (3.5in) for males; females can be slightly larger, but usually both sexes are smaller than these maximum sizes.
Food: Will accept dry formulations and deep-frozen and freeze-dried diets, but swimming livefoods are preferred.
Tank Conditions: *Alfaro cultratus* is a shy, often nervous, species, particularly in sparsely decorated aquaria. Dense thickets of vegetation should therefore be provided, along with some open swimming space. The water should be clear, well-filtered and, preferably, with some movement , e.g., generated by the outflow from a power filter or power head. The aquarium should also have a tight-fitting cover. The water should be around neutral in terms of pH and slightly to moderately hard. A small amount of salt can be added to the water ($1/2$ teaspoonful per 4.5–5 litres/1 Imperial gallon), but this is not essential.
Temperature: 24–28°C (75–82°F), the top end being suitable for breeding.
Breeding: Broods of up to 100 fry can be produced every 4–5 weeks. However, 20–30 fry per brood is more common.

A pair of Alfaro cultratus (Knife Livebearers) – male below.

Gambusia affinis **and** *G. holbrooki*
(Mosquito Fish)

THE MOSQUITO FISH used to be regarded as consisting of two subspecies, *Gambusia affinis affinis* and *G. affinis holbrooki*. Today, we regard them both as valid species in their own right, the Western Mosquito Fish (*G. affinis*) and the Eastern Mosquito Fish (*G. holbrooki*), some males of which can be black-spotted or totally black (melanic).

Together, they are almost certainly the most widely distributed fish in the world, being found in every continent except Antarctica. The reason for this wide human-mediated distribution is the propensity of these fish to consume large numbers of mosquito larvae, a factor that was seen, at one time, as the ultimate biological solution to eradicating the malarial mosquito.

However, not only does malaria still exist today, but wherever Mosquito Fish have been introduced, at least some of the local fish species have suffered.

Natural Range: (i) *Gambusia affinis* – Río Panuco Basin in northern Veracruz, Mexico, northwards to southern Indiana and eastwards to Alabama, including the Mississippi drainage and Texas. (ii) *G. holbrooki* – from central Alabama, eastwards to Florida and northwards along the Atlantic coastal drainage up to New Jersey. Numerous populations have been established throughout tropical and subtropical regions of the world (see main text).

Size: Up to 4cm (1.6in) for males; females up to 7cm (2.8in).

Food: A wide range of commercial foods is accepted, but livefoods are preferred.

Tank Conditions: Mosquito Fish are highly adaptable carnivores which will often attack the fin extensions of other, much larger, fish. They are best kept in a tank of their own planted with thickets of vegetation which offer shelter to adult individuals as and when they require it. Floating plants with feathery roots should also be provided as shelter, both for adults and, particularly, for fry. Water chemistry is not critical.

Temperature: From near-freezing, to over 30°C (86°F), with the mid-20s°C (77°F) being suitable, both for maintenance and breeding.

Breeding: Anything from 10–80 fry can be produced every 5–8 weeks during the breeding season.

Right: Gambusia holbrooki (Eastern Mosquito Fish), melanic form male. Below: A pair of G. affinis (western Mosquito Fish).

Limia melanogaster
(Blue/Black-Bellied Limia)

ALTHOUGH THE scientific name for this species, *Limia melanogaster*, translates as Black-bellied Limia (a reference to the large black abdominal patch exhibited by females), it is virtually universally known as the Blue Limia, an equally appropriate name when applied to well coloured specimens.

This is a very active species in which males are either constantly displaying to each other, or in front of females, or attempting to mate. Open aggression is, however, very rare, making the Blue Limia an excellent fish to keep, as long as suitable water conditions and an appropriate diet are provided.

Males will frequently attempt to mate with females of other species, especially – but not exclusively – other Limias, some of these matings resulting in fertile hybrids, whose physical characteristics appear to be influenced by the mother's own genetic make-up (see *Limia vittata* – page 236 – for fuller details).

Natural Range: Jamaica.

Size: Up to 4.5cm (1.8in) for males; up to 6cm (2.4in) for females.

Food: Wide range of commercial diets and livefoods accepted, but must include a vegetable component.

Tank Conditions: Blue Limias like grazing on encrusting algae. The sides and back of the aquarium should, therefore, not be scraped clean during routine maintenance, but left to develop some algal growth for the fish to feed on. An open swimming space should also be provided along the front, with plants arranged along the sides and back. *L. melanogaster* is an active, peaceful shoaler which should be kept in a group and can be housed with other species in a community aquarium. Although water chemistry is not too critical, alkaline, hardish water is best. The overall quality must also be good and there should be some water movement.

Temperature: 22–28°C (72–82°F).

Breeding: Broods of around 20 young are produced every 5–8 weeks. However, as many as 80 fry have been produced in a single batch and an interval of only 4 weeks between broods has been reported.

In suitable tank conditions, Limia melanogaster (Blue-Bellied Limia) is an excellent fish to keep.

Limia nigrofasciata
(Humpbacked/Black-Barred Limia)

Limia nigrofasciata (Humpbacked Limia) male above, and female left.

THE HUMPBACKED Limia (*Limia nigrofasciata*) is a lovely fish that lives up beautifully to both its common names when kept in appropriate conditions.

The characteristic hump is only exhibited by fully mature males, but both sexes carry the dark vertical body bars (although they are bolder in males) and possess an attractive yellowish base colour and net-like scale pattern. In addition, the ventral area of the body extending from behind the anal (belly) fin to the beginning of the caudal (tail) fin in males carries a series of keel-like scales not unlike those found in the Knife Livebearer (*Alfaro cultratus* – page 232).

Male Humpbacks are not quite as vigorous in their courting/mating activities as their Blue counterparts, but they still seek out females of both their own and other species. Hybridizations are, therefore, not uncommon in aquaria.

Natural Range: Restricted to a brackish pool (Etang Saumatre) and the northern part of Lake Miragoane in Haiti.

Size: Up to 5.5m (2.2in) for males; 6cm (2.4in) for females.

Food: A wide range of commercial diets and livefoods accepted, but must include a vegetable component.

Tank Conditions: This is a peaceful shoaling species which does well in a range of environments, as long as the water is not soft. Ideally, the pH should be between neutral and alkaline and the hardness moderate. Open swimming areas bordered by vegetation along the sides and back should be provided; encrusting algae should be allowed to grow on the sides and back. Although some populations are found in brackish water in Haiti, the addition of a small amount of salt (one teaspoonful per 4.5–5 litres/1 Imperial gallon) is not essential.

Temperature: 24–28°C (75–82°F).

Breeding: Up to 60 young can be produced in each brood at intervals ranging from as little as 4 weeks to as long as 10. Higher temperatures are said to result in more females than males.

Limia vittata
(Cuban Limia)

THE CUBAN Limia (*Limia vittata*) is able to hybridize with, at least, some other Limias. In a number of such crosses which I carried out between it and the Blue Limia (*L. melanogaster* – page 234), the results threw up a few interesting surprises.

In theory, all the hybrids should have been identical, irrespective of which parent was a male or a female. In practice though, the fertile first-generation (F1) hybrids ended up looking more like their mother than their father. The most obvious characteristics revealing this phenomenon were the number of spots and vertical bars. In hybrids where the mother was a *L. vittata*, the average number of spots on the caudal fin was 39, but if the mother was a *L. melanogaster* female, the average was a mere 12.3. Equally, if the mother was a Blue Limia, the hybrids had more body bars (average 7.8) than if the mother was a *L. vittata* female (average 4.9).

These results may indicate that a process known as cytoplasmic inheritance may be exerting an influence, but further studies are needed before any rock-solid conclusions can be derived.

Natural Range: Cuba: mostly in freshwater, but also in brackish and even marine conditions.

Size: Up to 6.5cm (2.6in) for males; up to 12cm (4.7in) reported for females, but usually smaller.

Food: Wide range of commercial diets and livefoods accepted, but must include a vegetable component.

Tank Conditions: The aquarium should be roomy, with swimming areas provided at the front and thick vegetation along the sides and back. As recommended for the two previous species, encrusting algae should be allowed to grow on the side and back panes as a natural source of plant food. The water should be well-filtered, neutral to alkaline and moderately hard. The addition of one teaspoonful of salt per 4.5–5 litres (1 Imperial gallon) may be found beneficial, but is not essential.

Temperature: 24–28°C (75–82°F).

Breeding: As many as 100 fry can be produced by large females every 4–6 weeks.

Limia vittata (Cuban Limia) enjoy a densely planted tank with plenty of algae as a natural food source.

Poecilia latipinna, P. sphenops, P. velifera
(Mollies)

Poecilia sphenops above and Poecilia velifera right are two of quite a few species of wild Molly available.

ALTHOUGH THERE are quite a few species of wild Molly (including one, *Poecilia formosa*, that consists entirely of females), only three can be regarded as aquarium fish. These are *Poecilia sphenops*, which is, basically, a short-finned variety, and the two Sailfin species, *P. latipinna* and *P. velifera*. I am dealing with all three under one main section because numerous crosses between them mean that many of today's aquarium Mollies are of mixed parentage.

The Green/Black or Sphenops Molly (*P. sphenops*) is the most robust of the three aquarium species. Its extensive geographical distribution has led to the evolution of numerous races and this, in turn, has led to about 45 different scientific synonyms for the species. Although a real expert might be able to distinguish and name many of these, the only two which are of any real significance to us as aquarists are the domesticated form and the Liberty Molly.

The Liberty Molly is, fundamentally, very similar to the wild-type in coloration, but has been selected over the years for the beautiful (short) dorsal fin that some of the males possess. It disappeared from circulation some time ago, but I have been very pleased to see it back in recent years, albeit in small numbers.

The domesticated form of the Molly is the one from which all the fancy 'Sphenops-type' varieties have been developed by exploiting the natural tendency of the species towards melanism (black pigmentation) and by selection of other mutations (inherited changes), such as the one that gives rise to the Lyretail and its numerous permutations. As a result, one can find Lyretails and normal short-finned types in a wide range of colours, from black at one extreme, through green, gold, mottled (marbled), orange-tailed, and others, to the pure albino form at the other.

Of the two Sailfin species, *P. velifera* (the Yucatán Molly) is the larger, growing to 18cm (7in) in length. However, most fish never get to this size, so distinguishing between the two species can be quite difficult without close examination.

Above: Hi-fin Black Molly.
Left: Black Molly, short-finned.

For the record, *P. velifera* has a fuller sailfin with 18–19 fin rays (compared with 14 for *P. latipinna*). In addition, the front edge of the dorsal fin originates nearer the head in *P. velifera*. Sailfins are available in a bewildering array of colours, with new ones appearing virtually every year.

As well as the above three species, a fourth type of Molly is sometimes available. It has characteristics of both *P. sphenops* and one or other of the Sailfins. Such fish are hybrids and tend to be larger than *sphenops*, with a dorsal fin which is somewhere between *sphenops* and the true Sailfins. They are fertile and, in some ways, exhibit the best of both worlds, in that they are substantially larger fish than *P. sphenops* and are tougher all-round than either of the Sailfins.

Wild Mollies, unlike the majority of other popular community fish, often come from coastal regions. They therefore inhabit waters that tend to contain a certain amount of salt. I have, for instance, seen Mollies in Florida estuaries in water with a specific gravity reading of 1.015, which is pretty salty. Indeed, it is quite possible to keep Mollies in perfect health under tropical marine conditions, as long as they are acclimatized properly.

In addition, some Molly species, particularly the Sailfins, are never at their best at temperatures lower than around 25°C (77°F). This temperature is near the top end of the range as far as many community tanks are concerned. Consequently, a temperature in the low 20s°C (around 72°F), which is fine for many other fish, is below that required by some Mollies. In time, this is likely to have a debilitating effect on the fish, which can, in turn, lead to all sorts of ailments.

In view of the above, a little extra effort should be put into the keeping of Mollies, which, given the conditions they require, are as hardy as most other aquarium fish, despite their reputation to the contrary.

Natural Range: (i) *P. latipinna*: North and South Carolina, Virginia, Florida, Texas and Atlantic coast of Mexico. (ii) *P. sphenops*: Texas to Mexico and down to Colombia, but also introduced into several exotic locations. (iii) *P. velifera*: Yucatán in Mexico.

Size: (i) *P. latipinna*: Around 10cm (4in) for males; around 12cm (4.7in) for females. (ii) *P. sphenops*: Up to 6cm (2.4in) for males; around 8cm (3.2in) for females. (iii) *P. velifera*: Up to 15cm (6in) for males; up to 18cm (7in) for females.

Food: All Mollies will accept a wide range of commercial diets and livefoods, but should also receive a regular vegetable supplement.

Tank Conditions: Mollies are shoaling fish which should be kept in groups. Males will display constantly and may become aggressive towards each other, especially if kept in twos. It is, therefore, better to keep either one male with several females, or a group of males with the females. This applies more to the Sailfin Mollies than to Sphenops-type varieties. Ample swimming space bordered by plants should be provided, along with good lighting. Close attention needs to be given to water chemistry, since Mollies often fare poorly if kept under 'average' community aquarium conditions. The water should be well filtered, alkaline and slightly to moderately hard with about one teaspoonful of salt added to every 4.5–5 litres (1 Imperial gallon).

Temperature: Sphenops-type varieties will be comfortable between 23-28°C (73-82°F), while for Sailfins the range should be between 25-28°C (77-82°F), or even a little higher.

Breeding: Sphenops Mollies can produce about 80 fry every 5–7 weeks. Sailfin broods are even larger, with more than 100 fry being produced at intervals of 6–10 weeks, depending on temperature and season.

Right: Lyretail Molly.
Below: Sailfin Molly.

Poecilia reticulata
(Guppy, Millions Fish)

THE GUPPY has been known scientifically as *Poecilia reticulata* since 1963 when two ichthyologists, Rosen and Bailey, published a major revision of livebearing fishes. Prior to that, it had been known by a variety of names, the most well-known of them being *Lebistes reticulatus*.

With respect to its common name, the Guppy, this is derived from *Girardinus guppii*, the name given to it by Günther in 1866 in honour of the Reverend Robert John Lechmere Guppy, who is sometimes referred to as the discoverer of this fish in Trinidad. He is, however, more likely to have rediscovered it, since the species was first scientifically described in 1859 by Peters, who based his findings on specimens from Caracas.

After the Mosquito Fish (*Gambusia affinis* and *G. holbrooki* – see page 233), the Guppy (*Poecilia reticulata*) is the most widely distributed of the livebearers. Being so widely distributed and occupying such diverse habitats

as ditches, streams and river tributaries, some of which are brackish, it is hardly surprising to find that wild Guppies are found in a variety of size and colour combinations in nature.

However different these wild varieties may be, they are nevertheless more similar to each other than to any of the varieties of fancy Guppies found in pet shops. All the wild stocks have short unspectacular fins. Yet they possess a kind of 'pure' beauty that makes them strong favourites among experienced livebearer enthusiasts. A particularly beautiful favourite is the type known as Endler's Livebearer.

Breeders and researchers have been exploiting the inherent genetic variability of the Guppy ever since its introduction to the European hobby in 1908, with the result that we now have endless strains that become progressively more elaborate with each passing year.

Poecilia reticulata (Guppy) Metalic Blue Guppy male, above, and male Snakeskin Guppy above right.

Poecilia reticulata (Guppy) male.

One of the centres of such Guppy development and production is Florida, with Sri Lanka also becoming a progressively stronger Guppy-developing country. Despite this, the Far East probably still produces more new Guppy varieties than any other region.

Poecilia reticulata (Guppy) female.

Natural Range: Widely distributed north of the Amazon: Dutch Antilles, Trinidad, Windward Islands, Barbados, Grenada, Antigua, Leeward Islands, St. Thomas, Venezuela and Guyana. In addition to this 'natural' distribution, this species is now found as established populations in numerous exotic locations from Alberta in Canada to Australia and Singapore.

Size: Up to 3cm (1.2in) for males; around 5cm (2in) for females. These sizes refer to wild-caught fish; cultivated varieties are generally larger.

Food: Wide range of small live, deep-frozen, freeze-dried and dry foods accepted, but the diet should include a vegetable component.

Tank Conditions: Guppies are peaceful shoaling fish which should be kept in a group. Males will display constantly, both towards each other and towards females, but no damage to fins results. Since commercial varieties possess enlarged fins, they should not be kept in the same tank as fin-nipping species such as Tiger Barbs (*Barbus tetrazona*). Open swimming space bordered by vegetation along the sides and back should be provided. Water chemistry is not critical, but the quality must be good, despite the undoubted hardiness of these fish. A small amount of salt may be found beneficial, particularly in the case of wild-caught specimens and for those reared in brackish conditions (one teaspoonful per 4.5–5 litres/1 Imperial gallon).

Temperature: 21–25°C (70–77°F) for general maintenance and breeding, although a much wider range is tolerated.

Breeding: As many as 193 fry have been recorded in a single brood, but, generally speaking, 30–40 fry are produced every 4-6 weeks.

Xiphophorus helleri
(Swordtail)

THE SWORDTAIL (*Xiphophorus helleri*) is one of several 'aquarium' species which is hardly ever seen in its original wild form in aquaria. This is a shame, because wild Swordtails, with their slim-lined bodies, short fins, magnificent straight swords and brilliant (and variable) coloration are truly beautiful fish.

The closest we come to the original article these days are the short-finned Green and Black-spotted Green varieties produced by some commercial breeders. In addition to these relatively basic varieties, today's Swordtails are found in innumerable colour and fin configurations.

Two major factors have contributed to this:

a) the species' inherent tendency towards variation (wild populations can range from green to red, with or without body speckling)

b) the ease with which *X. helleri* can hybridize with its closest relatives, in particular (from the hobby point of view) the Southern Platy or Moonfish (*X. maculatus*) and the Variatus or Sunset Platy (*X. variatus*) – see pages 244 and 245.

Given such excellent 'raw materials', it is little wonder that there are so many commercial varieties of Swordtail in existence today. Broadly speaking, these fall into three main groups:

i) short-finned fish which are similar in overall body shape to the wild form, but differ from it in coloration.

ii) high-finned varieties (Hi-fin) of the Simpson type, which have a sail-like dorsal (back) fin, but in which all the other fins are pretty similar to the wild form.

iii) the so-called Hi-fin Lyretail varieties, in which all the fins are highly developed and in which the caudal (tail) fin possesses ray extensions along the top and bottom edges, thus creating the 'lyre' for which these varieties are famous.

When choosing Swordtails, it is important to take into consideration the other fish with which they will share their aquarium. If these include fin-nipping species, such as Tiger Barbs (*Barbus tetrazona*), it would be sensible to avoid the more delicately finned Swordtail varieties.

A further point to bear in mind is that Swordtail males are generally aggressive towards each other. Therefore, choose only one male per tank or, alternatively, at least four to half a dozen. When kept in higher numbers, males are kept so occupied displaying to one another, that the risks of a single individual becoming the sole target of aggression are minimized.

In this species, it is only the males that bear the characteristic sword. In addition, as in all other

Xiphophorus helleri (Swordtail). This brilliantly coloured specimen is a Short-Finned Red male.

Wild type Swordtail.

Hi-fin Swordtail

poeciliids, the anal (belly) fin of the male is modified into the mating organ known as the gonopodium. Females have normal anal fins. The tip of the gonopodium is 'adorned' with tiny structures known as hooks and claws, and it is the precise arrangement of these that make mating possible only between Swordtails, or between them and their very closest relatives.

In the 'true' Lyretail varieties, the gonopodium – just like all the other fins – is much enlarged, making successful mating impossible, particularly since the hook, claw and blade arrangement may be highly reduced or be totally lacking. As a result, these Lyretail males represent an evolutionary dead-end, although they are quite fertile. There are, however, some Lyretails which do not exhibit extended development of the gonopodium and these are capable of mating.

The production of fully finned Lyretails, though, is only possible either by crossing a Lyretail female with a short-finned male, or by artificial insemination with sperm packets (spermatozeugmata) obtained from a Lyretail male. This latter technique is a highly specialized one and must only be carried out by a suitably experienced person.

There are many anecdotal reports of sex reversal in Swordtails, with females apparently becoming sexually viable males over a period of time. Despite these numerous reports, there is no incontrovertible scientific evidence that female-to-male reversal occurs in this species. Such fish are believed to be late-differentiating males.

Natural Range: Atlantic drainage of Central America. This species has become established in numerous locations, including Florida, Nevada, Wyoming, Arizona, California, Canada (Alberta), Hawaii, Puerto Rico, various locations outside the natural range in Mexico, South Africa, Sri Lanka, Australia and other regions.

Size: Up to 14cm (5.5in) for males (excluding sword); females up to 16cm (6.3in), but usually smaller.

Food: All commercial diets and livefoods are accepted.

Tank Conditions: The tank should be provided with a spacious open swimming area bordered by plants, along the sides and back. A tight-fitting cover should be installed (Swordtails are excellent jumpers). Bright illumination and well-filtered water will help show off the brilliant colours to best effect. Swordtails are tolerant of a wide range of water chemistry conditions, but alkaline, slightly hard water is preferred.

Temperature: 20–26°C (68–79°F).

Breeding: As many as 150 fry may be produced by large females every 4–6 weeks, although broods are generally smaller than this.

Xiphophorus maculatus and X. variatus
(Platies)

Xiphophorus variatus (Platy). Platies may often exhibit some characteristics of Swordtails, as they are closely related.

LOOKING AT today's colourful and highly developed Platies, it is often difficult to determine their precise identity. Some look almost as if they are true Southern Platies or Moonfish (*Xiphophorus maculatus*) or Sunset/Variatus Platies (*X. variatus*) in every sense other than coloration, but many look as if they possess characteristics of both species. Many even look as if they have some Swordtail (*X. helleri*) genes in them. One variety goes as far as having a respectable sword!

The reason why such confusion is possible in the first place is that Swordtails (see previous entry) and Platies are very closely related to one another, both belonging to the genus *Xiphophorus*. Because of their 'biological proximity', they can interbreed with the greatest of ease and produce viable hybrids in the process.

Such a state of affairs lends itself perfectly to commercial development, particularly when the original species themselves are highly variable in any case. The inevitable result of all this is that Platies are now available in a mind-boggling array of fin and colour configurations.

However, we must not forget that these coloured, often over-finned, delightful mutants are descended from real species, which can, fortunately, still be found in abundance in the wild.

There are numerous naturally occurring forms of the Southern Platy, some populations of which – such as that from Río Coatzacoalcos – are very beautiful indeed.

X. maculatus can be relatively easily distinguished from *X. variatus*, despite any additions of fancy finnage or colours which may have occurred. *X. maculatus* has a rather stumpy body, while *X. variatus* is more 'Swordtail-shaped' (minus the sword, of course). In addition, *X. variatus* usually carries a series of vertical bars on the sides of the body. Obviously, these characteristics apply only to individuals of pure *maculatus* and *variatus* parentage. Where they have been hybridized, intermediate characteristics occur and distinguishing criteria become blurred.

X. variatus, despite its name, is not as varied a species as *X. maculatus*. Several natural populations do, however, exist, the most attractive probably being that from the Río Axtla, which is closest in appearance to the more 'basic' of the cultivated varieties.

Two other fish which were formerly believed to be subspecies of *X. variatus* (namely *X. variatus xiphidium* and *X. variatus evelynae*) are now considered to be valid species in their own right: *X. xiphidium* and *X. evelynae*, respectively. Naturally occurring hybrids reportedly exist between *X. variatus* and *X. xiphidium* (*X. 'kosszanderi'* from the Río La Marina) and between *X. variatus* and *X. couchianus* (*X. 'roseni'*).

Natural Range: (i) *X. maculatus*: From Veracruz in Mexico to Belize and Guatemala. (ii) *X. variatus*: Atlantic slope of Mexico.

Size: (i) *X. maculatus*: Wild-caught males can be around 3.5cm (1.4in) in length; females, can reach 6cm (2.4in). (ii) *X. variatus*: Wild-caught males, around 5.5cm (2.2in); females around 7cm (2.8in). Cultivated varieties of both species, plus their hybrids, are generally larger.

A striking Red and Black Platy left, and a brightly coloured Sunset Platy below.

Food: Wide range of commercial diets and livefoods accepted, which should include a regular vegetable component.

Tank Conditions: The aquarium should be well lit and contain open swimming areas bordered by thick vegetation. Platies are peaceful community fish which should be kept as a shoal. Water chemistry is not too critical, but good quality neutral to slightly alkaline, slightly hard water is preferred.

Temperature: 18–25°C (65–77°F) recommended for *X. maculatus*; 16–27°C (61–81°F) reported for *X. variatus*. Both can be kept and bred at temperatures that fall within the *X. maculatus* range.

Breeding: Average broods of 50–60 fry are produced every 4–6 weeks, but larger broods have been reported for both species.

ANABLEPIDS

Anableps anableps
(Four-Eyed Fish, Four Eyes)

Anableps anableps (Four-Eyed Fish) only has two eyes, but is able to see above and below the water at the same time.

DESPITE ITS name, the Four-eyed Fish (*Anableps anableps*) has just two eyes. However, each eye is divided horizontally (and externally) by two elongated flaps of pigmented iris tissue which meet, but do not fuse, in front of the pupil, thus effectively splitting each eye into an upper and a lower half.

Internally, the eye lens is not round (as in other fish) but elongated, with rounded ends. It is aligned in such a way that one of the flatter surfaces is angled permanently upwards, i.e., into the air, and one of the rounded ends is directed permanently downwards, i.e., into the water.

This arrangement, allied to a split retina which can receive light rays from the air and water quite separately, allows Four-eyed Fish to see above and below the water surface simultaneously.

Natural Range: Freshwater and brackish habitats from southern Mexico to northern South America.

Size: Around 15cm (6in) for males; females up to double this size, but usually smaller.

Food: Will accept some floating deep-frozen, freeze-dried and dry commercial formulations, but floating livefoods are preferred.

Tank Conditions: Ideally, the tank should be long and only about half to three-quarters full to allow the fish to exhibit their characteristic behaviour of swimming just under the surface with only the top half of their eyes showing above water. On account of their brackish water requirements, the selection of plants that can be used is restricted to salt-tolerant species such as Java Fern (*Microsorum pteropus*), *Sagittaria* spp., some *Vallisneria* species and Amazon Swords, e.g., the Pygmy Chain Sword (*Echinodorus tenellus*). Driftwood, bogwood (or equivalent) can also be used as aquarium decor. The water should be alkaline and moderately hard with about one teaspoonful of salt per 4.5–5 litres (1 Imperial gallon).

Temperature: 22–30°C (72–86°F), but slightly lower and higher temperatures are also tolerated.

Breeding: Small broods (as few as six) of very large (3–4cm/1.2–1.6in) fry produced about twice a year.

Jenynsia lineata
(One-Sided Livebearer)

THE ONE-SIDED Livebearer (*Jenynsia lineata*) is so-named because the genital organs are deflected to one side in both sexes, making them either right-handed or left-handed.

Mating is only possible between fish of opposite 'indications', i.e., right-handed males can only mate with left-handed females and vice-versa. The same applies to the Four-eyed Fish (*Anableps anableps*) – see previous entry.

The fry of both anablepids are very large at birth, but are nourished in very different ways. In *Jenynsia*, the females ovulate and the embryos are then fed via special structures known as trophonemata. In *Anableps*, the females do not ovulate but retain the developing eggs within special 'sacs' – called follicles – within the ovary. Nevertheless, the developing embryos also receive nourishment and grow significantly during gestation.

Natural Range: Found south of the Amazon, from southern Brazil, through Uruguay, to the Río de la Plata in Argentina.

Size: Around 4cm (1.6in) for males; up to 12cm (4.7in) reported for females, but usually smaller.

Food: Will accept a wide range of commercial diets and livefoods; a regular vegetable component should be included.

Tank Conditions: *Jenynsia lineata* can be timid if kept in the company of boisterous tankmates. It does best either as a shoal in a species tank, or when kept with other peaceful fish. The tank should be heavily planted to make the fish feel secure. An open area can be left along the front, but this should not be over-large or exposed. The water should be alkaline and moderately hard with some salt added (about one teaspoonful per 4.5–5 litres/1 Imperial gallon), although this is not essential.

Temperature: 18–25°C (64–77°F) is recommended, but temperatures as low as 12°C (54°F) have been reported, while I have collected this species in Rio de Janeiro (Lago Rodrigo de Freitas) at a temperature of 34.4°C (94°F)!

Breeding: About 20 large fry are produced every 5–7 weeks.

Jenysia lineata (One-sided Livebearer) has to be careful in its choice of mate to ensure compatibility.

GOODEIDS

Ameca splendens
(Ameca, Butterfly Goodeid)

THE AMECA (*Ameca splendens*), more than any other single species, was responsible for bringing goodeids to the attention of aquarists during the early 1970s. Within a short time, interest in the family became widespread and, by the early 1980s, a high percentage of the 35-40 known species were being kept (and, often, bred) by members of specialist societies on both sides of the Atlantic.

Interest in goodeids among livebearer enthusiasts remains high today, yet surprisingly few species are available through general aquatic outlets on a regular basis. *Ameca splendens* is one such species and still rates as, perhaps, the top goodeid in terms of numbers sold, kept and bred. This is a hardy, lively fish which, in my view, deserves a place in every aquarist's tanks at one time or other.

Natural Range: Río Ameca and Río Teuchitlán in the Río Ameca basin in Jalisco, Mexico.

Size: Up to 8cm (3.2in) for males; females reported up to 12cm (4.7in), but usually smaller.

Food: All commercial diets and livefoods accepted; a vegetable component must be included.

Tank Conditions: This is a lively species which can be kept in a group. It is generally tolerant of other species, but some specimens can become fin nippers and are best kept away from fancy-finned species or varieties. The tank should have an open swimming area and thickets of plants. A cover of surface vegetation is also recommended as shelter for new-born fry. Good illumination and filtration should also be provided. Water chemistry is not too critical, but alkaline, medium-hard conditions help to bring out the best coloration, particularly in males.

Temperature: 20–29°C (70–84°F), with something in the region of 22–25°C (72–77°F) being advisable for general maintenance.

Breeding: Broods of over 40 very large fry can be produced ever 8 weeks or so during the breeding season. However, average broods are generally smaller than this.

Ameca splendens (Butterfly Goodeid) is a hardy, lively fish which every aquarist will enjoy keeping at some time.

Characodon lateralis
(Rainbow Goodeid)

The colourful Characodon lateralis (Rainbow Goodeid) is a shy fish which will seek shelter at the back of the tank.

THE RAINBOW Goodeid (*Characodon lateralis*) is one of the most colourful species in the family. When in good condition and kept in stress-free surroundings, males adopt a splendid reddish overall coloration, spangled with blue-green reflective scales and a yellow/golden throat, chest and abdominal area. There is also a longitudinal line of black spots extending from the tip of the snout to the caudal peduncle and all the fins have, at least, some red and yellow in them, plus a blackish edge.

Were these characteristics to be present in a lively, midwater, prolific, shoaling species, its popularity would be sky-high. However, because *C. lateralis* is a retiring fish that tends to seek the security of vegetation along the back of the aquarium and is a slow breeder, its availability is, unfortunately, restricted.

An equally attractive, but predominantly black, species, *Characodon audax* – most appropriately referred to as the Black Prince – is also sometimes available in limited quantities. Both species hybridize with one another and should therefore be kept apart at all times.

Natural Range: Widespread in the upper Río Mezquital in Durango, Mexico, although it is not abundant at any single locality.

Size: Around 4cm (1.6in) for males; around 5.5cm (2.2in) for females.

Food: Will accept freeze-dried, deep-frozen and dried foods, but prefers a livefood diet and should receive a regular vegetable supplement.

Tank Conditions: This is a shy, retiring species which should be kept as a shoal in its own aquarium. Alternatively, it may be kept with other quiet species. Heavy plant cover should be provided, along with relatively subdued lighting, best achieved by means of a thick layer of surface vegetation. Regular partial water changes are important, but not vigorous power filtration. The water should be slightly to moderately alkaline and medium-hard.

Temperature: 20–24°C (68–75°F).

Breeding: Small broods, usually numbering fewer than 20 fry, are produced at intervals of 8 weeks or so.

Xenotoca eiseni
(Orange-/Red-Tailed Goodeid)

Xenotoca eiseni (Red-tailed Goodeid) retains its wild colour characteristics well in captivity.

THE ORANGE-TAILED Goodeid (*Xenotoca eiseni*) occurs in several strikingly coloured forms in the wild, all based on an overall blue-orange/red theme, although one wild population also has golden scales on the anterior half of the body. These colours are retained well in aquaria, as today's commercial stocks – which are practically all captive-bred – testify.

As males grow older, they develop a thick-set body with a pronounced 'neck' hump which sometimes makes the head look a little small for the body (as in *Glossolepis* rainbows – see page 189). They also tend to become somewhat more intolerant and more prone to indulge in fin-nipping.

There are two other species in the genus, *X. melanosoma* and *X. variata* (the Jewelled Goodeid). The former is less colourful than *X. eiseni*, while the latter has a shallower body and looks a little like *Ameca splendens* (see page 248).

Natural Range: Nayarit: El Sacristán and Ríos Grande de Santiago and Leonel; Jalisco: Río Tamazula. All locations are in Mexico.

Size: Around 6cm (2.4in) for males; around 7cm (2.8in) for females. Larger sizes are sometimes reported.

Food: Wide range of commercial formulations and livefoods accepted; diet must include a vegetable component.

Tank Conditions: *X. eiseni* is an active species that needs to be provided with open swimming areas bordered by thick vegetation. This species exhibits fin-nipping tendencies, particularly with increasing age and is best kept away from tankmates with elongated fins. It does best in a roomy, well-lit species aquarium in which there are numerous shelters. The water should be well filtered and slightly agitated. Although a range of conditions are accepted, alkaline, moderately hard water is recommended.

Temperature: From as low as 15°C (59°F), to around 33°C (91°F) reported from the wild. Something around 25°C (77°F) is perfectly adequate, both for general maintenance and breeding.

Breeding: Although nearly 90 fry have been reported, a brood size of 30 or so is more common. The interval between broods can vary from around 7 to 9 weeks, depending on environmental conditions.

HALFBEAKS

Dermogenys pusillus
(Wrestling/Malayan Halfbeak)

THE WRESTLING Halfbeak (*Dermogenys pusillus*) is a slim-bodied predator, males of which are aggressive towards each other, to the point that they will fight for long periods (sometimes as long as 20 minutes). Although usually (but not invariably) no serious injuries are inflicted during these contests, it is not advisable to keep more than one male per tank.

When first born, the fry (which can measure as much as 1cm/0.4in in length) have almost equal-sized upper and lower jaws. However, the lower one will extend over a period of several weeks, eventually giving rise to the typical halfbeak shape.

Being such a widely distributed species, wild populations of Wrestling Halfbeaks exhibit considerable variation in coloration, some of which are regarded as subspecies by a number of ichthyologists. A commercially produced golden variety is also occasionally available.

Natural Range: Widespread in freshwater and brackish habitats in southeast Asia.

Size: Up to 6cm (2.4in) for males; females are larger, at around 8cm (3.2in).

Food: Although floating flaked food may be taken, the diet should consist predominantly of floating freeze-dried foods or livefoods.

Tank Conditions: This species tends to stick to the upper reaches of the water column, patrolling just under the surface for suitable floating prey items. Therefore, the tank should cater for this by having large areas of surface free of vegetation. The central area should also be clear, with vegetation distributed along the sides and back. Halfbeaks can be somewhat nervous and, if frightened by quick movements or loud vibrations, can easily damage the extended lower jaw against the sides of the aquarium. Alternatively, they may attempt to jump out of the aquarium; a tight-fitting cover is therefore essential. The water should be about neutral and slightly hard, with about one teaspoonful of salt to every 4.5–5 litres (1 Imperial gallon).

Temperature: 18–30°C (64–86°F).

Breeding: Broods of up to 40 relatively large fry – but usually 10-30 – can be produced every 4 to 8 weeks or so, depending on environmental conditions.

Dermogenys pusillus (Malayan Halfbeak).

Hemirhamphodon pogonognathus
(Long-Snouted/Nosed Halfbeak)

Hemirhamphodon pogonognathus (Long-Nosed Halfbeak) is very beautiful when viewed under good lighting.

THE LONG-NOSED Halfbeak (*Hemirhamphodon pogonognathus*) is a slender-bodied species which lacks spectacular coloration, but is, nevertheless, very beautiful when viewed under good lighting in water that meets its requirements.

In common with other members of its genus – and in contrast to *Dermogenys* halfbeaks – the teeth on the long, lower jaw (which is responsible for the common names) are clearly visible to the naked eye and constitute an unmistakable clue to the species' predatory habits.

Hemirhamphodon can also be distinguished by the structure of the males' anal fin (the andropodium) which possesses an extremely long leading edge and a strongly truncated rear one.

In addition to *H. pogonognathus*, there are two other species in the genus. Both are available from time to time, but not as frequently. *H. chrysopunctatus* (the Gold-spotted Halfbeak) is reported as growing up to 15cm (6in), but is generally only about 8.5cm (3.3in), while *H. phaiosoma* grows only to around 7.5cm (3in).

Natural Range: Found in a variety of flowing habitats in Malaysia, Singapore, Sumatra, the island of Borneo (including Kalimantan) and on the islands of Bangka, Belitung (Billiton) and Halmahera (Moluccas) in Indonesia.

Size: Up to 8cm (3.2in).

Food: May accept floating dried foods, but floating freeze-dried and deep-frozen foods, plus surface-swimming livefoods, are preferred.

Tank Conditions: The tank should provide open swimming surface space, along with a plant-free central area bordered by vegetation. Some floating plants may be included, but these must be prevented from taking over the whole of the surface (the same applies to aquaria housing any of the other halfbeak species). The water should be neutral to slightly alkaline and soft to slightly hard.

Temperature: 22–28°C (72–82°F)

Breeding: This is not an easy species to breed, with the large young being produced at the rate of a few a day over a period of up to 2 weeks, following a gestation lasting around 7–8 weeks.

Nomorhamphus liemi
(Celebes Halfbeak)

THE CELEBES Halfbeak (*Nomorhamphus liemi*), while originating in Sulawesi (formerly Celebes), is probably inaccurately named, since there is another species that is also found in Sulawesi and is scientifically known as *N. celebensis*.

Within the species *N. liemi*, two different morphs are known, despite its somewhat restricted distribution: the males of one type have predominantly red fins edged in black, while, in the other, the fins are predominantly black. Fully mature males of both kinds have a pronounced black, fleshy, downward-pointing hook on the lower jaw.

The red-/black-finned variety is often regarded as belonging to the subspecies, *N. liemi liemi*, and the darker type as *N. liemi snijdersi*; both are equally impressive and well worth keeping and breeding.

Natural Range: Found in the highlands of Maros in southern Sulawesi, Indonesia.

Size: Around 6cm (2.4in) for males; females are considerably larger, up to 10cm (4in) being reported. Some reports, however, state that both sexes measure about 8.5cm (3.3in).

Food: Although some floating dry formulations may be accepted, this species prefers freeze-dried, deep-frozen foods and, particularly, livefoods.

Tank Conditions: *Nomorhamphus* halfbeaks are, like the other members of the family, ideally suited for life just under the water surface. Allowances must, therefore, be made for this requirement by keeping a substantial area of the aquarium surface clear of vegetation. There should also be a clear open area along the front, with submerged plants being arranged along the sides and back. Some thickets should be provided as shelter for fry, which (as in other halfbeaks) run the very real danger of being eaten by their parents. The water should be well filtered and well oxygenated, ranging from slightly acid to sightly alkaline and soft to medium-hard . Coming from mountain regions, no salt is required for this species.

Temperature: 22–26°C (72–79°F), the lower end being preferred.

Breeding: Up to ten large fry can be produced over several weeks, following a gestation of between 4 and 8 or 9 weeks.

Nomorhamphus liemi (Celebes Halfbeak).

Index

Acanthophthalmus (Pangio) myersi 181
Acanthopsis choirorhynchus 182
Acara
　Blue 122
　Brown *see* Acara, Port
　Golden Dwarf 142
　Port 127
Aequidens pulcher 122
Alfaro cultratus 232
Algae Eater, Chinese
　see Loach, Sucking
Ameca 248
Ameca splendens 248
American Flagfish 208
Anableps anableps 246
Ancistrus hoplogenys 99
Angelfish 148
Anostomus, Striped 70
Anostomus anostomus 70
Aphyocharax anisiti 71
Aphyosemion
　Steel-Blue 203
　Gardner's *see* Aphyosemion, Steel-Blue
Aphyosemion
　australe 202
　gardneri 203
Apistogramma agassizii 123
Aplocheilichthys macrophthalmus 204
Aplocheilus annulatus 205
Archer Fish 219
Archocentrus nigrofasciatus 124
Argentine Pearl 206
　Black-Finned 207
　Dwarf *see* Argentine Pearl, Black-Finned
Argus Fish *see* Scat
Arowana, Silver 228
Astronotus ocellatus 125
Astyanax fasciatus 72
Aulonocara nyassae 126
Auratus
　see Cichlid, Malawi Golden

Badis *see* Chameleon Fish
Badis badis 224
Balantiocheilos (Balantiocheilus) melanopterus 49
Barb
　Black-spot 52
　Checker 55
　Cherry 59
　Cuming's 51
　Filament *see* Barb, Black-spot
　Golden *see* Barb, Green
　Green 57
　Half-striped *see* Barb, Green
　Island *see* Barb, Checker
　Odessa 54
　Purple-headed *see* Barb, Ruby
　Rosy 50

　Ruby 53
　Schubert's *see* Barb, Green
　Tiger 58
　Tinfoil 56
Barbatus *see* Corydoras, Bearded
Barbus
　conchonius 50
　cumingi 51
　filamentosus 52
　nigrofasciatus 53
　'odessa' 54
　oligolepis 55
　schwanenfeldi 56
　semifasciolatus 57
　tetrazona 58
　titteya 59
Batfish, Silver *see* Mono
Bedotia geayi 188
Belontia signata 157
Betta
　Crescent 158
　Emerald 159
　Peaceful *see* Betta, Crescent
　One-spot 161
Betta
　imbellis 158
　smaragdina 159
　splendens 160
　unimaculata 161
Black Widow *see* Tetra, Black
Blind Cave Fish *see* Characin, Blind Cave Fish
Blockhead, African 151
Bloodfin 71
Blue-eye
　Australian 193
　Pacific *see* Blue-eye, Australian
Botia
　macracantha 183
　sidthimunki 184
Brachydanio
　albolineatus 60
　rerio 61
Brachygobius xanthozona 196
Bream, Butter *see* Mono
Brichardi
　see Lamprologus, Fairy
Brochis
　Common *see* Catfish, Emerald
　Emerald *see* Catfish, Emerald
　Giant 100
Brochis
　britskii 100
　splendens 101
Bunocephalus coracoideus 102
Bushfish, Spotted
　see Ctenopoma, Leopard
Butterflyfish 229

Catfish
　Angel 119
　Banjo 102
　Bronze *see* Corydoras, Bronze

　Emerald 101
　Flag-Tailed 109
　Frying Pan *see* Catfish, Banjo
　Ghost *see* Catfish, Glass
　Glass 113
　Midget Sucker
　　see Otocinclus, Dwarf
　Sailfin Suckermouth
　　see Pleco, Spotted
　Short-bodied
　　see Catfish, Emerald
　Spotted Bristle-nosed 99
　Stick *see* Catfish, Twig
　Stripe-Tailed
　　see Catfish, Flag-Tailed
　Sturgeon *see* Whiptail, Royal
　Twig 110
　Upside-down 120
　Whip-tailed 117
Chameleon Fish 224
Chanda ranga 217
Characin, Blind Cave Fish 72
Characodon lateralis 249
Chromide, Orange 132
Cichlasoma portalegrensis 127
'Cichlasoma' - Red Parrot 128
Cichlid
　African Peacock 126
　Agassiz's Dwarf 123
　Banded *see* Cichlid, Severum
　Butterfly *see* Cichlid, Ram
　Checkerboard 131
　Cheeseboard *see* Cichlid, Convict
　Convict 124
　Eye-spot
　　see Cichlid, Severum
　Festive 140
　Flag 138
　Golden-eyed Dwarf
　　see Acara, Golden Dwarf
　Jewel 134
　Keyhole 129
　Lemon 144
　Lyretail Checkerboard
　　see Cichlid, Checkerboard
　Malawi Golden 139
　Nyassa Blue *see* Cichlid, Zebra
　Parrot 128
　Peacock-Eye *see* Oscar
　Pearl 133
　Purple *see* Krib
　Ram 141
　Ramirez's Dwarf
　　see Cichlid, Ram
　Red-Finned *see* Cichlid, Trewavas'
　Red Parrot
　　see Cichlid, Parrot
　Severum 135
　Trewavas' 137
　Triangle *see* Uaru
　Velvet *see* Oscar
　Zebra 147

　also *see* Cichlid, Convict
Cleithracara maronii 129
Colisa
　fasciata 162
　labiosa 163
　lalia 164
　sota 165
Combtail 157
Copella arnoldi 73
Corydoras
　Bandit 107
　Bearded 104
　Bronze 103
　Dainty 105
　Dwarf *see* Corydoras, Dainty
　Leopard 106
　Masked *see* Corydoras, Bandit
　Peppered 108
　Sailfin *see* Catfish, Emerald
Corydoras
　aeneus 103
　barbatus 104
　habrosus 105
　hastatus 105
　julii 106
　metae 107
　paleatus 108
Ctenopoma
　Leopard 166
　Spotted *see* Leopard
Ctenopoma acutirostre 166
Cynolebias
　bellotti 206
　nigripinnis 207
Cyrtocara moorii 130

Danio
　Pearl 60
　Zebra 61
Demon Fish *see* Devil Fish
Dermogenys pusillus 251
Devil Fish 150
Dianema urostriata 109
Dicrossus filamentosus 131
Discus 152
Distichodus, Long-nosed 74
Distichodus lusosso 74
Dojo *see* Loach, Japanese Weather
Dolphin, Malawi Blue 130
Dormitator maculatus 197

Earth Eater *see* Devil Fish
Eel
　Asian Fire *see* Eel, Fire
　Fire 215
　Lesser Spiny 214
　Spotted Fire *see* Eel, Fire
Elephantnose 225
　Elephantnose, Peter's
　　see Elephantnose
Epalzeorhynchus
　bicolor 62
　kallopterus 63

Erpetoichthys calabaricus 213
Etroplus maculatus 132

Farlowella, Royal
   see Whiptail, Royal
Farlowella acus 110
Festivum *see* Cichlid, Festive
Fighter
   Emerald *see* Betta, Emerald
   One-spot *see* Betta, One-spot
   Siamese 160
   Smaragd *see* Betta, Emerald
Finger Fish *see* Mono
Firemouth 154
Four-Eyed Fish 246
Four Eyes *see* Four Eyed Fish
Fox, Flying 63

Gambusia
   affinis 233
   holbrooki 233
Gasteropelecus sternicla 75
Geisha Girl *see* Medaka, Japanese
Geophagus brasiliensis 133
Ghostfish *see* Catfish, Glass
Glassfish, Indian 217
Glossolepis incisus 189
Glyptoperichthys gibbiceps 111
Gnathonemus petersii 225
Goby
   Bumblebee 196
   Empire 198
   Fat Sleeper *see* Goby, Striped
   Knight 199
   Peacock 200
   Spotted *see* Goby, Striped
   Striped 197
Goodeid
   Butterfly *see* Ameca
   Orange-Tailed 250
   Rainbow 249
   Red-Tailed *see* Goodeid,
     Orange-Tailed
Goramy *see* Gourami, Giant
Gourami
   Amethyst
     see Gourami, Two-spot
   Banded *see* Gourami, Indian
   Blue *see* Gourami, Two-spot
   Brown *see* Gourami, Two-spot
   Chocolate 174
   Common *see* Gourami, Giant
   Croaking 179
   Dwarf 164
   Giant 170
     also *see* Gourami, Indian
   Gold *see* Gourami, Two-spot
   Honey 165
   Honey Dwarf
     see Gourami, Honey
   Indian 162
   Kissing 167
   Lace *see* Gourami, Pearl
   Lavender
     see Gourami, Two-spot
   Leeri *see* Gourami, Pearl
   Licorice
     see Gourami, Licquorice

Liquorice 171
Moonbeam
   see Gourami, Moonlight
Moonlight 176
Mosaic *see* Gourami, Pearl
Opal (Platinum)
   see Gourami, Two-spot
Opaline (Cosby)
   see Gourami, Two-spot
Pearl 175
Snakeskin 177
Splendid Dwarf
   see Gourami, Licquorice
Spotted Pointed Tail
   see Paradise Fish, Ornate
Striped *see* Gourami, Indian
Thick-lipped 163
Thin-lipped
   see Gourami, Moonlight
Two-spot 178
Three-spot
   see Gourami, Two-spot
Gudgeon
   Carp *see* Goby, Empire
   Empire *see* Goby, Empire
   Peacock *see* Goby, Peacock
Guppy 240
Gymnocorymbus ternetzi 76
Gyrinocheilus aymonieri 185

Hairfin *see* Gourami, Two-spot
Halfbeak
   Celebes 253
   Long-Nosed *see* Halfbeak,
     Long-Snouted
   Long-Snouted 252
   Malayan
     see Halfbeak, Wrestling
   Wrestling 251
Hasemania nana 77
Hatchetfish, Common 75
Headstander
   see Anostomus, Striped
Helostoma temmincki 167
Hemichromis bimaculatus 134
Hemigrammus
   caudovittatus 78
   erythrozonus 79
   rhodostomus 80
Hemiodopsis gracilis 81
Hemiodus, Slender 81
Hemirhamphodon pogonognathus
   252
Heros severus 135
Hoplo, Spotted 112
Hyphessobrycon
   bentosi 82
   erythrostigma 83
   herbertaxelrodi 84
   pulchripinnis 85
Hypseleotris compressa 198

Iriatherina werneri 190

Jenynsia lineata 247
Jordanella floridae 208
Julidochromis regani 136
Julie

Regan's *see* Julie, Striped
   Striped 136
Jurupari *see* Devil Fish

Killifish, Clown 205
Knifefish, Clown 226
Krib 145
Kribensis *see* Krib
Kryptopterus bicirrhis 113

Labeotropheus trewavasae 137
Laetacara curviceps 138
Lamp-eye
   Big-eye
     see Panchax, Lamp-eye
   Iridescent
     see Panchax, Lamp-eye
Lamprologus *see* Cichlid, Lemon
   Fairy 143
   Lyretail *see* Fairy
Lepthoplosternum pectorale 112
Limia
   Black-barred *see* Limia,
     Humpbacked
   Black-Bellied *see* Limia, Blue
   Blue 234
   Cuban 236
   Humpbacked 235
Limia
   melanogaster 234
   nigrofasciata 235
   vittata 236
Livebearer
   Knife 232
   One-Sided 247
Loach
   Chain 184
   Chinese Weather *see* Loach,
     Japanese Weather
   Clown 183
   Dwarf *see* Loach, Chain
   Horse-faced 182
   Japanese Weather 186
   Kuhli 181
   Long-nosed *see* Horse-faced
   Myers' *see* Loach, Kuhli
   Slimy *see* Loach, Kuhli
   Sucking 185
Loricaria, Whip-tailed
   see Catfish, Whip-tailed
Lumphead
   African *see* Blockhead, African
   Blue
     see Dolphin, Malawi Blue
Lyretail *see* Lyretail, Cape Lopez
   Cape Lopez 202

Macrognathus aculeatus 214
Macropodus opercularis 168
Malpulutta
   see Paradise Fish, Ornate
Malpulutta kretseri 169
Medaka
   Golden *see* Medaka, Japanese
   Japanese 227
Megalamphodus megalopterus 86
Melanochromis auratus 139
Melanotaenia

boesemani 191
   maccullochi 192
Mesonauta festiva 140
Metynnis, Plain *see* Silver Dollar
Metynnis hypsauchen 87
Micralestes interruptus 88
Microgeophagus ramirezi 141
Millions Fish *see* Guppy
Minnow, White Cloud
   Mountain 68
Misgurnus anguillicaudatus 186
Moehkhausia, Yellow-banded
   see Tetra, Red-eyed
Moenkhausia
   pittieri 89
   sanctaefilomenae 90
Mollies 237-8
Mono 221
Monodactylus argenteus 221
Moon Fish *see* Mono
Moorii *see* Dolphin, Malawi Blue
Mosquito Fish 233
Mouthbrooder
   Egyptian 146
   Nile *see* Egyptian

Nannacara anomala 142
Nannostomus beckfordi 91
Nematobrycon palmeri 92
Neolamprologus
   brichardi 143
   leleupi 144
Neon, Black 84
Nomorhamphus liemi 253
Nothobranch
   Günther's 209
   Rachow's 210
Nothobranchius
   guentheri 209
   rachovi 210
Notopterus chitala 226

Oryzias latipes 227
Oscar 125
Osphronemus goramy 170
Osteoglossum bicirrhosum 228
Otocinclus
   Dwarf 114
   Golden *see* Otocinclus, Dwarf
Otocinclus affinis 114

Pachypanchax playfairi 211
Pacu *see* Silver Dollar
Panaque
   Pin-striped *see* Panaque, Royal
   Royal 115
Panaque nigrolineatus 115
Panchax
   Comet *see* Killifish, Clown
   Lamp-Eye 204
Lyretailed
   see Lyretail, Cape Lopez
   Playfair's 211
   Rocket *see* Killifish, Clown
Pantodon buchholzi 229
Paracheirodon
   axelrodi 93
   innesi 93

Paradise Fish 168
  Brown Spike-tailed
    see Paradise Fish, Day's
  Ceylonese *see* Combtail
  Day's 173
  Ornate 169
  Spike-tailed 172
Parasphromenus deissneri 171
Pelvicachromis pulcher 145
Pencilfish, Golden 91
Penguin Fish 97
Perch, Climbing
  see Ctenopoma, Leopard
Pim, Angelicus 116
Pimelodella, Angelicus
  see Pim, Angelicus
Pimelodus pictus 116
Piranha
  Natterer's *see* Piranha, Red
  Red 96
  Red-bellied *see* Piranha, Red
Platies 244-5
Pleco
  Emperor *see* Panaque, Royal
  Spotted 111
Poecilia
  latipinna 237
  reticulata 240
  sphenops 237
  velifera 237
Pompadour *see* Discus
Pristella maxillaris 94
Pseudocrenilabrus multicolor 146
Pseudomugil signifer 193
Pseudosphromenus
  cupanus 172
  dayi 173
Pseudotropheus zebra 147
Pterophyllum scalare 148
Puffer, Green 218
Pyrrhulina
  Banded
    see Pyrrhulina, Striped
  Striped 95

Pyrrhulina vittata 95
Rainbowfish
  Australian *see* Rainbowfish,
    McCulloch's
  Black-Lined *see* Rainbowfish,
    McCullochís
  Boeseman's 191
  Celebes 194
  Dwarf *see* Rainbowfish,
    McCulloch's
  McCulloch's 192
  Madagascan 188
  Red 189
  Threadfin 190
Rasbora
  Big-spot
    see Rasbora, Two-spot
  Clown *see* Rasbora, Two-spot
  Harlequin 64
  Glowlight 66
  Red-line
    see Rasbora, Glowlight
  Red-striped
    see Rasbora, Glowlight
  Scissortail 67
  Three-lined
    see Rasbora, Scissortail
  Three-spot
    see Rasbora, Two-spot
  Two-spot 65
Rasbora
  heteromorpha 64
  kalochroma 65
  pauciperforata 66
  trilineata 67
Ricefish, Japanese
  see Medaka, Japanese
Rineloricaria fallax 117

Sailfish, Celebes
  see Rainbowfish, Celebes
Satanoperca jurupari 150
Scalare *see* Angelfish
Scat 222

Silver/Striped 223
Scatophagus
  argus 222
Selenotoca multifasciata 223
Serrasalmus (Pygocentrus)
  nattereri 96
Shark
  Bala Tri-colour 49
  Malaysian
    see Shark, Bala Tri-colour
  Red-tailed Black 62
  Silver *see* Shark, Bala
    Tri-colour
Silver Dollar 87
Snakefish
  Reed 213
  Rope *see* Snakefish, Reed
Sphaerichthys osphromenoides 174
Steatocranus casuarius 151
Stigmatogobius sadanundio 199
Sturisoma panamense 118
Swordtail 242-3
Symphysodon 152
Synodontis
  Angel *see* Catfish, Angel
  Polka Dot *see* Catfish, Angel
  Upside-down *see* Catfish,
    Upside-down
Synodontis
  angelicus 119
  nigriventris 120

Tanichthys albonubes 68
Tateurndina ocellicauda 200
Telmatherina ladigesi 194
Tetra
  Bentos 82
  Black 76
  Black Phantom 86
  Bleeding Heart 83
  Blind Cave Fish *see* Characin,
    Blind Cave Fish
  Buenos Aires 78
  Cardinal 93

Congo 88
  Copper *see* Tetra, Silver-tipped
  Diamond 89
  Emperor 92
  Glowlight 79
  Jumping *see* Tetra, Splashing
  Lemon 85
  Neon 93
  Red *see* Tetra, Black
  Red-eyed 90
  Rosy *see* Tetra, Bentos
  Rummy-nosed 80
  Silver-tipped 77
  Splashing 73
  Spraying *see* Tetra, Splashing
  White *see* Tetra, Black
  X-ray 94
Tetraodon fluviatilis 218
Thayeria obliqua 97
Thorichthys meeki 154
Toxotes jaculator 219
Trichogaster
  leeri 175
  microlepis 176
  pectoralis 177
  trichopterus 178
Trichopsis vittatus 179

Uaru 155
Uaru amphiacanthoides 155

Waroo *see* Uaru
Water Goldfinch *see* Tetra, X-ray
Whiptail
  Hi-fin *see* Whiptail, Royal
  Royal 118

Xenotoca eiseni 250
Xiphophorus
  helleri 242-3
  maculatus 244
  variatus 244
X-ray Fish *see* Tetra, X-ray

Bibliography

Bailey, Mary and Gina Sandford
(1995) *The Ultimate Aquarium*
Lorenz Books
ISBN 1-85967-081-4

Dawes, John (1991)
Livebearing Fishes – A Guide to Their
Aquarium Care, Biology and
Classification **Blandford**
ISBN 0-7137-2152-9

Dawes, John (1996)
Tropical Aquarium Fishes
New Holland (Publishers) Ltd.
ISBN 1-85368-578-X (hardback)
1-85368-579-8 (paperback)

Nelson, Joseph S. (1994)
Fishes of the World (3rd Edition)
John Wiley & Sons, Inc.
ISBN 0-471-54713-1

Reihl, Rüdiger and Hans A Baensch
(1987) *Aquarium Atlas*
Hans A Baensch ISBN 3-88244-050-3

Sandford, Gina (1995)
An Illustrated Encyclopedia of
Aquarium Fish
Apple Press ISBN 1-85076-597-9

Schäfer, Frank (1997)
All Labyrinths – Betta, Gouramis,
Snakeheads, Nandids
Verlag A.C. S. GmbH
ISBN 3-931702-21-9

Scheel, Jorgen J. (1990)
Atlas of Killifishes of the Old World
T.F.H. Publications, Inc.
ISBN 0-86622-668-0

Stawikowski, Rainer (1993)
The Biotope Aquarium
T.F.H. Publications, Inc.
ISBN 0-86622-519-6